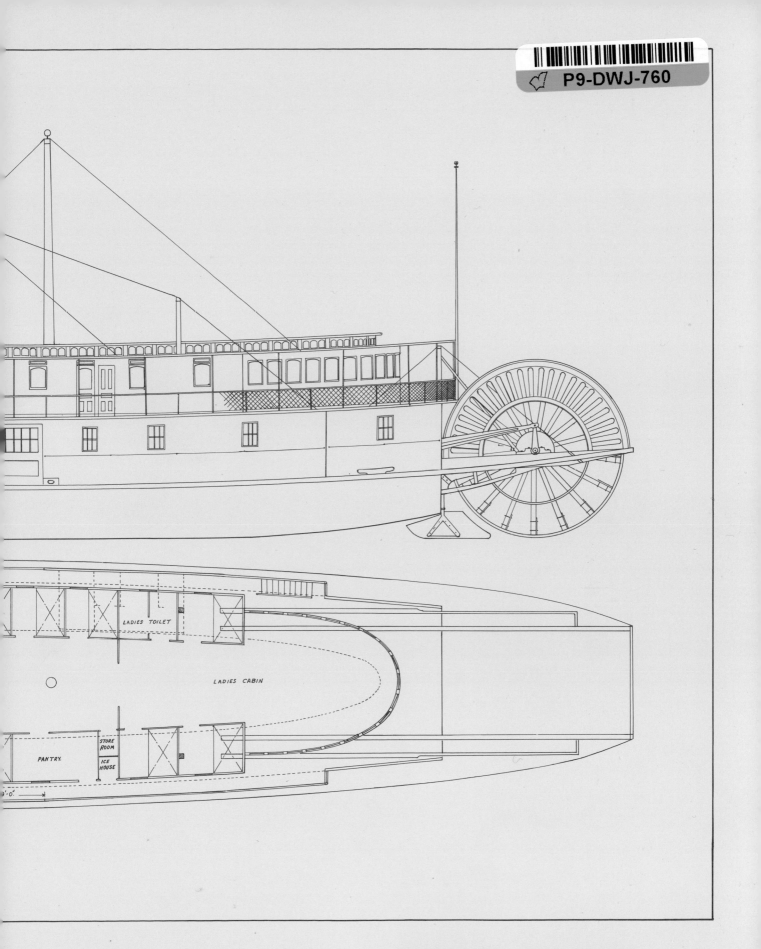

LADIES TOILET

LADIES CABIN

PANTRY.

STORE ROOM

ICE HOUSE

STEAMER KOKANEE

As Designed by Captain James W. Troup / July 1895

Sternwheelers and Steam Tugs

The sternwheeler *Bonnington* was the pride of the Canadian
Pacific's British Columbia Lake and River Service when she was
built in 1911 at Nakusp on the Arrow Lakes. She was the largest
and most elegant sternwheeler yet seen on the lakes and rivers
of southeastern British Columbia and had passenger accommodations equal to some of the best coastal steamships. This painting, by Harlan Hiney, depicts the *Bonnington* soon after entering
service and is based on a photograph by CPR Chief Steward
F. A. Buchholz. — AUTHOR'S COLLECTION

Sternwheelers and Steam Tugs

AN ILLUSTRATED HISTORY OF
THE CANADIAN PACIFIC RAILWAY'S
BRITISH COLUMBIA
LAKE AND RIVER SERVICE
BY ROBERT D. TURNER

Published by
SONO NIS PRESS
Victoria, British Columbia

1984

Canadian Cataloguing in Publication Data

Turner, Robert D., 1947-
    Sternwheelers and steam tugs

    Bibliography: p.
    Includes index.
    ISBN 0-919203-15-9

    1. Paddle steamers — British Columbia —
History.   2. Steam-navigation — British Columbia —
History.   3. Canadian Pacific
Railway Company — History. I. Title.
HE635.Z7B788   386'.22436'097114   c83-091323-8

First printing February 1984
Second printing July 1985

*Published with assistance from the British Columbia Heritage Trust and
the Canada Council Block Grant Program*

Published by
SONO NIS PRESS
1745 Blanshard Street, Victoria, B.C., Canada v8w 2j8

JACKET ILLUSTRATION AND FRONTISPIECE: The *Bonnington*, one of the
largest and most luxurious of the CPR's Lake and River Service
steamers on the Columbia River, shortly after entering service in 1911.
The painting is by Harlan Hiney and was specially commissioned
for *Sternwheelers and Steam Tugs*.

The *Princesses, Empresses* and *Sternwheelers* series of books by
Robert D. Turner was designed at Morriss Printing by Bev Leech.

Printed and bound in Canada by
MORRISS PRINTING COMPANY LTD.
Victoria, British Columbia

FOR MOLLY AND SARAH

Nakusp on Upper Arrow Lake was the centre for steamer operations on the Arrow Lakes run. Framed by a backdrop of the Monashee Mountains, the sternwheelers *Bonnington* (right) and *Minto* and the passenger tug *Columbia* rest quietly near the Nakusp shipyard in a scene from the declining years of the Lake and River Service. — ED VIPOND COLLECTION

ACKNOWLEDGEMENTS

My interest in the history of the Canadian Pacific's stern-wheelers began at an early age when my father told me about the *Minto, Bonnington* and other CPR vessels on the Arrow Lakes and how these steamers had been a part of his boyhood years at Burton City and Nakusp. Both he and my grandfather took pictures of the sternwheelers and it was using their negatives that I learned some of the magic of photographic printing and enlarging. My grandparents homesteaded a fruit ranch at Burton in the years before World War I and later, with their two sons, moved to Nakusp where they lived until the early 1940's. I found the appeal of the sternwheelers irresistible and determined that I would learn more about them.

I soon realized that a book was warranted and gradually built a file of material on the vessels and the stories that evolved around them. Many people eventually contributed to this history of the Lake and River Service. Some worked on the boats or lived in the communities they served. Others, working in museums and archives, contributed through their dedication to saving the records of the past. To all of them, I extend my sincere thanks for their help and encouragement.

Former Lake and River Service employees who helped me by recalling their years with the company and by loaning me photographs, diaries and other documents were: Bill Curran, retired CP Rail conductor whose late father was shipyard foreman. Bill also worked on the boats and was a conductor on the Slocan Lake trains; Chief Engineer Lawrence Exton; Chief Engineer George Donaldson, whose father was also a chief engineer on the sternwheelers; Bill Merrifield, shipyard carpenter; Chief Engineer John Millar; Captain Walter Spiller; Purser William Triggs; Chief Engineer Charles Verey; Chief Steward David Webster; and the late John Williams, chief engineer. Similarly, Dr. R. S. Goodwin, purser of the *Kaslo*, later assistant superintendent of the KR&N at Kaslo and whose father worked at the Mirror Lake shipyards; and Earl Marsh and Superintendent Engineer Hugh Tumilty, both of the B.C. Coast Steamship Service helped with insights and information. In later years, the BCCSS was directly involved in Lake and River Service operations and inspections.

Others who assisted with photographs, information, and their enthusiasm and advice include: Clinton Betz, Arthur Broomhall, Steve Cannings, Peter Chapman, Dr. W. B. Chung, Hugh Fraser, Roy Green, John E. Gregson, Norman Gidney, Ned Hanning, Pat Hind, Jim Hope, Mark S. Horne, Philip C. Johnson, W. Gibson Kennedy, Mrs. Ray Kosiancic, Bradley Lockner, Jack McDonald, Gordon Mercer, L. S. Morrison, Peter Ommundsen, Robert W. Parkinson, Margaret Rapatz, the late Eric Sismey, the late J. D. Spurway, Lloyd Stadum, Roy L. Troup (grandson of captain James Troup), Albert and Ruth Turner, Arthur Urquhart, Gerald E. Wellburn, Wilbur C. Whittaker, Charlie Yingling, Brian Young and Ken Young.

The staffs of many public and private institutions greatly contributed to this book and their help is much appreciated. I would like to acknowledge the following: Alaska Historical Library, Juneau; Archives of the Canadian Rockies, Banff; R. N. Atkinson Museum, Penticton; British Columbia Legislative Library, Victoria; British Columbia Provincial Museum, Modern History Division (BCPM), Victoria; Chilliwack Museum and Historical Society, Chilliwack; CP Rail, Nelson; Cominco, Trail; Cranbrook Archives, Museum and Landmark Foundation, Cranbrook; Eastern Washington State Historical Society, Spokane; Federal Archives and Records Center, GSA, Seattle; Glenbow-Alberta Institute, Calgary; Interior Photo Bank (IFB), Kelowna; Kelowna Centennial Museum, Kelowna; Maritime Museum of British Columbia, Victoria; Minnesota Historical Society, St. Paul; Moyie Museum (Kootenay Lake Historical Society); Nelson Centennial Museum, Nelson; Oregon Historical Society, Portland; Provincial Archives of British Columbia (PABC), Victoria; Public Archives of Canada (PAC), Ottawa; Puget Sound Maritime Historical Society (PSMHS), Seattle; Rossland Historical and Museum Association, Rossland; Summerland Museum, Summerland; Vancouver City Archives (VCA), Vancouver; Vancouver Maritime Museum (VMM), Vancouver; Vancouver Public Library, Historic Photograph Section (VPL), Vancouver; Vernon Board of Museum, Archives and Art Gallery, Vernon; and the Yukon Archives, Whitehorse.

My friends Omer Lavallée and Dave Jones of Canadian Pacific Corporate Archives (CPCA) were particularly helpful in finding elusive and long forgotten material on the Lake and River Service. Their support was very much appreciated. Harlan Hiney, that talented artist, and a good friend, once again took great care with the cover painting for this book.

My thanks go as well to my friends at Crystal Finish Photo Service for their careful printing of many of the photographs.

My colleagues and friends, Dave Parker and Peter Corley-Smith, at the Provincial Museum read the manuscript and contributed sound editorial assistance. Other friends who graciously read the manuscript and helped fill in elusive details or photos were: Len McCann, the Curator at the Vancouver Maritime Museum; Bob Spearing, historian and tug authority; Dave Wilkie, railway photographer and historian; and Ed Vipond, formerly with the CPR and a lifetime enthusiast of the Lake and River Service. My brother Bill was a constant source of needed advice and provided word processing facilities. My mother, always enthusiastic, helped with proofreading. Nancy, my wife, helped in ways beyond measure in all phases of the book from sympathetic editing to considered advice.

Finally, special thanks are due to my friends at Sono Nis Press and the Morriss Printing Company for their help and interest in this book. As usual it is both fun and an education to work with such talented people.

PREFACE

THE STERNWHEELED STEAMBOAT — the sternwheeler — was a vessel uniquely capable of navigating the formidable, swift-flowing, often treacherous rivers of western North America. On the Pacific Coast sternwheelers were used from California to Alaska and made a lasting contribution to the histories of the regions they served. In British Columbia, these vessels provided what was often the first reliable, reasonably economical transportation within large parts of the province. In a very direct way, they made settlement, agriculture and industry possible in areas that otherwise would have been virtually inaccessible.

Their greatest assets were sturdy construction, shallow draught — it was said some of them could "float on dew" — and the driving force of their paddlewheels. In the hands of an experienced captain and crew, these boats could be navigated through rapids and shallows that the timid of heart would have considered impassable. But sometimes even the sturdiest sternwheeler and the most skilled of crews would lose to the rivers; the bones of many fine vessels, rotting on the banks, was the price of a moment's carelessness or bad luck.

In southeastern British Columbia, range upon range of high, rugged mountains stretch across the entire southern boundary of the province, forging enormous barriers to travel. The Coast, Cascade, Monashee, Purcell, Selkirk and Rocky mountains, all running generally north and south, made overland transportation across the breadth of the province an arduous, trying, expensive ordeal. The rivers, particularly the Fraser, the Columbia and the Kootenay, provided the best and sometimes only feasible routes through the great mountain ranges. Often swift, sometimes plagued by shallows, the rivers were nonetheless the easiest routes of travel. In some places where they broadened, deep, fjord-like lakes formed; the Arrow, Okanagan and Kootenay lakes made travel easier. The sternwheeler was the ideal vessel to navigate these waterways.

The sternwheelers came to southeastern British Columbia comparatively late, few being in operation before the 1890's. Some were primitive, crudely-built craft that would have made a trained shipwright cringe with distaste; others were outstanding examples of shipbuilding craftsmanship. But their years of prominence were short and by 1920, their numbers were in rapid decline. Many changes had occurred during these few decades and the sternwheelers had often helped make feasible the developments — usually the railways — that replaced them.

Two companies stand out in the story of sternwheelers in southeastern British Columbia. The first, the Columbia and Kootenay Steam Navigation Company, developed from a primitive, hardly credible, frontier operation of one awkward vessel into a flourishing venture with a fleet of modern, well-appointed steamers. Its sternwheelers served the Columbia River and Arrow Lakes from Revelstoke in the north to Little Dalles, Washington in the south. On Kootenay Lake, its steamers made Nelson a centre of mining and commerce. The second company, and ultimately the successor to the Columbia and Kootenay Steam Navigation Company, was the Canadian Pacific Railway.

Since its completion as a transcontinental route in 1885-86, the Canadian Pacific has been the transportation giant of southern British Columbia; sternwheelers, and steam tugs and barges provided the railway with a means of tapping the rich lands to the south of its sparsely settled main line. In 1893, the CPR built its first sternwheeler to serve the Okanagan Valley. Just four years later, with the development of branch lines in the Kootenays and encroachment from American railroads from Spokane, the CPR purchased the entire operations of the Columbia and Kootenay Steam Navigation Company and set out to expand and develop steamship services on the Okanagan, Columbia and Kootenay waterways.

Steamers like the *Rossland, Slocan, Kootenay, Minto* and *Moyie* brought new standards of speed, elegance and reliability to the Okanagan and West Kootenays. In 1898, however, the CPR turned its attention and energies to the north and built a fine fleet of sternwheelers for operation on the Stikine River as part of a scheme to provide an all-Canadian route to the Klondike. In just a few months the venture was in ruins and the fleet an expensive, unwanted embarrassment.

In contrast, the operations in the south prospered and before World War I new vessels, including the fast sternwheelers *Kuskanook* and *Okanagan*, a fleet of powerful tugs, and the magnificent sternwheelers *Bonnington, Nasookin* and *Sicamous*, had been built. These last three vessels were the largest steamers ever to operate in southeastern British Columbia and among the finest sternwheelers ever constructed in the Northwest. Sadly, decline followed rapidly on the heels of success and by the 1930's road and railroad construction had made the sternwheelers and the tugs and barges virtually unnecessary. By the end of the decade, only two sternwheelers remained, the *Minto* and the *Moyie*, persistent anachronisms that endured into the 1950's. The tugs and barges continued to perform important, though much reduced, services into the 1970's until they too were replaced by more modern and efficient technologies. By 1980, only the modest tug and barge service on Slocan Lake remained.

In the booming days of the 1890's, the sternwheelers embodied excitement and adventure. Gold rushes, steamboat races, picnic excursions, moonlight cruises, white-water running, fires and groundings were all part of their traditions — the traditions of youth. Just a few generations later, the last, tired steamers were gone from the rivers of the Interior. Sedate, unhurried vessels, they had been bypassed and all but forgotten by a world much too busy and impatient to enjoy the luxury of an evening cruise on a steamboat parting the stillness of the Arrow Lakes or the leisurely pace of the *Moyie* steaming to Kaslo on a spring morning.

CONTENTS

Sternwheelers
and
Steam Tugs

The speedy steamer *Kokanee*, shown here at Nelson about 1896, was a product of the skilled design work of Captain James W. Troup, a man with an eye for fast, beautiful vessels. The *Kokanee* was the Columbia and Kootenay Steam Navigation Company's answer to any competition on Kootenay Lake and her owners were not disappointed. Behind the *Kokanee*, nearly hidden but for her smokestack, is the sternwheeler *Nelson*.
— CPCA

CHAPTER I

EARLY STEAMBOATING
IN THE KOOTENAYS
AND THE OKANAGAN

Pioneer Steamboating:
The Columbia and Kootenay
Steam Navigation Company

IN THE LATE 1880's and early 1890's, the rugged West Kootenay District of British Columbia was a remote, sparsely settled area. The major routes into this vast land were from Revelstoke in the north, where the Canadian Pacific Railway crossed the Columbia, and from the south, up the Columbia and its tributaries from Washington. In between there were overland trails — notably the Dewdney Trail, intended to help open the interior, leading along the southern border of the province — but the distances were great and the routes arduous and difficult. The mountains, tall and rugged, seemed to stretch endlessly across the entire southern part of the province.

Steamboats operating on the major lakes and rivers offered an easier and more reliable alternative to packing overland, and several enterprising men set out to provide these services. However, despite several early limited operations, it was not until the late 1880's that more permanent services began.

The first sternwheeler on the Arrow Lakes-Columbia River route was the *Forty-Nine*, built in 1865 at Colville Landing (Marcus), Washington. She ran intermittently for only a few years before being withdrawn. The small steamer had been built at the time of a short-lived gold rush on the Big Bend of the Columbia (north of the present site of Revelstoke) and after the collapse of the rush, there simply had not been enough traffic to justify running her. The construction of the Canadian Pacific Railway in the 1880's produced a second opportunity for steamboats to operate on the route, but it, too, was brief. In 1884, the small steam launch *Alpha* operated up the Columbia taking supplies to Farwell (later renamed Revelstoke) for railway construction. The *Alpha* was an unusual teak-hulled boat, built at Hong Kong in 1882. She had been shipped to Spokane Falls (later Spokane), Washington and then carried overland to the Columbia, just south of the border near what was to become Marcus. The next year, a considerably larger vessel, the sternwheeler *Kootenai*, was built at Little Dalles, Washington Territory, by Henderson and McCartney, who were contractors for the CPR. The supply business for the railway was short-lived and in any case, the *Kootenai* ran aground on September 4, 1885, effectively ending her services for the time being. She was repaired but was not to be used for some years to come.

The year 1888 marked the real beginning of sustained service on the Columbia downstream of the Big Bend.* Three enterprising businessmen, J. Frederick Hume, William Cowan and Captain Robert Sanderson, formed the Columbia Transportation Company to operate steamboats on the Columbia River route. The three men brought with them a number of skills, including business abilities, but they were certainly not shipwrights. The vessel they built, named the *Dispatch*,† was anything but beautiful. She had an unusual catamaran hull, the two parts apparently being somewhat asymmetrical, and a boxy wooden cabin with a small wheelhouse perched on top. At the time of her construction, her owners lacked funds to pay the freight on her second engine so her first trips down the river required some unusual procedures. Every time the single engine stopped, it would be on centre at the end of its stroke, without the second engine to start the wheel rotating. Consequently, the crew and passengers would have to climb up onto the paddlewheel to turn it off centre so that the engine could begin to rotate it.

The *Dispatch* was a small vessel, only 54 feet (16.5 m) long and just over 20 feet (6.1 m) wide overall. She measured only 37 gross tons but was reasonably tough and serviceable if not comfortable. Her first trip down the Columbia commenced on August 9, 1888 under Captain Sanderson. She was to provide a useful service for several years to come. As mining activity in the West Kootenays gradually expanded, there was a steady increase in traffic and the little company proved successful. In what appears to have been a seperate operation, Hume and Sanderson acquired the little steamer *Marion*, which had been operating from Golden on the Upper Columbia. She was shipped over to Revelstoke and entered service on the Arrow Lakes.

Even with two vessels on the route, the service was still primitive to say the least and could only be considered a beginning. George Mercer Dawson, of the Geological Survey of Canada, who was responsible for early surveys of vast areas of western Canada during his noteworthy career, travelled up the Columbia on the *Dispatch* in July 1889. His diary entries

J. Fred Hume, one of the three founders of the Columbia Transportation Company, brought a background of successful merchandising to the new company. He developed interests in both Revelstoke and Nelson and later entered provincial politics, eventually serving as Minister of Mines.
— *The British Columbia Mining Record*

The little steamer *Dispatch* was hardly an auspicious beginning for regular steamboat service on the Columbia River between the Canadian Pacific Railway's main line at what is now Revelstoke and the vast, and potentially rich, country to the south. Makeshift, and barely adequate, she was nonetheless a start. This photograph taken by George Mercer Dawson of the Geological Survey of Canada shows the little steamer in July 1889 at a landing on the Columbia. Cordwood for fuel and what appears to be sacks of ore are piled on her deck. Just aft of the wheelhouse, a single chair awaits any passenger wishing a better view or more air.
— PAC, PA-38001

The *Dispatch* was an unusual catamaran craft, with two separate, narrow hulls supporting the rudimentary superstructure. Her cabins provided only the most basic accommodations for passengers. The forward part was not even fully enclosed, canvas serving to keep out the worst of the weather but probably few of the mosquitoes.
— VPL, 19986

---

* The story of steamboating on the Upper Columbia, focusing around the town of Golden, and of operations on the Kootenay River in the East Kootenays, is beyond the scope of this book since it is not directly related to the development of the CPR's British Columbia Lake and River Service.

† In some sources, the name is spelled *Despatch*, but most records from that period use *Dispatch*.

for the trip provide some unusual insights into early travel on the Arrow Lakes:*

"9 July. At Landing [Sproat's] all day. The 'Dispatch' & 'Marion' Steamers both arrived Early this Am. Arranged to go back to Revelstoke in the first named as wished to get Some information about lakes from Capt. Sanderson, who knows them well. Steamer at first timed to leave about noon but afterwards postponed till morning. Got lat. & time obsns., Sun & polaris, but otherwise a lazy day. Got a Couple of photos [including the one reproduced] & paced traverse to 'town' to Connect it with my obsn. point, near Mr Sproats House. A fine & warm day.

"10 July. Up Early & left about 6.30 by Steamer. Tied up for night at 10.30 about five miles up the Upper Arrow Lake, on West Side [this would be approximately 60 miles or 100 km north of Sproat's]. Day very fine & scenery certainly equal to any we have seen on Kootanie Lake, particularly on the length of river Connecting the two lakes. . . . Through kindness of Captain got a few soundings along the lower lake which proves not to be remarkably deep. Primitive steamboating, the 'accomodation' Consisting of a little board Shed or 'Cabin' at Stern of Steamer. This contains a few I fear dirty bunks, a stove with pantry, a chinaman [who was presumably the cook and steward] & a table, & serves for sleeping, eating etc etc!"

George Dawson's somewhat derogatory remarks about the *Dispatch* were accurate, as she was indeed a "primitive" stern-wheeler. However, vessels like the *Dispatch* and the *Marion*, which was very similar, made it possible for entrepreneurs, settlers and miners to develop the region. They also proved that steamboat services were both essential in the region and economically viable, justifying the much more significant investments required for vessels like the *Lytton* and *Columbia* that were soon to follow.

Fred Hume and his partners lacked capital for significant expansion of their fleet and it was clear that more backers for the service were needed. These were found in Captain John Irving, the veteran riverboat and coastal steamship captain and entrepreneur; J. A. Mara, businessman, steamboat operator from the Thompson-Shuswap area, and member of Parliament; and Frank S. Barnard, whose father had founded the British Columbia Express Company. All three men had experience in steamboating, as well as the necessary capital and political influence. With their backing, expansion of the service to the Kootenays was possible. A new company, the Columbia and Kootenay Steam Navigation Company (C&K SN), was formed with capital of $100,000 to operate steamers on both the Columbia River and on Kootenay Lake, where mining activity was expanding rapidly.

The first step towards securing the growing traffic down the Columbia was to build, or at least acquire, more vessels. To do this, the C&KSN contracted Alexander Watson, a highly skilled shipbuilder from Victoria, to construct a new vessel at

* Spelling and punctuation are Dawson's.

CERTIFICATE OF INCORPORATION.

CERTIFICATE OF INCORPORATION.

WE, the undersigned, hereby certify that we desire to form, under the provisions of the "Companies' Act, 1878," Part II., a company, hereinafter mentioned:—

1. The corporate name of the company shall be the "Columbia and Kootenay Steam Navigation Company, Limited Liability."

2. The objects for which the company are formed are:—

(a.) The building, purchase, chartering, navigation and maintenance of steamboats for the carrying of passengers, goods, chattels, wares, ores and merchandise, and for the towing of logs on the Columbia River, the Kootenay River and the Kootenay Lake.

(b.) The purchase, renting and holding of such lands, wharves, docks, warehouses and other buildings as may be found necessary for the purposes of the company.

3. The capital stock of the company shall be $100,000, divided into 1000 shares of $100 each.

4. The time of the existence of the company shall be twenty years.

5. The number of the Tustees shall be three, and their names are John A. Mara, of Kamloops, J. Fred Hume and Robert Sanderson, of Revelstoke, who shall manage the affairs of the company for the first three months.

6. The principal place of business of the company shall be at Revelstoke.

7. A stockholder shall not be individually liable for the debts of the company, but the liability of a stockholder shall be limited to his proportion (based upon the amount of his respective shares) to assessments legally levied, and the charges thereon if advertised as delinquent during the time that he is a stockholder, upon a share or shares of which he is the holder, as shown by the stockholders' register book of the company; assessments and charges thereon, when taken collectively, shall not exceed in the aggregate the value in dollars printed or shown upon each share when issued.

Dated at Revelstoke this twenty-first day of December, A.D. 1889.

| Made, signed and acknowledged by John A. Mara, J. Fred. Hume, Wm. Cowan and Robert Sanderson in presence of J. A. Gilker. | J. A. MARA, J. FRED. HUME, WILLIAM COWAN, JNO. IRVING, ROBERT SANDERSON, F. S. BARNARD. |

Made, signed and acknowledged by the above named John Irving in the presenc of
C. Dubois Mason, Notary Public, &c., Victoria.

Made, signed and acknowledged by the above named F. S. Barnard in the presence of
Charles Wilson, Notary Public.

Filed (in duplicate) 21st January, 1890.
C. J. LEGGATT,
ja23   Registrar of Joint Stock Companies.

— *B.C. Gazette*, January 23, 1890.

C&KSN OFFICIALS

Frank S. Barnard

J. A. Mara

John Irving

Revelstoke. Another vessel was found in the form of the old *Kootenai*, out of service since 1885 or 1886 at Little Dalles, but still basically sound. She was refitted and readied for service. In payment, her owners were given $10,000 in promissory notes. This may seem like an excellent bargain for the C&KSN, but in truth, the owners of the steamer had everything to gain and little to lose in the transaction. Sitting on the bank of the Columbia, slowly falling apart, the *Kootenai* would have been worthless in a few years in any case.

A contemporary of the *Dispatch*, the steamer *Marion* was certainly no more refined. Her cabins had little room for her few passengers, but in a land still wild and largely unexplored, she provided an essential service to the prospectors, miners, merchants and settlers who began moving into the Kootenays in the early 1890's. — PABC, 31750

On December 21, 1889, six men, J. A. Mara, J. Fred Hume, William Cowan, John Irving, Robert Sanderson and Frank S. Barnard, incorporated the Columbia and Kootenay Steam Navigation Company. It was a successful venture and wrought great changes to transportation in the West Kootenays. Barnard, Mara and Irving brought capital, influence and a background in transportation to the enterprise. Barnard, with his father, had gained fame with their B.C. Express Company. J. A. Mara brought business talents to the company and in addition he had operated steamboats on Kamloops Lake. Mara and Barnard also happened to be brothers-in-law. John Irving, although young, was a seasoned riverboat captain and manager of the Canadian Pacific Navigation Company. Irving, Mara and Barnard also became successful politicians. Barnard eventually was appointed Lieutenant-Governor of British Columbia.
— PABC, 4837, 3518 / *The British Columbia Mining Record*

The steamer *Lytton*, built under the supervision of Alexander Watson, was to be an important addition to the Columbia and Kootenay Steam Navigation Company's fleet. She was laid down in December 1889 at Revelstoke but construction was delayed because of ice conditions and work could not be resumed until April. Launched the following month, she was ready for service by the beginning of July 1890.

The *Lytton* was not large by later standards and measured 131 feet (39.9 m) long by 25 feet, 6 inches (7.8 m) in beam. With steam up, but no cargo aboard, she drew only 19 inches (48 cm) of water. With a cargo of 60 tons (54.4 tonnes), as she might carry on a typical voyage on the Columbia, she still drew only 2 feet, 6 inches (0.8 m) forward and 2 feet, 2 inches (0.6 m) amidships. Such a shallow draft made her a versatile vessel for navigating in the shallows of the Columbia.

In building the *Lytton*, Alexander Watson had recruited, as *The Kootenay Star* reported, the best ship's carpenters he could find in Victoria. His crew also included John Patterson, as construction engineer, whose responsiblity it was to install the *Lytton*'s engines, which were second hand, and mate them with the many new components required. The best wood available was used throughout in the *Lytton*'s construction. In fact, some delays had been experienced in obtaining lumber of high enough quality for the work. In total, the cost of the vessel was $38,000.

By later standards, the *Lytton* was neither luxurious nor particularly large, but she was a significant and welcome addition to the vessels available for service on the Columbia at the time. There was nothing unusual in her design that made her stand out from other sternwheelers of the period. She had three decks, the first being devoted to housing the boiler, which was situated in the traditional forward position approximately beneath the pilothouse. At the after end of the vessel were the engines. The remainder of this deck was for freight and cordwood fuel. Immediately above was the passenger deck, which included a lounge forward, a dining saloon with clerestory roof, and staterooms. Above the passenger deck was the pilothouse and officers' accommodations.

The steamer's first trip down the Columbia began on July 2, 1890. The newly-completed vessel steamed down from the docks near the Canadian Pacific's bridge across the Columbia River, to the Revelstoke smelter dock. There, 65 tons (nearly 59 tonnes) of track-building supplies, including rail, bolts and fish plates were loaded on board. These were for the construction of the Columbia and Kootenay Railway being built between Sproat's Landing at the junction of the Columbia and Kootenay rivers, and Nelson on Kootenay Lake. On her first trip down the Arrow Lakes, the *Lytton* carried a distinguished group of officials from both the steamship company and the Canadian Pacific Railway. These included J. A. Mara and his partner Frank Barnard, who were anxious to see how their new steamer performed, and a CPR party which arrived

The *Lytton Joins the C&KSN Fleet, 1890*

The C&KSN made arrangements to provide a connecting service between the Canadian Pacific Railway at Revelstoke and the Spokane Falls and Northern at Little Dalles, Washington in 1890. By September 1892, the railroad had been extended north seven miles (11.3 km) to what became Northport and the steamers made connection there. In this photograph, the *Lytton* is just off the landing at Northport about 1897.
— EASTERN WASHINGTON STATE HISTORICAL SOCIETY

The directors of the Columbia and Kootenay Steam Navigation Company were astute enough to realize that vessels like the *Dispatch* were totally inadequate to meet the anticipated growth in traffic south of Revelstoke. One of their first steps was to have the new sternwheeler *Lytton* built at Revelstoke. She was ready for service in July 1890 and is pictured above, right, her foredeck piled high with cordwood, taking on passengers and cargo at the head of Upper Arrow Lake. — MAYNARD PHOTO, PABC, 234

Other vessels were needed and the C&KSN was able to purchase the American sternwheeler *Kootenai*, unused for some years, at a bargain price and return her to service. She was basically a freight boat, but most welcome. This photograph by Richard Maynard shows her at Robson with the steamers *Columbia* (built in 1891) and the *Lytton*. — PABC, 235

on train No. 2. In the latter group were such notables as President William C. Van Horne and R. B. Angus.

The *Lytton* sailed at 11:30 a.m. on July 3, 1890 to the cheers of many Revelstoke residents who crowded the landing and also the nearby steamer *Kootenai*. The new vessel performed well, although there were of course a few "running-in" problems that were to be expected on any new vessel. Starting out, steam pressure in the boiler was 90 pounds (620 kp), but this dropped to 80 (550 kp) by the time she was well under way and then to 60 (410 kp) by the time they reached the mouth of the Illecillewaet River, five miles (8 km) downstream. Before they reached the upper end of the lake, they had to stop to allow a journal on the paddlewheel to cool off and for the engineers to make some minor adjustments. The delay gave the dignitaries time for lunch. A further 40-minute stop was made to take on wood for fuel and the steamer reached the head of Upper Arrow Lake at 2:30 p.m. Her average speed for the 28-mile (45-km) run had been 14 miles per hour (22.5 km/h) aided by the current in the river which varied from three to seven miles per hour (about 5-11 km/h).

The *Lytton* completed the run down Upper Arrow Lake by 6:30 that evening. Half an hour was spent "wooding-up" before proceeding down the 16 miles (25.8 km) of narrow river channel separating the Upper and Lower Arrow Lakes. The Lower Lake was reached at 8:10 but because the last load of wood was particularly wet, steam pressure had dropped in the boiler to only 40 pounds (275 kp). The remaining 75 miles (120 km) to Sproat's Landing was steamed in five and one-half hours. The average speed for the trip, allowing for delays, was calculated at 12 1/3 miles per hour (19.8 km/h), which was quite satisfactory.

At this time, Sproat, or Sproat's Landing, was a growing town as construction of the railway to Nelson proceeded. The town boasted the Genelle sawmill with six boarding shacks for its employees, a railway depot and express office, government building and post office, three restaurants, the Kootenay House Hotel, a drug store, a hardware and grocery store, Lemon's General Store, two or three log and frame houses, a few tents, and, as *The Kootenay Star* noted, "Joe Wilson's corral of pack horses."

After breakfast the next morning, most of the dignitaries on the *Lytton* rode on horseback to inspect progress on the railway which was to open to traffic the following May 28. After taking on more cordwood, the *Lytton* steamed north for Revelstoke later that morning. She managed to maintain 90 lbs (620 kp) pressure in the boiler and aside from a 30-minute stop to allow a bearing to cool and to pick up two passengers, the return trip was uneventful. Her actual steaming time was 13 hours, 45 minutes for the 150-mile (240 km) trip and she averaged about 11 miles per hour (17.7 km/h) working upstream. She arrived at Revelstoke at 12:30 a.m. on Friday. J. A. Mara commented to the reporter from *The Kootenay*

The Canadian Pacific's crossing of the Columbia River at Revelstoke required a major bridge. To permit a steamboat to navigate upstream to the "Big Bend" country to the north, one span in the bridge had to be raised. In this photograph, the work is nearly completed as a westbound passenger train crosses over the river. — PABC, 77670

The railroad connection from Northport via the Spokane Falls and Northern to Spokane proved to be an important link for the C&KSN. It meant through traffic to and from the north as well as an important route for the ores from the burgeoning Kootenay mines. — EASTERN WASHINGTON STATE HISTORICAL SOCIETY

Star that, "On the whole, she is quite satisfactory as far as tested. She had not the boiler capacity of the *Kootenai*, and as we do not care to push her on the first trip, her speed may not be quite up to her competitor's. When her bearings are more even, friction will be reduced and with a few alterations, she will improve in steaming capacity. Our policy is to employ the most efficient and experienced men that can be obtained to fill the various positions of trust."

Her crew included: Captain Frank Odlin; Chief Engineer E. Hattersley; Purser G. C. Tunstall, Jr.; Steward G. F. Henly; two firemen; a watchman; a Chinese cook whose name was recorded only as Charlie; and eight deckhands.

Mara was pleased with the operations of the Company to date and noted that:

"Business has been good, fully up to our expectations, although the river did not open as early as usual. We have taken to date — passengers 1,325; animals, 63; tons of freight, 1,275 [1,157 tonnes]. Future prospects are encouraging. By August 1st., the Spokane Northern R.R. will be completed to Little Dalles and we expect good trade between that point and Revelstoke. There will be a competition of rates between the CPR and the "Northern" and connections that will give us a carrying trade from both of these sources . . . With our comfortable and well furnished boats, we expect a considerable tourist trade in the near future. The present mining outlook is exceedingly favourable for Kootenay."

The railroad Mara alluded to in his comments, the "Spokane Northern," was actually called the Spokane Falls and Northern. It was built by Daniel Chase Corbin from Spokane Falls to the Columbia at Little Dalles. Corbin, a railroad builder, had his eyes on the rich potential of the West Kootenay mines and hoped to push his railroad northwards to Nelson on the shores of Kootenay Lake. In the meantime, however, a connecting steamboat service was established between Revelstoke and Little Dalles providing a direct service between the Canadian Pacific Railway and the Spokane Falls and Northern. The connection with the SF&N meant that a through route existed to the Northern Pacific Railroad and shortly, to the Great Northern at Spokane. Corbin had travelled to Victoria in mid-July to formalize arrangements with the C&KSN for the connecting steamer service which would not only add through traffic to his line but would also give him the access he wanted to the West Kootenay mining country.

With the completion of the railroad, Corbin ran a special train on August 15, 1890, from Spokane Falls to Little Dalles with businessmen, their families and other guests. The *Lytton* was to meet the train, inaugurating the through service between Revelstoke and Spokane. However, the *Lytton* had her troubles on the run down from Revelstoke. Low-hanging branches damaged her smokestack and she was delayed en route by a crowd of prospectors trying to reach the new ore

9

deposits just discovered in the mountains behind Trail Creek on the Columbia below Sproat's Landing. The net result was that the *Lytton* left Sproat's Landing 10 hours late and it was 5:30 p.m., instead of early in the morning, before she steamed to the landing at Little Dalles. Nonetheless, her welcome was warm and after cargo and passengers were disembarked and northbound merchandise and travellers were safely aboard, she steamed back up the river. The first, more-or-less reliable north-south link from the Canadian Pacific Railway through the Kootenays to Spokane was complete.

The first season's operations of the C&KSN were a marked success. The *Lytton* operated until November 15, 1890 and made 42 trips down the Columbia, including 13 round trips to Little Dalles. The *Kootenai* made 27 trips running between May 13 and August 12 before being laid up due to low water and a slackening of business. In addition the *Dispatch* made four trips. Overall, the steamers logged 23,252 miles (37,419 km) and carried 4,500 tons (4,082 tonnes) of freight, 150,000 feet of lumber and timber, 19 railway cars and a locomotive and tender. Unfortunately, passenger totals were not recorded.

The greatest single barrier to efficient communication between the growing mining communities on Kootenay Lake, centring at Nelson, and the Columbia, was the series of waterfalls downstream from the West Arm of Kootenay Lake on the Kootenay River. These cascades, highlighted by beautiful Bonnington Falls, precluded any navigation on the river and required a long and costly diversion overland by pack trail. The solution that quickly presented itself to the merchants and businessmen at Nelson was the construction of a short railway between Sproat's Landing and Nelson.

Nelson, like most towns in the Kootenays, owes its existence to the discovery of ore deposits. The Silver King Mine on Toad Mountain proved a lucrative find in 1886 and two years later, the town of Nelson was founded becoming one of the major centres of the West Kootenays. Nelson's rail connection to the world was chartered as the Columbia and Kootenay Railway (C&K) in 1889. The British Columbia government agreed to provide a land grant of 200,000 acres (80,940 ha), while the federal government granted a construction subsidy of $112,000. The 28-mile (45-km) line was built by the Canadian Pacific and opened for traffic on May 31, 1891.

The CPR noted, in its Annual Report for 1891, that it acquired the line " . . . to prevent the invasion by foreign lines of the Kootenay District, to British Columbia — a district rich in precious metals and other resources." It was, in reality, much more than just a small, isolated branch line. It was a stop-gap measure, but it really represented the beginning of CPR expansion in the Kootenays and would eventually lead to the construction of a railway across the southern expanse of British Columbia.

The construction of the Columbia and Kootenay Railway from the Columbia River at Robson to Nelson by the CPR bypassed an impassable section of the Kootenay River. The 28-mile (45-km) railway line was opened on May 31, 1891 and was an immediate boost to the settlement and commercial development of the district. Here, a C&K mixed train is crossing the Kootenay River near Nelson. The isolated line was the CPR's first branch line in the Kootenays and it was some years before the CPR incorporated the short standard gauge route into a more extensive rail system spanning southern British Columbia. — PABC, 45897

New Rail Connections and New Steamers

The charter of the Columbia and Kootenay
Steam Navigation Company provided for the
operation of steamers on Kootenay Lake. In 1891,
the first of what was to become an impressive
fleet of sternwheelers and steam tugs was placed
in service. She was the *Nelson*, a somewhat
enlarged and improved version of the *Lytton*.
Her engines were second-hand, probably salvaged
from the steamer *Skuzzy* (II) which had in turn
received the engines of her famous predecessor,
the original *Skuzzy*, the only sternwheeler to have
battled upstream through Hell's Gate on the
Fraser River. — PABC, 14257

With the opening of the C&K, a railway that CPR President Van Horne called " . . . a railroad from nowhere to nowhere," Nelson had fairly direct and reliable connections to the CPR main line at least during the seasons of good navigation on the Columbia. Growth in the Kootenays at this time was rapid, and with the improved rail connections, the future looked more promising than ever. To provide the tonnage necessary to handle the traffic on the Columbia the C&KSN ordered a new steamer to be built at Little Dalles and at the same time, expanded its operations onto Kootenay Lake by building a substantial sternwheeler at Nelson.

The new vessel ordered for the Columbia River service was to supplement the *Lytton* on the route from Little Dalles to Revelstoke. The other new steamer, to be built at Nelson, was to operate on Kootenay Lake from Nelson, at the end of track of the C&K Railway, to Bonners Ferry, Idaho. She was also to serve various other points on Kootenay Lake. At Bonners Ferry she would eventually connect with the Great Northern Railway (GN), which was to pass through Bonners Ferry on its route to the coast. GN, on reaching Bonners Ferry, would thus have water access — though not rail access — to Nelson and the other mining centres on Kootenay Lake. The C&K SN's plans were to have a profound effect on the quality of service available on Kootenay Lake.

The new Kootenay Lake sternwheeler, which was to be called the *Nelson*, was a dramatic improvement over the *Galena*, a little 80-foot steamer, built at Bonners Ferry in 1888 and then the largest steamer operating regularly on Kootenay Lake. The *Nelson* was a typical Columbia River sternwheeler, not unlike the *Lytton* in design. She was built at Nelson, a town rapidly growing with the completion of the railway and eventually to become the centre of the C&KSN's steamer operations. The *Nelson* was built by David Stephenson, being laid down in the spring of the year and launched on June 11. One month later, *The Miner* reported that she was nearing completion:

"Work has been somewhat retarded during the past two weeks on account of rain, but the machinery is all in place, the wheel is finished, three life-boats have been built, and the state-rooms are all but complete. Interior finishing work is being done and the cabins, pilot house, officers quarters and rooms for the crew are well under way. The boat presents a handsome appearance and will take front rank among river steamers in British Columbia and be a credit to her builder."

The *Nelson* measured 131.6 feet (40.1 m) long by 26.4 feet (8 m) in breadth. Her gross tonnage was 496. Her engines were second-hand, probably from the old CPR construction era sternwheeler *Skuzzy** and rebuilt at the Albion Iron Works

* For details of the steamers *Skuzzy* (I) and *Skuzzy* (II), see Appendix V.

Prior to the completion of the *Nelson* by the C&KSN, transportation on Kootenay Lake was quite primitive. Facilities at Kootenay Landing, at the southern end of Kootenay Lake were certainly far from elaborate but included the small tarpaper-covered Kootenay Landing Hotel and H. William's Restaurant. — PABC, 1622

The *Galena*, a screw-driven steamer, was one of the most important vessels on Kootenay Lake before the *Nelson* was placed in service. The *Galena* was modest by later standards, but she did have a small cabin for passengers and reasonable freight capacity. At Nelson, supplies are being unloaded onto wagons. A steamer wharf has yet to be built. — PABC, 57800

— *The Kootenay Star*, June 6, 1891

in Victoria. They were powerful enough to give the *Nelson* sufficient speed to surpass any other vessels then on the lake. Her cargo deck provided ample space for freight while the saloon deck had lounges both fore and aft, a comfortable dining area and overnight cabins. She was licensed to carry 125 day passengers.

On July 25, *The Miner* reported that work on the *Nelson* was progressing well:

"The pilot house has been completed, the smoke stack put up and the wheel covered. Carpenters are now finishing the interior and painters are busily engaged in putting the boat in proper colors. The dining room and ladies cabin will be in white, the boiler deck in Prussian blue, and the engineer's room will be grained, while outside of the eaves, on the upper deck the colour will be Paris green."

Captain D. C. McMorris had been appointed master while William Simmons was to be mate and August Manentean pilot.

After some delays installing and finishing her machinery, the *Nelson* entered service later in the summer. She proved to be a fine, efficient vessel and remained the stalwart on Kootenay Lake until 1896 when the *Kokanee* was completed. The *Nelson* began a twice-weekly service between her namesake city and Bonners Ferry as well as providing two trips a week to Ainsworth and way points.

While work had been underway at the Nelson shipyard on the *Nelson*, the second new steamer was progressing under the direction of Alexander Watson, who had built the *Lytton* the year before. This new vessel, which was named the *Columbia*, was somewhat larger than the *Nelson*. Her gross tonnage was 534 and she measured 152.5 feet (46.5 m) in length and 28 feet (8.5 m) in breadth. Her depth of hold was 6.25 feet (1.9 m). She was described in *Lewis & Dryden's Marine History* as "the finest sternwheeler ever [i.e., by 1891] constructed so far inland."

The *Columbia* was an attractively designed vessel, of typical layout and pleasingly proportioned. She was basically a refined, somewhat larger version of the *Lytton* and was similar to the *Nelson*. Her engines were old, but serviceable, having been built in 1877 by the firm of Harlan and Hollingsworth of Wilmington, Delaware. They appear to have been powerful, however, as her early voyages showed. She made her first regular trip from Little Dalles on Thursday, August 20, 1891, leaving at 1:00 p.m. and reaching Robson between seven and eight in the evening, which was said to be about one hour better time than the *Lytton* would normally have made on the run.

The *Columbia* was registered in the United States and was placed under the command of Captain John C. Gore. She was said to have cost $75,000 to complete. However, the C&KSN now had two fine new steamers in operation and the invest-

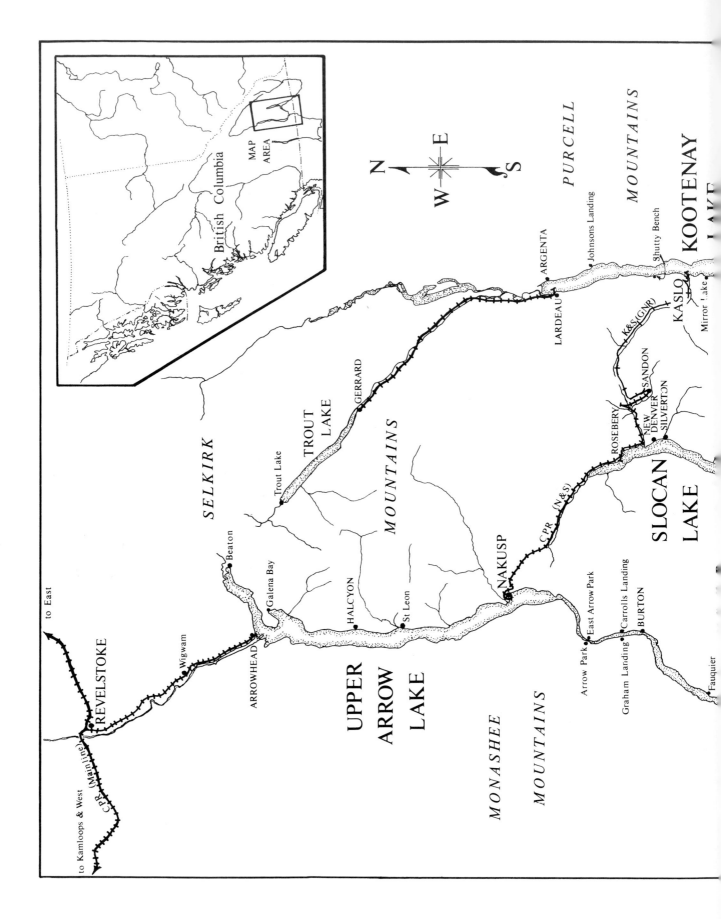

14

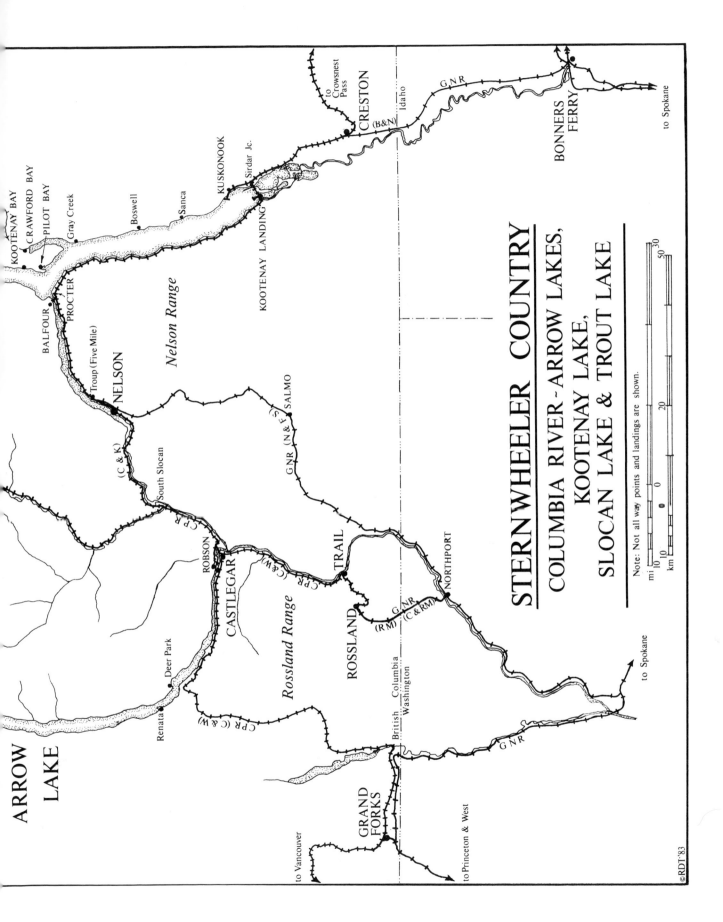

STERNWHEELER COUNTRY

COLUMBIA RIVER ~ ARROW LAKES, KOOTENAY LAKE, SLOCAN LAKE & TROUT LAKE

Note: Not all way points and landings are shown.

ARROW LAKE

Renata

Deer Park

KOOTENAY BAY
CRAWFORD BAY
PILOT BAY
Gray Creek
Boswell
Sanca
KUSKONOOK
Sirdar Jc.
KOOTENAY LANDING

BALFOUR
PROCTER
Troup (Five Mile)
NELSON
Nelson Range

to Crowsnest Pass
CRESTON
(B&N)
Idaho
G N R
BONNERS FERRY
to Spokane

SALMO
GNR (N & F)

ROBSON
CASTLEGAR
Rossland Range
TRAIL
ROSSLAND
NORTHPORT

South Slocan
(C & K)
CPR
CPR (C&W)
G N R (C & RM)
(RM)

British Columbia
Washington
Columbia

CPR (C&W)
GRAND FORKS
G N R
to Spokane

to Vancouver
to Princeton & West

©RDT '83

mi 10 · 0 · 20 · 30
km 10 · 0 · 50

The *Nelson*, above, on Kootenay Lake about 1891 with a large excursion crowd aboard. — CANADIAN PACIFIC

The *Columbia*, a slightly enlarged version of the *Lytton*, was built at Little Dalles, Washington Territory and was registered in the United States. Both vessels were constructed by Alexander Watson, one of British Columbia's most experienced sternwheeler builders. In the photograph at right, the *Columbia* (nearest inshore) and the *Lytton* are docked at Revelstoke in the summer of 1891. The similarity of the two vessels to the *Nelson* is quite evident. Later in 1891, the *Columbia*'s cabins were enlarged as shown on page 19. — PABC, 14253

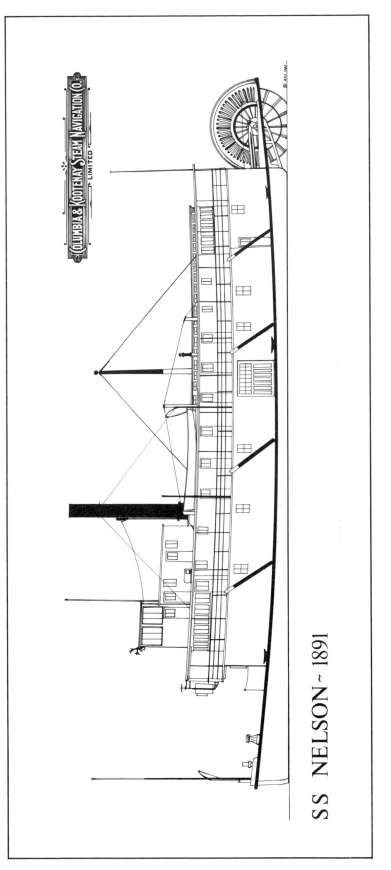

COLUMBIA & KOOTENAY STEAM NAVIGATION CO. LIMITED

S S NELSON ~ 1891

17

ment was undoubtedly a good one from the Company's perspective. Prospects for increasing traffic seemed bright.

With the *Columbia* in service, the C&KSN was able to schedule two round trips a week between Revelstoke and Little Dalles using the *Columbia* and the *Lytton*. This left the *Kootenai* and the old *Dispatch* available for freighting and any extra business that might develop. In addition, the *Dispatch* was useful for snag-pulling and emergencies.

The completion of the *Nelson* for Kootenay Lake and the *Columbia* for the Columbia River route put the C&KSN in a far better position to capitalize on the growth in mining and commerce in southeastern British Columbia and effectively extended its influence all the way from Revelstoke on the CPR main line in the north to Little Dalles in the south and Bonners Ferry in the east. But the sternwheeler network had its weaknesses, notably occasional winter freeze-ups or low water. Therefore, improved vessels and further branch line construction were required before the Kootenay district had a truly reliable transportation system. To illustrate the importance of the sternwheeler service for the Kootenays, when operations had to be stopped during the winter months, mail from Revelstoke to Nelson had to be routed via Victoria and then, on a once a week schedule, across Washington to Marcus. From there it was carried up the Columbia or by trail to Sproat's Landing. It was a 10-14 day delivery instead of the two-day service when the boats were running.

That fall, with low water on the Columbia River, the *Lytton* handled traffic between Revelstoke and Robson. This gave the Company time to withdraw the *Columbia* and modify her cabins. A small "Texas," or upper cabin deck was added, raising the pilothouse one deck higher, and her system of hogposts was modified and strengthened. Electric lights were added to her passenger accommodations and she emerged as clearly the finest vessel on the Upper Columbia. The construction work was carried out at Revelstoke and time was taken to finish the vessel in a more careful and complete manner. It was not uncommon for steamers to be placed in service before all finishing work on the cabins was complete so that the revenues could be gained from a heavy summer's traffic.

In March 1892, Captain James William Troup, a 37-year-old steamer captain, river pilot, skilled ship designer and businessman, arrived at Robson on the *Lytton* and took the connecting C&K train to Nelson. There he was to assume the duties of Manager of the C&KSN. His appointment may well have been one of the most propitious decisions the owners of the Company ever made, for his talents were to help shape the future of steamer service probably to a greater extent than any other person's.

Captain Troup, a native of Portland, Oregon and a riverboat captain since the age of 19, had worked for both J. A. Mara and John Irving in the 1880's and had won their respect as a particularly skilful steamer captain. For Captain

Robson, B.C., near the confluence of the Columbia and Kootenay rivers, became an important trans-shipment point for all freight moving up or down the Columbia to or from the main line of the CPR at Revelstoke. In addition, traffic destined for downstream points on the Columbia also passed through Robson. Here the C&KSN's sternwheelers met the trains of the Columbia and Kootenay Railway. In the upper photo, all three of the C&KSN's major vessels on the Columbia River route are docked as passengers, freight and mail are transferred. The *Lytton*, in the distance; the *Columbia*, in the middle; the *Kootenai*, in the foreground.
— NEELANDS BROS. PHOTO, PABC, 3771

The size of Robson belied its importance to the Kootenays. In this view of the town, from across the Columbia, the *Lytton* is at the wharf while the smaller *Illecillewaet* steams upstream.
— PAC, PA-51390

In 1892, Captain James W. Troup was appointed to manage the C&KSN. Although only 37, he was an experienced captain, talented designer and good administrator. This portrait is from 1873.
— OREGON HISTORICAL SOCIETY, 11235

Irving he had worked as master of the big and cantankerous sidewheeler *Yosemite* on the run from Victoria to New Westminster and also commanded the sternwheeler *William Irving* on the Fraser. For Mara he had been master of the steamers *Peerless* and *Spallumcheen*, operating on the Thompson River and on Kamloops and Shuswap lakes in 1884 and 1885 during construction of the Canadian Pacific Railway.

To both employers he proved himself highly competent. J. A. Mara wrote to him, "I have much pleasure in testifying that during the two seasons you have been on this line, you have given the utmost satisfaction to the Owners for your skill in successfully handling the *Peerless* in lower water than she had previously been run, for your strict attention to business, and the courtesy you have always shewn to the travelling public."

Troup had left Mara's employment to become superintendent with the Oregon Railway and Navigation Company steamer operations. Apparently Mara remembered the young man well and urged him to return to British Columbia. Troup did so and devoted the rest of his life to building the steamer services, first in the Kootenays and later on the Coast.

The task ahead for Troup was formidable: new vessels were required; the vagaries of weather, water levels and river channels had to be countered; traffic controlled; crews recruited; and the public satisfied. The services were still irregular. For example, that winter the Columbia had been blocked by ice and then low water had meant a long closure to navigation. Only the *Dispatch* and Captain Sanderson's *Marion* had been running. On Kootenay Lake, the *Nelson*'s services had been greatly restricted. She had not been operating down the West Arm nor upriver beyond the head of the lake towards Bonners Ferry. The job ahead for Troup was to be full of challenge.

To try to overcome some of the problems of low water navigation, Troup designed a new sternwheeler and the shipyard at Revelstoke was busy that fall building a replacement for the *Dispatch*, which had never been a particularly successful vessel. Since the major investment in the *Dispatch* was the engines and boiler, scrapping the makeshift catamaran hulls and cabin was not much of a loss. Her replacement was the small steamer *Illecillewaet*. She was designed, it was said, to "float on dew." Launched from the shipyard on October 30, she was ready for service that winter.

Like her predecessor the *Dispatch*, the *Illecillewaet* was anything but beautiful and was designed for freighting. Her hull was basically a flat-bottomed barge with a blunt bow, reinforced with railroad steel for ice-breaking. Cabin work, built of cedar "V-joint," was rudimentary. At a modest 98 gross tons, she was only 78 feet (23.8 m) long by 15 feet (4.5 m) in width and four feet (1.2 m) in depth. She was, in fact, little more than a self-propelled barge but aesthetic drawbacks did not in any way impair her functional abilities and she proved to be a very useful boat, particularly during low water

— *The Miner*, Nelson, July 30, 1892

— *The Miner*, Nelson, December 31, 1892

With the discovery of rich ore deposits inland from the Columbia near what is now Rossland, the town of Trail developed into an important trans-shipment point on the Columbia. Until railroad connections were completed to the north and south, the sternwheelers were the only economical and reliable means of transport to the district. The steamer at the landing is the *Illecillewaet*. — PABC, 10045

The S.S. Aberdeen
First of the CPR's Okanagan Sternwheelers

periods when others could not have operated. Moreover, it was beneficial to have a small boat available for services that would not pay the expenses of a larger steamer with a bigger crew and higher operating costs.

Railway construction, directly affecting the sternwheelers, was also carried out in 1893 when the CPR built a branch line south from Revelstoke along the eastern bank of the Columbia to a point called Wigwam 17 miles (27.5 km) downstream. The purpose of the line was to bypass part of the shallow section of the river above the head of Upper Arrow Lake, facilitating the steamer service to the south. The branch was extended three years later to Arrowhead, eliminating the need for the steamers to navigate up the river beyond the lake. After the Arrow Lake Branch was completed by the CPR in 1896, the only time a sternwheeler was required to steam up to Revelstoke was if the branch line was temporarily closed for some reason.

West of the Kootenays, in the Okanagan Valley, the Canadian Pacific Railway also had been pushing southwards. There, it seized the opportunity to provide its own steamer service from the head of Okanagan Lake to the rich lands to the south. In the Okanagan, if not in the Kootenays, the CPR planned to provide, and therefore control, its own connecting service.

For a man of the land, anxious to farm or raise cattle, the sight of the Okanagan Valley with its rich alluvial bottomlands and benches must have been a welcome change indeed from the stark and inhospitable beauty of the mountains that dominate so much of the British Columbia landscape.

The main line of the Canadian Pacific Railway did not penetrate the Okanagan; it passed about 50 miles (80 km) to the north along Shuswap Lake and the South Thompson River. It was logical, however, that a branch line should be built southwards to tap this rich valley and provide an outlet for the produce of the land that seemed to await settlement and cultivation. The Railway was anxious to see such areas develop as quickly as possible. Hundreds of miles of thinly populated territory along the main line produced little revenue and consequently the development of branch lines or connecting steamboat services was of paramount importance to the future of the CPR and, it could be said, to Western Canada.

In 1886, a charter was granted to the Shuswap and Okanagan Railway to build a rail line from Sicamous Narrows on the CPR main line to Okanagan Lake. The route was to follow the shores of Mara Lake and the Shuswap River in a southwesterly direction, past Swan Lake to the head of Okanagan Lake near what is now the city of Vernon.

In 1890, the CPR reached an agreement to lease the line on its completion and in this way acquired the charter for a branch line that was to prove not only lucrative for the Com-

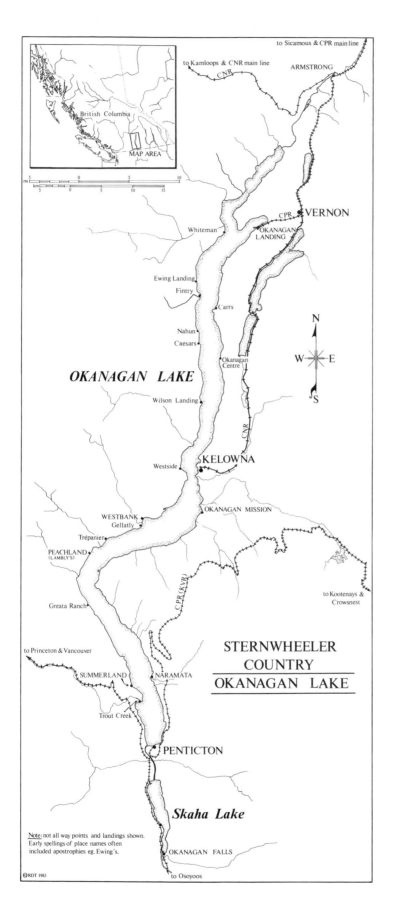

to Sicamous & CPR main line

to Kamloops & CNR main line

ARMSTRONG

CNR

British Columbia

MAP AREA

mi 5   0   5   10
km 5   0   10   15

CPR   VERNON

Whiteman   OKANAGAN LANDING

Ewing Landing
Fintry

Carrs

Nahun
Caesars

OKANAGAN LAKE

Okanagan Centre

N
W E
S

Wilson Landing

CNR

Westside   KELOWNA

OKANAGAN MISSION

WESTBANK
Gellatly

Trépanier

PEACHLAND
(LAMBLY'S)

CPR (KVR)

to Kootenays & Crowsnest

Greata Ranch

to Princeton & Vancouver

STERNWHEELER
COUNTRY
OKANAGAN LAKE

SUMMERLAND   NARAMATA

Trout Creek

PENTICTON

Skaha Lake

Note: not all way points and landings shown.
Early spellings of place names often
included apostrophes eg. Ewing's.

OKANAGAN FALLS

©RDT 1983

to Osoyoos

The launch of the Canadian Pacific Railway's steamer *Aberdeen* at Okanagan Landing on May 22, 1893 was a cause for considerable celebration. She was a first-class vessel and the farmers, settlers and merchants of the Okanagan Valley had cause to be pleased. For the first time a large, modern steamer would be available to connect communities all along Okanagan Lake with the rail head of the CPR at Okanagan Landing.

— PABC, 2180

Captain D. T. Shorts was one of the pioneers of steamboating on Okanagan Lake. — ERIC SISMEY

pany but particularly important to the settlement of the Okanagan. The line was completed as far as Okanagan Landing in June 1892, opening up the entire length of Okanagan Lake to direct access via steamer to the Canadian Pacific.

Before the arrival of the CPR at Okanagan Landing — and the construction of the Canadian Pacific's first sternwheeler — rudimentary service had been provided on Okanagan Lake by various individuals. Typically, the operations were small, undercapitalized, and decidedly unreliable. They were certainly not the transportation linkages needed to promote and maintain the development of the region as an agricultural area. Prominent among the early operators was Captain D. T. Shorts, a persistent and enterprising individual, who, at least initially, also had a strong back. He began his transportation business in the Okanagan with the 22-foot (6.7-m) boat *Ruth Shorts*. This vessel was rowed or sailed by Captain Shorts down Okanagan Lake as business warranted with a return trip taking perhaps nine days. In 1886, with some financial backing, he acquired a kerosene-burning vessel, the *Mary Victoria Greenhow*, which was an improvement, except for the difficulty of obtaining sufficient kerosene to keep her running. Converted to burn wood, she was more versatile, but she herself burned later in the year. Captain Shorts persevered and the next year began operating the small steamer *Jubilee* which he ran with apparent success for two seasons until she sank through the ice during the thaw in the spring of 1889. More makeshift vessels followed. Using the machinery from the *Jubilee*, Captain Shorts powered his barge, christening it the *City of Vernon*. A small steamer, *Red Star,* unofficially renamed *Okanagan*, was resurrected from the Spallumcheen River by another entrepreneur and also operated after 1889 in competition with Captain Shorts. Raising more capital, Shorts then built the twin-screw steamer *Penticton*, a decided improvement over anything previously seen on Okanagan Lake. With this vessel, a reasonably reliable schedule could be maintained for the growing communities in the southern Okanagan. Settlement in the area was increasing, but it had lacked the impetus of any rich mineral strikes to cause a real boom. Still, the increase in travel anticipated with the completion of the branch line made it clear that a modern, reliable transportation service on Okanagan Lake would be an asset.

Work for the CPR on a modern sternwheel steamer to service Okanagan Lake began under the supervision of Edwin G. McKay early in 1893. It was based on designs of John F. Steffen of Portland, Oregon. Horace Campbell, also of Portland, designed the engines for the steamer although they were built by the British Columbia Iron Works in Vancouver. The boiler was fabricated at the Canadian Pacific's locomotive shops in Montreal and rated at 175 pounds per square inch (1,200 kp) operating pressure.

23

In design and construction, the new vessel, to be christened *Aberdeen*, was a typical Columbia River sternwheeler and could have been the product of one of the yards on the Lower Columbia. In *Lewis & Dryden's Marine History of the Pacific Northwest*, she was described as "the finest inland steamer set afloat in the Northwest in 1893 . . . and like everything else in connection with the equipment of [the CPR], is up to date in every particular."

The launch of the *Aberdeen* on May 22, 1893, was a cause for celebration by people from all the surrounding communities. The ceremonies took place early in the afternoon and a large crowd was on hand to witness the event. Some took the train from Vernon, while others chose to walk to the shipyard at Okanagan Landing. The launch was flawless and amid the cheers of the crowd, the *Aberdeen* slid down the ways. *The Vernon News* headlined the story "Afloat on the Briney" in typically enthusiastic prose, despite the fact, or perhaps because of it, that there was far more champagne in evidence than salt water.

The *Aberdeen* was very similar to the *Nelson* in overall layout, although her pilothouse was placed further aft. She measured 146.2 feet (44.6 m) by 29.9 feet (9.1 m) and her depth of hold was 6.8 feet (2.1 m). Her gross tonnage was 544 — 48 tons larger than the *Nelson*. She was licensed to carry a maximum of 250 passengers and her main freight deck could accommodate 200 tons (180 tonnes) of cargo.

Her accommodations were a vast improvement over anything afloat on Okanagan Lake and were typical of first-class vessels of the period. The main deck was devoted primarily to the boiler, machinery, crews' accommodations (for eight) and freight. The saloon deck was reached by the standard staircases leading up from the bow at the front of the freight deck. Forward was the smoking room, with large windows providing fine views of the passing scenery. Immediately aft was the purser's office and a spare room. The dining saloon was centrally located with staterooms along both sides. The 11 staterooms, the stewardess' room, a pantry with dumb waiter, and the ladies' toilet were all located along the outside of the saloon deck. Aft was the ladies' cabin. At the time of her launch, work on the cabins had not been completed, and carpenters and painters were busy doing the finishing work before she entered regular service. However, the final touches of this work could not be done until the following year; the woodwork had to be allowed to shrink fully before the last coat of paint and gilt stripping were applied. Spacious, sheltered open-deck areas were provided both forward and aft on the saloon deck so that passengers could enjoy the fine weather typical of the Okanagan Valley from spring through the fall. Officers' accommodations were provided behind the pilothouse. Captain J. Foster, former mate of the coastal liner *Islander*, was given command of the *Aberdeen* and R. Wil-

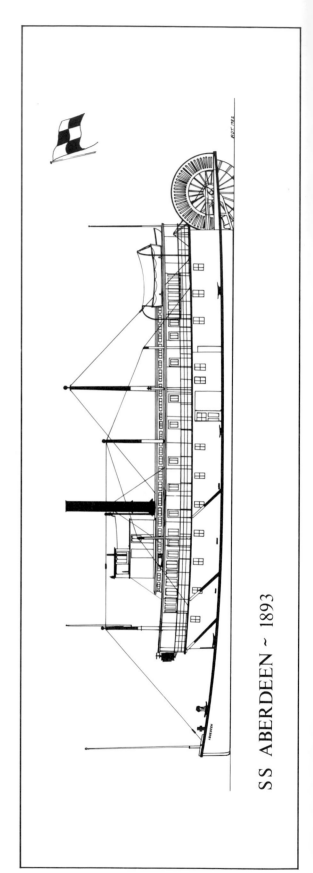

SS ABERDEEN ~ 1893

The *Aberdeen* may not have been as graceful or as elegant as some of the later steamers to be built for service on Okanagan Lake, but her importance to the communities throughout the district was great. Even though she was a bit boxy in appearance, her picturesque qualities were undeniable. — VERNON BOARD OF MUSEUM AND ARCHIVES

Penticton, at the southern end of Okanagan Lake, became the centre for a rich agricultural area and a trans-shipment point for the southern end of the valley as far as the United States border. Before the completion of the Kettle Valley Railway to Penticton in 1914, the sternwheelers and tugs and barges were the main means of communication and transport. Here, the *Aberdeen* is docked at Penticton about 1900.

— VERNON BOARD OF MUSEUM AND ARCHIVES

Okanagan Landing, just west of Vernon, at the head of Okanagan Lake, was chosen by the CPR as the terminal for steamers operating to the south. It became the site of a shipyard, transfer barge slip and a fairly large railway yard for handling the traffic to and from the Okanagan Valley. Views in later chapters show the ultimate development of the facilities but in this scene, recorded soon after the *Aberdeen* was placed in service, the terminal is still quite modest in size.

— PABC, 41045

1893-1894: Competition, Calamity and Construction in the Kootenays

liams was first mate. H. Fawcett was purser while W. B. Couson was chief engineer.

The construction of any vessel of this size resulted in work for many local businesses, particularly those supplying mouldings, lumber and fittings. Finishing lumber products, for example, were milled at Armstrong by Hammel and McCloud, and many local men were employed at the yard during the peak of activity prior to her launch.

With the *Aberdeen* working on Okanagan Lake, the quality of service for residents was dramatically improved. Captain Shorts ran the steamer *Lucy* (formerly *Okanagan*) briefly before selling her to work on Kootenay Lake. He had previously sold the *Penticton*, which had been withdrawn by 1894. Thus, the *Aberdeen* had a virtual monopoly on the passenger trade on Okanagan Lake; there were no comparable vessels to compete with her. The small, privately-owned steamer *Fairview* was built in 1894 and operated on the Okanagan River and occasionally on the Lake as well, but whatever competition she provided for the CPR was offset by her availability as a temporary relief vessel for the *Aberdeen*. The CPR steamer settled down to a routine averaging three trips a week down the lake. She maintained a steady, reliable service for the remainder of the decade. The basically placid, uneventful career of the *Aberdeen* was in marked contrast to the story, which follows, of the C&KSN's steamers in the Kootenays during the remaining years of the 1890's.

In the Kootenays in 1893, events were proceeding at a rapid pace. For the Columbia and Kootenay Steam Navigation Company, the year looked promising. The fleet was in better shape than ever before. On the Columbia River route, there were the new, first-class passenger steamers *Columbia* and *Lytton* and the just completed *Illecillewaet*, with the older, but serviceable *Kootenai* for freight. On Kootenay Lake, there was the new *Nelson*. Traffic was ample to keep all of the boats busy.

Even in their most optimistic moods, the directors of the C&KSN must have known that competition of a serious nature would eventually develop on some of their routes. On both the Columbia and Kootenay Lake routes there were small, independent steamers that took some of the business but they posed no serious threat and probably freed the C&KSN steamers from making some unprofitable runs. One such vessel was the small sternwheeler *City of Ainsworth*, built at its namesake city in 1892. More serious competition developed the next year when the Bonners Ferry and Kaslo Transportation Company was formed to place a large, first-class sternwheeler on Kootenay Lake. This vessel, the *State of Idaho*, was built at Bonners Ferry and entered service in May 1893. She was a fine-looking boat of just over 500 gross tons but her economic performance did not equal her appearance and the Company was soon in

27

financial difficulty. So bad did conditions become, that her owners had to keep her north of the border to avoid seizure by creditors. However, the *State of Idaho* continued in service between Kaslo and Nelson, competing with the C&KSN's *Nelson*.

The C&KSN had responded to the increasing competition on Kootenay Lake by purchasing the steamer *Spokane* which had been built in 1891 at Bonners Ferry to aid in the construction of the Great Northern Railway being built across northern Idaho and Washington towards the coast. Taken to Nelson, the steamer was refitted and lengthened before entering service in April 1893. With two fine steamers available, the C&KSN was in an excellent position to handle any trade or competition that came its way.

Competition from the *State of Idaho* did not last long as the unfortunate steamer ran aground near Ainsworth Hot Springs just before daybreak on November 10, 1893, and was severely damaged. She appeared to be in such bad condition that she was judged to be a total loss and was sold to one of her passengers for a reported $350.00. After considerable effort, she was raised and towed to the shipyard at Mirror Lake, just south of Kaslo where, over the next year, repairs were carried out for her new owners, known as the Alberta and B.C. Exploration Company.

The story of her grounding was carried in considerable detail in the local press. One report, published a week later in *The Miner* added a lighter note:

"It is reported of one of the crew of the wrecked steamer *State of Idaho* that when the steamer ran full steam ashore on the rocks recently breaking her bottom in the middle he was thrown out of his berth by the force of the concussion. Mistaking the concussion for one of the steamer's famous wharf landings, he crept back into his berth with the remark 'I wonder when that wheelman will be able to make a wharf comfortably.'"

If fate was hard on the owners of the *State of Idaho*, it was no kinder to the C&KSN over the next few years, for two of their vessels were involved in a series of crippling accidents. The first of these put the *Lytton* out of service on July 26, 1894 when, while moving a barge of railway construction materials near Nakusp, she was caught in a sudden summer storm and driven ashore. She remained safely afloat but had to be withdrawn for emergency repairs at the Nakusp shipyard. This sort of accident was more annoying than disastrous but worse was to come.

Bad luck seemed to be haunting the C&KSN that summer for on August 2, 1894, the *Columbia*, lying at a wood pile just north of the British Columbia-Washington border, was swept by fire. "The fire was discovered about 1:30 a.m.," reported *The Kootenay Mail*, "and in ten minutes the vessel was a total wreck." Fire had apparently started in the crews' quarters; it was believed that one of the deckhands had left a burning

The steamer *State of Idaho* provided the first serious competition for the C&KSN on Kootenay Lake when she entered service in 1893. She was built at Bonners Ferry, Idaho and was a fine vessel but her operations were trouble-plagued. She ran aground in November 1893 and was severely damaged although eventually returned to service as the *Alberta*. — PABC, 1609

Throughout the 1890's, the *Lytton* continued on the Columbia River route, proving to be one of the luckier vessels in the fleet. She is shown here transferring cargo. While the location is uncertain, it may be Wigwam, on the Columbia south of Revelstoke. To bypass the section of difficult river navigation between Revelstoke and the head of Upper Arrow Lake, the CPR built a branch line along the river. Initially the end of track was Wigwam but later, it was extended to Arrowhead. Navigation on the Columbia was marked by extremes of water levels. High water peaked in mid-June and fell slowly through the summer and fall. Low water from November to March made operations difficult and in the early years, service was suspended during the winter months. For steamers like the *Lytton*, river navigation between Revelstoke and Arrowhead was difficult and time consuming, as it was south of Robson to Northport. Between Robson and Northport, there were shallows and fast water runs that, for a steamer working upstream required warping or lining up. For better control going downstream, the paddlewheel could be run in reverse to slow the boat. Winter ice and snags were also persistent problems. Rapids included the Tincup and Kootenay, upstream from Trail, and the Rock Island and Telegraph, downriver towards Northport. On the Arrow Lakes, ice accumulated above and below the narrows connecting the two lakes, in the lower reaches of Lower Arrow Lake, and around Arrowhead and the northern parts of Upper Arrow Lake. The *Lytton* worked the Columbia River route for over a decade and survived all of these obstacles: a truly remarkable feat. — PABC, 236

pipe in his pocket when he had gone to bed. "The fire spread so rapidly," the report went on, "that those onboard had barely time to escape with such clothing as could be grabbed in their haste." Completely gutted, the hull sank in eight feet (2.5 m) of water. It was hoped that the boilers might be salvageable, but otherwise, the steamer was considered a total loss. She had been insured for only $15,000. Fortunately, no one was injured, but the C&KSN's finest vessel could not be easily replaced. That fall, the *Lytton* was once again in trouble, running aground above Arrowhead, and again had to be withdrawn briefly from service. Unfortunately, the loss of the *Columbia* was not the last disaster to strike the Company, but it was given a brief respite.

During this period, the C&KSN had been providing a reliable and profitable service on both of its major routes. The *Lytton* and *Columbia* had held the main passenger and freight service between Wigwam (where the branch line from Revelstoke ended) and Northport. This route also provided the vital connections to Nelson, via the Columbia and Kootenay Railway at Robson, and to Rossland at Trail Creek. The *Kootenai* and the *Illecillewaet* carried on a busy freighting business with the growing volume of railway construction (detailed later in this chapter) in the district. The *Illecillewaet* also provided a service around the north end of Upper Arrow Lake to Beaton and the trail heads leading into the Trout Lake mining district to the southeast. At the same time, on Kootenay Lake, the *Nelson* was making two trips a week to Bonners Ferry and three to Kaslo. The *Spokane* had been diverted to unexpected duty that year when she was used to replace the wharf at Kaslo which had been carried away by the record flood waters that spring. (Kaslo had had a devastating year in 1894, first suffering badly from a fire and then having the lower part of the town flooded out just a few months later.)

Despite the problems and setbacks, in the space of just five years, the C&KSN had become a vital link between the major railway systems, essential to many settlements and mining developments in the West Kootenays, and a profitable business. The fleet had grown from the very makeshift *Dispatch* to include several fine steamers, but more were needed.

The *Columbia* had to be replaced as quickly as possible. There was no alternative to new construction. It was clear as well that with a fleet of this size, a permanent shipyard staff was required to maintain the vessels, and to construct new steamers and barges. To build a new steamer to replace the *Columbia* and to oversee the shipyards at Nakusp and Nelson, Captain Troup hired the experienced team of Thomas J. Bulger and his sons, James M. Bulger and David T. Bulger, all of Portland.

Just as the C&KSN management had shown wisdom in hiring James Troup, so too did Troup show his judgement in recruiting the Bulger family. They were all skilled shipwrights and their talents were to be demonstrated in the construction of many fine vessels. In 1894, Tom Bulger was 67 years old, and he brought with him a great deal of practical experience. Born at St. Johns, Newfoundland in 1827, he grew up to learn the shipbuilding and sailing trades. In 1859 he had built his own ship which he sailed to California, only to see her wrecked nearly in sight of the Golden Gate. He moved north to Portland and from then until 1894 he was engaged exclusively in building river steamers and deep-sea vessels on the Columbia and also on Puget Sound. His sons also learned the trades well and when Tom Bulger retired in 1903 and returned to Portland, they remained in British Columbia, James as superintendent of the Nelson shipyards, and David as foreman of the yards at Nakusp.

Troup and the Bulgers began work that winter on the design of a new steamer to replace the unfortunate *Columbia*. The new vessel was to be the finest steamer yet seen in the Kootenays and her construction would mark both the high standard of boats the C&KSN intended to maintain as well as reflecting the rapid developments that had occurred in steamboating in the Kootenays in less than a decade.

While steamboating continued at a busy pace during the early 1890's, further developments were occurring in railroad construction in the Kootenays. The details of the corporate and political dealings behind the advent of these lines were of great importance to the region in general and the C&KSN in particular. The first of these was Daniel Corbin's Nelson and Fort Sheppard (N&FS), which was built during 1893, connecting the Spokane Falls and Northern with Nelson via a twisting, mountain-climbing route that eliminated any water connections and gave a direct rail link with Spokane. As far as the C&KSN was concerned, this line was not a disadvantage and the extra traffic the railway generated was welcome. The CPR, unhappy with competition for the trade to and from Nelson, barred access of the N&FS to Nelson. The CPR had received exclusive access to the Nelson waterfront from the late Premier, John Robson, so Corbin had to content himself with ending his tracks near the city limits.

A connecting service with the C&KSN was established soon after the railway's completion at Five Mile Point where the N&FS reached the shore of Kootenay Lake. Construction of the railway proceeded throughout 1893 and the line was completed late in December 1893 with just days to spare in meeting the terms of its charter. Late completion could have resulted in a loss of land grants and subsidy.

Meanwhile, charters had been granted for two other railway projects that were to affect the C&KSN in quite different ways. One, the Nakusp and Slocan Railway (N&S), was planned to connect Nakusp with the new ore discoveries in the Slocan Valley, another long, narrow valley about midway between the Arrow Lakes and Kootenay Lake. Very rich deposits of silver-copper ore were discovered there and several

The Nelson and Fort Sheppard Railway reached the shore of Kootenay Lake at Five Mile Point where a steamer landing was constructed. There, the Columbia and Kootenay Steam Navigation's sternwheelers connected with the trains to and from Spokane. The completion of the railway was seen by many people as a positive step for the Kootenays but the line ran south to the United States and better Canadian routes into southeastern British Columbia were still desired. Docking arrangements were not elaborate as the *Nelson* meets a N&FS train at Five Mile in this scene from the mid-1890's. — PABC, 642

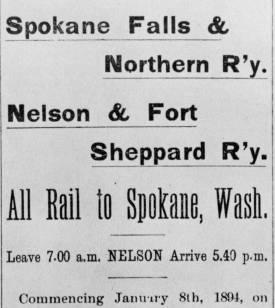

— *The Miner*, Nelson, December 8, 1893

One Step Forward and Three Steps Back: 1895

communities had sprung up, almost overnight, it seemed. These included Silverton and New Denver on Slocan Lake itself, and Sandon, several miles inland.

The Nakusp and Slocan Railway was chartered in 1893 and construction was begun from Nakusp, resulting in heavy traffic for the sternwheelers bringing in rail and other materials. Work continued at a slow pace throughout 1894 and 1895; the line opened for traffic between Nakusp and Sandon on December 12, 1895. Like the Columbia and Kootenay Railway, this new branch line also was leased by the CPR so that the giant railway company was gradually extending its influence into the mining districts of the Kootenays.

By this time, the rich mines of the Slocan Valley had also attracted other interests and in April 1892, a charter had been granted to the Kaslo and Slocan Railway Company (K&S), to build a line, as the name implies, from Kaslo on Kootenay Lake westward to the Slocan Valley. However, work did not begin until 1894 when, with the charter amended to permit the construction of a three-foot (0.9 m) gauge line, work began. The line was backed financially by the Great Northern Railway, which had seen in this venture an opening to the rich Slocan mining district. The little line twisted and climbed its way to Sandon over a precarious route that would have made an engineer from the legendary Rio Grande Southern of Colorado feel at home, if not comfortable. The 29-mile (47-km) long line reached the bonanza town of Sandon and was opened for traffic on November 20, 1895. The combination of the K&S and the steamers operating on Kootenay Lake down to the rail head at Bonners Ferry gave the Great Northern reasonably direct access to the heart of the Kootenay mining district.

If 1894, with the loss of the *Columbia*, had been a bad year for the Columbia and Kootenay Steam Navigation Company, 1895 was worse. On a positive note, construction got underway at Nakusp on a replacement for the *Columbia*, and traffic in general was brisk. The economic depression that had hit North America in 1893 following the repeal of the Silver Purchase Act by the United States government had certainly had an adverse effect on the economy of the Kootenays, but the district had come through the depression reasonably unscathed. Railway construction had not slowed and mining development had continued around Kootenay Lake, in the Slocan, and at Rossland. The outlook was bright for the coming years and the immediate need of the C&KSN was more tonnage.

While work was progressing on the new steamer at Nakusp, the *Spokane* was being readied for service after being used as a temporary wharf at Kaslo. On March 21, 1895, for unexplained reasons, fire broke out and quickly spread throughout the boat. Prompt action by the crew and the steamer *City*

Kaslo was one of the major centres on Kootenay Lake in the 1890's and an important stop for the sternwheelers. Like many frontier towns, Kaslo suffered an extensive fire but before the town had recovered from the damage, the high water of 1894 flooded the lower sections of the business district. With water still flooding the streets, the *Nelson* is able to ease into shore well above her usual docking place. A photographer is about to record the flood damage on his plate camera.
— MOYIE MUSEUM

The *Spokane* was the second large steamer acquired by the C&KSN for service on Kootenay Lake. She had been built to carry supplies for construction work on the Great Northern Railway and after lengthening was a welcome addition to the C&KSN's fleet. For a time she was used as a floating dock at Kaslo. The *Nelson* is shown getting under way in the background.
— PAC, PA-16037

While at Kaslo being readied to return to service, the *Spokane* caught fire on March 21, 1895. The fire spread throughout her cabins and only the hull could be saved. The other steamer is the *City of Ainsworth*, whose crew tried to help save the ill-fated steamer. — PABC, 40571

of Ainsworth saved the vessel from sinking but only the hull could be saved. Once again, fire had claimed one of the C&KSN's vessels; two had been lost in less than a year.

Not long after, in May, the *State of Idaho*, renamed the *Alberta*, was finally returned to service. Now under the ownership of the newly-formed International Navigation and Trading Company, she was capable of providing serious competition to the C&KSN's *Nelson* for the important trade on Kootenay Lake. The combination of the completion of the Kaslo and Slocan Railway and the return of the *Alberta* meant that traffic from the Slocan could be handled all the way to Bonners Ferry without any use of C&KSN steamers at all.

Meanwhile, construction on the new steamer had been proceeding rapidly at the Nakusp shipyard. While an enlarged version of the *Columbia* might have kept pace with the traffic for a time, Captain Troup had more ambitious plans. He wanted something better. Since both the freight and the passenger businesses were booming, Troup, in a characteristic action, decided to build a new steamer that would surpass in both size and quality any vessel yet seen on the Upper Columbia River.

Captain James W. Troup was not one for taking half measures in steamship design although he was far from being an impractical man. Indeed, his career was highlighted by a succession of ships that demonstrated his instinctive ability to understand the qualities needed in steamships to best capitalize on the traffic conditions. His vessel designs tended towards the fast and the elegant although there were of course some utilitarian exceptions. They also developed reputations for good, reliable performance and long service lives. The only major vessel that would seem to be an exception to this generalization was the coastal liner *Victorian*, built at Portland in 1891. This elegant wooden-hulled coastal liner had engines that were simply too powerful for her wooden hull, causing vibration, damage and excessive fuel consumption. Over the years she went through a succession of owners, never finding, it appears, a profitable niche in west coast shipping. Captain Troup also learned from his mistakes for none of his later vessels have been described as anything but successful.

The new steamer designed for the Arrow Lakes route was a dramatic development over any other vessels in the Columbia and Kootenay fleet. Prior to 1895, the *Columbia*, of 534 gross tons, was the largest vessel on the Arrow Lakes, while the *Spokane*, of just under 400 tons, had been largest on Kootenay Lake. At 1,083 gross tons, the new vessel was more than double the size of any other steamer in the Company's service. Not only was she larger in tonnage, but she was also better equipped and more luxuriously appointed throughout. She had two passenger decks above the freight and machinery deck providing much greater and more luxurious accommodations. The saloon deck itself had 17 staterooms, a parlour measuring

18 x 44 feet (5.5 x 13.4 m), a dining room 17 x 38 feet (5.2 x 11.6 m) and a smoking room 17 x 34 feet (5.2 x 10.4 m). More staterooms were located above the saloon deck on the cabin, or "Texas" deck, although the central part of the Texas deck was kept open and fitted with balconies on either side giving the central dining room, immediately below, a deckhead height of 17 feet (5.2 m). A clerestory around the ceiling of the saloon provided extra lighting through coloured glass windows.

The main deck had room for 15 carloads of freight or approximately 300 tons (270 tonnes). Her two single cylinder engines had a bore of 20 inches (50.8 cm) and a stroke of 72 inches (182.9 cm). She was equipped with three steam pumps, a double steam capstan and a dynamo to provide electricity for the 130 incandescent lights on board. For night operations she had two searchlights and one boom light. These were useful when cargo was to be loaded and also to light the shoreline during landings or in navigating difficult parts of the river.

The steamer, which was launched on July 1, 1895 at Nakusp and christened, quite appropriately, the *Nakusp*, was 171.0 feet (52.1 m) long by 33.5 feet (10.2 m) in breadth and 6.3 feet (1.9 m) in depth. Her cabin work, although incomplete at the time of her launching, was carefully constructed and showed considerable care and expertise in its execution. Unfortunately, work on finishing her cabins was delayed when a fire at the Brunette mills at New Westminster destroyed the entire order of moulding work for the new vessel. Troup was forced to make an unexpected trip to the coast to make arrangements for replacing the lost materials.

The *Nakusp*, like the other C&KSN steamers, was painted white with a black funnel. The effect was attractive and pleasing. The sternwheeler reflected the talents of both Captain Troup and Tom Bulger, her builder. By late August 1895, the *Nakusp* was in service on the Columbia, in time to capture at least part of the summer trade.

Next, it was the old *Kootenai* whose luck ran out. On December 3, 1895, she ran hard aground near Bannock Point on Upper Arrow Lake and although she was floated off, was considered not worth repairing. While the loss of the *Kootenai* did not compare with the burning of either the *Columbia* or the *Spokane*, it was still a serious loss particularly when combined with the other losses to the fleet. By the end of the year, the tally stood at three ships lost for one replacement built. Moreover, there was now serious competition on Kootenay Lake.

The year still held one more card — the weather. In December the *Nakusp* was cut off when the narrows froze over, barring her way to Nakusp. While this in itself was not uncommon, tragedy occurred on January 3, 1896, when the small tug *Arrow*, which was trying to break a channel through the narrows, capsized, drowning her captain and engineer.

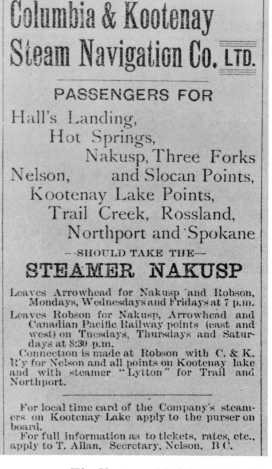

— *The Kootenay Mail*, March 6, 1897

The Magnificent Nakusp

While earlier vessels built for the Columbia and Kootenay Steam Navigation Company had been practical, utilitarian vessels, the *Nakusp* of 1895 was lavish. She was the largest steamer yet seen in the Kootenays and completely eclipsed her predecessors. In terms of gross tonnage, she was twice as large as any other steamer in the fleet. The upper photograph shows her under way on the Columbia with a large crowd on board. The pilot is clearly visible at her wheel. The scene below captures crew members loading cordwood for fuel in what was a time-consuming and laborious task. By the end of the decade, however, coal from the Crowsnest Pass coalfields was used as fuel on the steamers.
— PABC, 726, 22159 (J. J. THOMPSON)

The *Nakusp*'s dining room was the highlight of the steamer's interior and featured a double staircase leading to the balconies surrounding the central saloon. Electric lighting and clerestory windows kept the room bright and cheerful. — STEELE & CO., PABC, 62946

While the *Nakusp* was the queen of the fleet she was not excused from the mundane duties of carrying freight. Her freight deck could accommodate 15 carloads and she was also used, as shown in the photograph at right, to push freight barges. — PABC, 60017

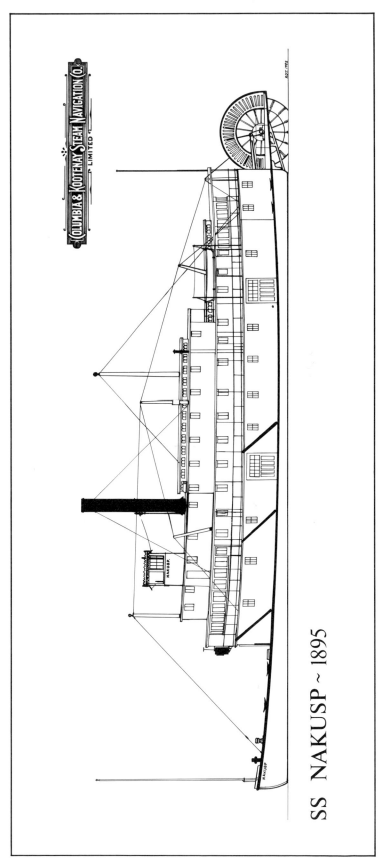

SS NAKUSP ~ 1895

The loss of the *Arrow* was hardly a propitious note on which to begin the new year, but fortunately 1896 was not to have the bad luck in store for the C&KSN that the previous year had.

With a now desperate need for new C&KSN vessels just to replace the recent losses, it was clear that 1896 would be a busy one for Thomas Bulger and his sons. A major vessel was required on each of the main routes, and with the completion of the Nakusp and Slocan Railway and the extension of the branch line from Revelstoke to Arrowhead, the CPR was anxious to move rail cars by transfer barge directly to Nakusp. This new service would require a tug and new barges. Moreover, in February 1896, a smelter was completed at Trail Creek creating more traffic, including shipments of coal, moving over the Columbia River route.

At the Nakusp shipyard, work was pushed to build a replacement for the *Kootenai*. The new boat, the *Trail*, was designed as a freighter with limited passenger accommodations. Her engines probably came from the *Kootenai* but she appears to have had a new boiler; Nelson's newspaper, *The Miner*, reported on April 11 that the *Nakusp* had brought one down from Arrowhead for the new sternwheeler being built at Nakusp. The report noted that: "J. McCain, in charge of the house work is making good progress. Chief Engineer Stephens and staff have a large portion of the machinery in place [and] the caulking will be completed this week . . . " She was launched on May 7, 1896, and was ready to begin freight service on June 11. While lacking the elegant interior and fittings of the passenger steamers, the *Trail* was nonetheless an attractive vessel. She was in many ways an enlarged and improved version of the *Kootenai* and was similar in overall appearance. The *Trail* measured 165 feet (50.3 m) long by 31 feet (9.5 m) in breadth and 5 feet (1.5 m) in depth. Her gross tonnage was 633, making her the biggest vessel in the fleet next to the *Nakusp*.

No sooner had the *Trail* been launched than work began on a large barge which was launched early in June. Construction then started on a second, and before the year was over a large tug, named the *Columbia*, had also been built. This vessel was the first and only screw-driven tug built for the C&KSN, but many others were to follow for the Canadian Pacific after it acquired the C&KSN fleet. The *Columbia* was 77 feet (23.5 m) long by 15 feet (4.6 m) in breadth and had a depth of 6 feet (1.8 m). At 50 tons, she was not a large vessel, but she was powerful and better able to handle the large railway transfer barges and freight barges than were the sternwheelers.

Meanwhile at the Nelson shipyard, another sternwheeler was taking shape. This vessel, which was named *Kokanee* at her launching on April 7, 1896, was a departure in design from the other sternwheelers in the fleet. She was quite small

1896: Rebuilding and Competition — the Kokanee *and the* International

With the completion of the Nakusp and Slocan Railway from the Columbia River to the Slocan Valley there was an increasing need to move freight between Nakusp and Arrowhead to the north. To provide for this growth, the C&KSN built the screw-driven tug *Columbia* at Nakusp in 1896. — PABC, 51868

The year 1896 saw the completion of the beautiful and speedy sternwheeler *Kokanee*. She was designed by Captain Troup and built at the C&KSN's Nelson shipyard for passenger and freight service on Kootenay Lake. Her hull was of the lake boat design, deeper and more rounded than the riverboat type designed for shallower waters. The upper photo shows her next to a railway transfer barge loaded with sacks of ore. Note how the bow has been enclosed with canvas, as a protection from the weather. In the lower photograph, the *Kokanee* is shown in more festive circumstances decorated with branches and flags. — PABC, 75819, 1477

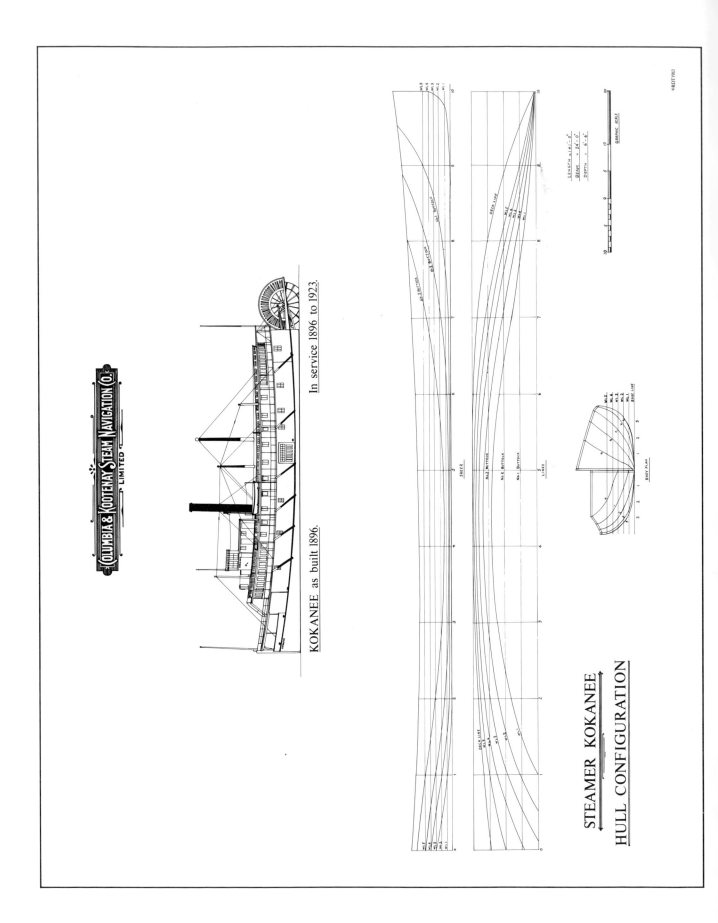

COLUMBIA & KOOTENAY STEAM NAVIGATION CO.
LIMITED

KOKANEE as built 1896.

In service 1896 to 1923.

STEAMER KOKANEE
HULL CONFIGURATION

The Nakusp shipyards completed work on the freight steamer *Trail* in 1896. She was built to replace the old *Kootenai* on the Columbia River route and was an important addition to the fleet as mining and railway development continued to provide heavy traffic for the sternwheelers. Captain Troup was sufficiently pleased with the design of the *Trail* to use it as the basis for several more very similar vessels built in 1898 for service on the Stikine River. Unfortunately, because of her utilitarian duties, photographs of the *Trail* are uncommon.

— PABC, 40373

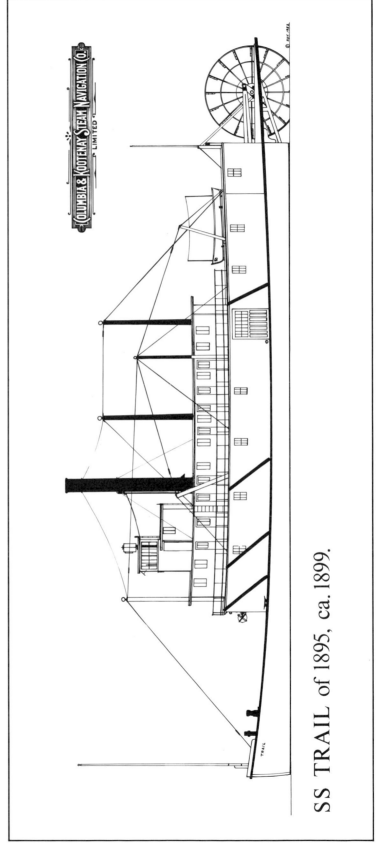

COLUMBIA & KOOTENAY STEAM NAVIGATION CO. LIMITED

SS TRAIL of 1895, ca. 1899.

The dining saloon of the *Kokanee* was centrally located with doors leading off both sides to passenger staterooms. The table service featured linen and silver in the best traditions of the era. The dining saloon of the *International*, the *Kokanee*'s rival, was somewhat unusual in being placed to one side of the boat and having large picture windows. This was an appealing design feature on routes as scenic as those on Kootenay Lake. — PABC, 737

Nelson grew quickly in the 1890's to become the major centre of the Kootenay Lake region. This scene from about 1896 shows both the *International* and the *Kokanee* at the steamer wharf with the city covering the lower slopes of the surrounding hills. — PABC, 5245

The *Alberta*, formerly the *State of Idaho*, was returned to service on Kootenay Lake in 1895 and until the completion of the *International* was the International Navigation and Trading Company's only steamer. She was a useful and well-built sternwheeler and comparable to the *Nelson* but she was soon outperformed by the C&KSN's new *Kokanee* and the IN&T's *International*. — PABC, 95566

compared to the *Nakusp* and at 348 gross tons measured 143 x 25 x 6 feet (43.6 x 7.6 x 1.8 m). She had the deeper, more rounded, lakeboat hull form and she was fast.

"It is doubtful if a more graceful or better appointed boat can be found in British Columbia," commented *The Miner*. "She was designed by Captain Troup and built under the supervision of Thomas J. Bulger, of Portland, John McCain acted as foreman joiner, and the painting and interior decorations were under the care of A. L. Johnson."

On May 2, 1896, the *Kokanee* sailed on her trial trip carrying a large crowd of excursionists on an extended run to the major points on Kootenay Lake. Five days later, she had a chance to show her speed. Leaving Kaslo one hour after her rival, the *Alberta*, the new steamer worked up to speed and beat the *Alberta* to Nelson by ten minutes. The *Kokanee*'s time, including stops at both Ainsworth and Pilot Bay, was only two hours and fifty-five minutes.

The International Navigation and Trading Company was by no means ready to give up without a good fight and had itself ordered a new steamer which it hoped would successfully challenge the *Kokanee*. This new sternwheeler was built at the Mirror Lake shipyard just south of Kaslo. The frames arrived at Mirror Lake early in April and construction started soon afterwards. Work progressed throughout the summer and the new boat was ready for her trials late in October 1896. Named the *International*, she was an attractive vessel, quite different in appearance from the *Kokanee*, and somewhat larger. She measured 160 feet, 4 inches (48.9 m) in length, nearly 20 feet (6.1 m) longer than the *Kokanee* while being only 9 inches (23 cm) wider. Her gross tonnage was 525.

From the start, it seemed that the *Kokanee* and *International* were destined to be rivals. The *Kokanee* was Nelson's pride, a product of the local shipyard, and the C&KSN was headquartered there. Similarly, the *International* was the favourite in Kaslo, the rival city for prominence in Kootenay.

Both were fine steamers. Certainly little had been spared in the construction of the *International* and she was an attractive and elegant vessel. She was fitted with new engines from the Iowa Iron Works, and the boiler was supplied by John Inglis of Toronto. Her hull was described as clean cut and modern. *The Kootenaian* of Kaslo described her accommodations in its edition of November 21, 1896:

"In the forward room are the offices of the purser, a lavatory and neatly fitted writing room, for the use of passengers. The central compartment is the general sitting room and is finished in oak, tipped with gold. The windows are of the Pullman car pattern and mirrors are fitted into intervening spaces. The after room is arranged on one side for a dining room with convenient pantry and on the opposite side are a number of staterooms comfortably furnished and roomy. The entire upper deck of the boat presents many new points of construction in the way of steamboat architecture and is quite up to date."

38 Mon May 15 1899
Engine room S.S. International
Kaslo to Nelson & return

Arrive	Left	Time Running	Time at Ldg	Landings	Remarks
Am	6·05			Kaslo	Bright Morni...
6·18	6·25	·13	·07	Shipyard	fresh, Co...
6·57	7·01	·32	·04	Woodbury	
7·14	7·18	·13	·04	Ainsworth	
7·46	7·50	·28	·04	Pilot Bay	
8·04	8·07	·14	·03	Balfour	
8·19	8·59	·12	·40	Ralstons	7½ Cords Wood
9·06	9·09	·07	·03	Wests Landing	Weather fin...
9·51	9·55	·42	·04	Six Mile Pt	
9·59	10·10	·04	·11	Five Mile Pt	
10·33	10·43	·23	·10	Nelson	
11·05	2·37	·22	3·32	Five Mile Pt	
2·58		·21		Nelson	
				Return Trip	
Pm	4·31		1·33	Nelson	
4·53	5·14	·22	·21	Five Mile Pt	
6·22	6·25	1·08	·03	Balfour	
6·41	6·45	·16	·04	Pilot Bay	berry
7·12	7·17	·27	·05	Ainsworth	
8·13		·56		Kaslo	

Total Wood taken 7½ Cords
Supplies etc
1 Spool Copper Wire 1/16"
Byns & Co
Nelson

44

The International Navigation and Trading
Company's time card taking effect on
February 1, 1897. Note the 5:30 a.m. departure
time from Kaslo.

The city of Kaslo, top left, on a sheltered bay on
the northwest shore of Kootenay Lake was the
home port for the *International* and also the
eastern terminus of the Kaslo and Slocan
Railway. — MOYIE MUSEUM

The *International*, middle left, at the KR&N
(which took over the IN&T) wharf at Kaslo. A
large excursion crowd is boarding the steamer.
—PABC, 1553

The small sternwheeler *City of Ainsworth*, lower
left, operated on Kootenay Lake from
1892 until she foundered in 1898. She was owned
by the Nelson and Lardo Steam Navigation
Company. — PABC, 68994

The engine room log of the *International*,
recorded by Chief Engineer James Donaldson,
shows a typical run from Kaslo to Nelson and
return. — GEORGE DONALDSON COLLECTION

The Miner of the same date noted one more point of significance, namely that, "The forward cabin or smoking room is
most comfortable and in here may be found the cup that
cheers..." *The Miner* also reported that the new vessel
seemed pretty well matched with the *Kokanee* and commented, "In build the *International* looks somewhat like the
Kokanee but draws only 3.5 feet [1.07 m] while the latter
draws 4 feet [1.22 m]. This is said to be due to the fact that
the *Kokanee* is double frame while the *International* has but
a single frame."

While the accommodations of the two steamers were comparable, the real test seemed to be in which was the faster. As
the *International* neared completion, speculation had grown.
"All sorts of opinions are advanced," noted *The Kootenaian*,
"on the respective merits of the boats. The two ships have the
same boiler capacity, and while the new boat's engines have
one inch less stroke, they are described by engineers as being
vastly superior to those of the *Kokanee*, besides which her
wheel is larger by about three feet..."

How often the two boats raced is difficult to say, but at
least two encounters were reported by the papers. *The Miner*
reported late in November that, "While the *International* was
coming to Nelson... the *Kokanee* came abreast of her at Five
Mile Point and when the dock was reached, the latter was
some distance in the lead. This, however is not taken as a test
as the *International* was not forced to its greatest speed."

A few weeks later, the December 12 issue of *The Kootenaian* noted that "in a short race yesterday morning in the
vicinity of Nelson, the steamer *International* outran the *Kokanee* by two lengths. The broom may now be shifted to another
masthead..."

In the long run, however, it appears to have been the *Kokanee* that, rightly or wrongly, retained the reputation as the
"flyer." In later years, after bigger and faster boats had made
their appearance on Kootenay Lake, the *Kokanee* still held
her own. It may have been simply that the *Kokanee* looked
like the faster boat because her design imparted a feeling of
speed.

As 1896 drew to a close, with steamboat races prominent in
people's minds, the Columbia and Kootenay Steam Navigation Company would soon cease to exist; an agreement had
been reached with the Canadian Pacific Railway over the sale
of the C&KSN's entire operations in the Kootenays. The CPR
was anxious to secure and expand its position in the district
and acquiring the C&KSN's holdings was the simplest way.

Race between Rivals — The *International* and the *Kokanee*.
The International Navigation and Trading Company's powerful
sternwheeler *International* and the Columbia and Kootenay
Steam Navigation Company's speedy *Kokanee* were both
completed in 1896 and they were born rivals. While they differed
in design and styling, they were fairly evenly matched and which
boat ultimately was the fastest is difficult to establish clearly.

They raced on several occasions in the fall of 1896 without a clear winner apparently being recognized. But perhaps in the end, the question of speed was secondary to the spirited competition that surrounded the races. Before long, both boats were overshadowed by larger, faster vessels but for a few short years the *International* and *Kokanee* were the finest steamers on Kootenay Lake. The *Kokanee* retained a reputation for speed and survived long after the 1909 retirement of the *International*. Her hull waterlogged and her services no longer needed, the *Kokanee* was stripped of useful parts in 1923 and her hulk sold for use as a hunting and fishing lodge. — MOYIE MUSEUM

The magnificent sternwheeler *Kootenay* was the first vessel to join the Canadian Pacific's fleet of riverboats following its purchase of the Columbia and Kootenay Steam Navigation Company. She was a slightly enlarged version of the *Nakusp* and with the two vessels available, the CPR was able to provide a daily service on the Arrow Lakes route when traffic warranted. R. H. Trueman exposed this glass plate portrait of the *Kootenay* just off Arrowhead. — VCA

CHAPTER II

CPR STEAMBOATS
IN THE KOOTENAYS

*The CPR Buys the
Columbia and Kootenay
Steam Navigation Company*

IN 1897, THE Canadian Pacific Railway purchased the entire assets of the comparatively tiny, but vital, Columbia and Kootenay Steam Navigation Company (C&KSN) to give itself complete control over the steamer connections between its main line railway and its Kootenay branch lines. This was a logical extension of CP's transcontinental railway system.

The purchase included the C&KSN's entire fleet and all related shipyards and other facilities on the Arrow and Kootenay lakes. At that time, the fleet comprised the following vessels: on the busy Columbia River route, the tug *Columbia* and the sternwheelers *Illecillewaet, Lytton, Nakusp* and *Trail*; and on Kootenay Lake, the sternwheelers *Nelson* and *Kokanee*. In addition, there were 10 barges for freight.

It appears that by the time the C&KSN sold out to the CPR, Mara, Barnard and Irving had bought out Hume and Sanderson, the original founders. The sale to the CPR was undoubtedly profitable to the C&KSN and also eliminated the possibility of the CPR building its own vessels for Columbia River and Kootenay Lake service. The purchase took effect on February 1, 1897 and with that move, CP's steamer operations grew overnight from the *Aberdeen* on Okanagan Lake to an impressive and modern fleet of steamers operating on the three major water routes in southeastern British Columbia. The CPR was at last its own master in controlling these vital water routes to the rich mining districts of the Kootenays.

The sale had been under negotiation in 1896 and in the Canadian Pacific's Annual Report for the year the purchase was announced. The report noted:

"The Company has been at a great disadvantage in reaching the traffic in the mining districts of Southern British Columbia in having to depend upon steamboat connections controlled by other parties. The rapid growth of the traffic, the high rates exacted, and the inadequate service performed, led your Directors recently to negotiate for the purchase of the entire property of the Columbia and Kootenay Navigation Company consisting of seven steamboats, ten barges, mechanical shops, office buildings, water-houses, etc., and to put under contract for immediate construction three additional steamers for service on the Arrow and Slocan Lakes. You will be asked to approve the expenditure of $280,000 for the boats purchased and under contract, and for a tug-boat and barges that will probably be required.

"In the event of the establishment of direct rail connections with the mining districts, both for the east and the west, this steamboat property will still have ample occupation, for the extraordinary system of navigable waters in Southern British Columbia afford for many years to come the most feasible means of connection with many of the important mining sections."

The very nature of the topography of the Kootenays almost guaranteed the longevity of the steamboat operations since the cost of railway construction to some parts of the region would have been astronomical. The C&KSN's boats formed a vital link and the CPR could not and would not do without it.

Few would argue that the C&KSN had not gone after the available business vigorously or that it had not built up an impressive fleet of vessels in the seven years since its service began. However, the Canadian Pacific had even greater plans for their operations in the Kootenays. Prompting the CPR was the booming trade in the area, the expansion of the interests of Daniel Corbin's railroads centred at Spokane and the growing influence of F. Augustus Heinze, a tough American mining promoter who had built a smelter at Trail. Topography suggested a natural flow of commerce to the south focusing on the rapidly growing transportation business and industrial centre of Spokane. Couched in the careful language of directors' reports to stockholders, the CPR's 1896 Annual Report emphasized the perceived threat to the Canadian Pacific:

"But even with these important additions to its facilities for handling the traffic of the mining districts, your company will continue at a disadvantage in competing with the American lines (which have already reached Nelson, Rossland and other important centres in these districts) until it shall have direct railway connections of its own. Until then, the greater part of the mining traffic will be beyond its reach, and will continue to be as at present, carried by the American lines southward.

"Your Directors are strongly of the opinion that any delay in securing your interests in that direction will be extremely dangerous — that unless your Company occupies the ground, others will, the demand for shipping and travelling being most urgent. The Directors feel that they cannot too strongly urge the immediate construction of a line from Lethbridge to a connection with your Columbia and Kootenay Railway at Nelson, a distance of 325 miles [523 km] and anticipating your approval they have already taken steps towards commencement of the work on the opening of the spring."

The construction of the railway line through the Crowsnest Pass into southern British Columbia, which this report announced, was to have a profound effect on the history and development of the province in general and, inescapably, the Company's sternwheelers. In fact, the extension of the railway to Nelson was not completed for over 30 years. In the interim, sternwheelers and tugs and barges were used to close the final gap in the railway route — from the southern end of Kootenay Lake along the western shore to the end of track east of Nelson. The story of this aspect of the Lake and River Service is developed in later sections of this book.

Rivalry and Canadian Pacific Expansion in the Kootenays

The Canadian Pacific Railway's interest in the Kootenays had matured slowly and had been prompted by both competition and the incredibly rich mining developments around Rossland, Trail, Nelson, and in the Slocan. The mines at Rossland were proving to be unbelievably rich, with output and dividends increasing substantially. The Le Roi mine, treasure of the Rossland camp, and other rich claims were producing fortunes in silver-copper-gold ores. In 1894 production from the Rossland mines had been a modest 1,856 tons (1,684 tonnes), valued at $75,510. The next year production had jumped approximately ten times, and for 1897, the year the CPR bought out the C&KSN, 68,804 tons (62,415 tonnes) of ore had been mined, valued at $2,097,280. In 1898, it rose still higher to 111,282 tons (100,953 tonnes) worth $2,470,811.

A key to successful mining of the ores was access to smelters and in February 1896, F. Augustus Heinze had opened his smelter at Trail Creek Landing on the Columbia. Later that year, Heinze also completed the narrow gauge Columbia and Western Railway (known during its construction as the Trail Creek Tramway) to connect the Rossland mines with his smelter. Twisting, turning and switchbacking over grades in excess of four percent, the line climbed from the Columbia River up to the mountainside mines of Rossland. The rickety little line looked too fragile and makeshift to function properly, but it did, and at a profit.

Heinze had ambitious plans for the district, including expansion of his smelter and additions to his railway. In 1897, he extended the railway from Trail up the west bank of the Columbia River to a point called Robson West, or West Robson, opposite the CPR's docks and the Columbia and Kootenay Railway at Robson. This new line was standard gauge and Heinze had plans and a provincial charter in hand to extend it west towards the Boundary district of Grand Forks and eventually to the Okanagan. Capital was required, however, and Heinze had trouble raising it.

Meanwhile, Daniel Corbin of Spokane had extended a rail line from Northport, the terminal of his Spokane Falls and Northern Railway, to Rossland. As usual, there were legal complications crossing the international boundary. To overcome these difficulties, the American end of the line became the Columbia and Red Mountain while the Canadian component was called the Red Mountain Railway. The railway

In February 1896, F. Augustus Heinze opened a smelter at Trail Creek Landing on the Columbia and later completed a rail line connecting the smelter with the mines at Rossland. The smelter became a major industry in the region and an important source of business for the sternwheelers. Coal was shipped down the Columbia for the plant and ore was also brought in on the river. The smelted ores were a valuable cargo destined for refineries in the east and the United States. In 1898, in a further expansion of its interests in the Kootenays, the CPR purchased the smelter and Heinze's railway lines. In this photo, the *Lytton* is docked below the town during low water on the Columbia. Note the temporary track leading down over the gravel river banks to the steamer. — COMINCO

Arrowhead, on Upper Arrow Lake and at the end of the CPR branch line from Revelstoke, became an important community. By 1910, the town had a population of 500.

— PABC, 91900

reached Rossland in December 1896. Part of Corbin's overall scheme was the construction of a smelter at Northport, Washington and this facility was "blown in" on January 1, 1898, providing direct competition for Heinze and his smelter at Trail. The completion of the rail route to Northport had an important effect on the sternwheelers as well since it provided much cheaper, more reliable transportation between Rossland-Trail and Northport. After the railway was built, sternwheeler service was eliminated south of Trail. Similarly, the completion of the Columbia and Western from Trail to Robson made the sternwheeler service from Robson to Trail redundant.

CPR concern over Heinze's plans grew, since the route planned for his Columbia and Western extension approximated the CPR's own plans for building westwards. At first Heinze and the CPR were at loggerheads, but after Heinze had suffered financial setbacks in Montana and had not been able to secure financing for the Columbia and Western, he finally agreed to sell his smelter and railway interests to the Canadian Pacific. The total price for the Trail smelter, the Columbia and Western and its land grant was $806,000. This purchase was probably one of the best investments the CPR ever made. It led directly to the development of the highly profitable Consolidated Mining and Smelting Company — Cominco. With the purchase, taking effect on February 11, 1898, the CPR had greatly enhanced its position in the Kootenays. Significantly, the connections to Trail were improved while at the same time a troublesome steamer route was eliminated.

The situation was complicated in 1898 when the Great Northern acquired control of the Spokane Falls and Northern (SF&N) and both the lines to Rossland and to Nelson (the Nelson and Fort Sheppard). By this purchase James J. Hill's Great Northern became firmly established in the West Kootenays. Notably, after its purchase of the C&KSN, the CPR terminated steamer service to Five Mile Point where connections had been made with the Nelson and Fort Sheppard. The CPR had no wish to provide business for its competitor.

The GN purchase had become complicated by J. P. Morgan trying to acquire control of the line on behalf of the Northern Pacific. The NP had acted to stop what it thought was a CPR bid for control of the SF&N. Unknown to the NP, it was James J. Hill of the GN who was behind moves to acquire the SF&N and the result was that the two closely affiliated American lines had actually been, in effect, bidding against each other. However, the matter was straightened out, and GN control secured in an agreement between the lines on July 1, 1898. Corbin, who had sold his interests to the Northern Pacific, apparently unaware of the GN moves, might not have acted so readily had he realized Hill's involvement. In any case, the Great Northern was now well established in the Kootenays and, driven by Hill, was eager to extend its influence.

Access to the Kootenays was still very indirect for the Canadian Pacific and traffic for the Kootenays still had to move all the way up the Columbia to Arrowhead and Revelstoke before reaching the main line. With the construction of a rail line through the Crowsnest Pass to the Kootenays, traffic to and from the east would be greatly facilitated, but movement to the west would remain a problem until construction could be pushed west. In 1898, wasting little time, the CPR began building west toward the Boundary district, using its newly-acquired Columbia and Western charter.

The line was pushed through the Monashees, over what became known as Farron Hill, and through to the Kettle River at Cascade. There, a spectacular wooden trestle carried the tracks to the west bank where they continued on to Grand Forks. From there they again climbed over the mountains to Greenwood and finally to Midway on the Washington border. This line, completed in November 1899, tapped a district rich in both mining and agriculture and was to be a lucrative source for traffic.

Until rail connections were secured to the west, all of the traffic to and from the Boundary country was funnelled through Robson West, either for transfer up the Columbia to the main line or to move east via the Columbia and Kootenay to Nelson and, ultimately, the new line through the Crowsnest Pass. Initially, a barge service was operated across the Columbia between Robson and Robson West but in 1902 a bridge was completed across the river which greatly facilitated the movement of rail traffic, and eliminated the need to ferry rail cars across the river. Steamers continued to call at both locations for passengers and freight.

Without connections through to the west coast from Midway, the westward extension of the Columbia and Kootenay was only a dead-end, albeit profitable, branch line. Building through to the main line, however, was a far from easy matter. Using the charter of the Kettle Valley Railway which the CPR acquired via a 999-year lease, a connection was completed through to Penticton in 1914. Moving westward, tracks reached Princeton in 1915. Connections were then completed to Merritt, and from there, via existing trackage, with the main line at Spences Bridge. Finally, a more direct route via the Coquihalla Pass to Hope was finished in 1916. Until this system was completed, all CPR traffic to or from the West Kootenays and large parts of the Okanagan had to pass, at some point, over the Lake and River Service. If Kootenay traffic did not move on the Columbia, either via Robson or the alternate Slocan Lake Route (described more fully in the next section), it moved over Kootenay Lake and the Crowsnest Pass railway. Okanagan traffic moved via the Lake and River Service to the end of track at Okanagan Landing, and after 1914, to Penticton. In 1897, however, when the CPR began to expand its sternwheeler fleet, few people would have foreseen this rapid expansion of rail lines that was to occur.

Many small communities grew along the lakes and rivers of the West Kootenays. Many owed their existence to mining although agriculture took on increasing importance. Ainsworth, on the west side of Kootenay Lake, was perhaps typical. However, the town had the advantage of natural mineral springs which gave it added importance as a stop for tourists or the sick. These scenes show the town itself and teamsters delivering sacks of ore to the steamer dock to await shipment. — PABC, 62006, 60056

The mining boom town of Sandon was the centre of the rich mining district of the Slocan. It was served by two railways, the narrow gauge Kaslo and Slocan, at right, and the standard gauge, CPR-controlled Nakusp and Slocan, in the foreground. — GLENBOW ARCHIVES

The New Sternwheeler Program of 1897

The announcement that the Canadian Pacific would build at least three new vessels was very welcome to people throughout the West Kootenays. It was a most significant step in improving the services on the Arrow Lakes route and providing a first-class vessel for the expanding traffic in the Slocan country. There was an air of excitement and prosperity in the Kootenays in the late 1890's that was infectious. The developments in the transportation systems of the region seemed to more than support anyone who might have been branded overly optimistic about the future prospects for southeastern British Columbia.

Highly significant to the success of the CPR's plans was the skilled labour force that had been developed by the C&KSN. Particularly important were the shipyard crews under the supervision of Thomas Bulger at Nakusp. When the CPR announced its plans for three new vessels, it was clear that the shipyard workers would be busy indeed.

The first was a large, attractively designed riverboat almost identical in appearance to the *Nakusp*. She was named, quite appropriately, the *Kootenay* and was launched at Nakusp in April 1897. The *Kootenay* had, in fact, been under construction before the official takeover date of the C&KSN by the Canadian Pacific. At 1,117 gross tons, she was just slightly larger than her near sister ship the *Nakusp* and measured 184 feet (56 metres) long by 33 feet (10 metres) breadth and 6 feet (1.8 metres) in depth. At this time she was the largest steamer on the Upper Columbia. Like the *Nakusp*, the *Kootenay* had four decks, counting the wheelhouse. Two of these provided passenger accommodations, including two large lounges and the dining saloon, while the freight deck had ample capacity for fuel and cargo. Her engines had come from the sternwheeler *William Irving* which had been wrecked on the lower Fraser River on June 20, 1894, near Farr's Bluff. As the *Irving* was considerably smaller than the *Kootenay*, the new CPR steamer was somewhat underpowered and consequently not very fast. The handicap did not prove to be too serious for the *Kootenay* as she was to continue in operation on the Arrow Lakes route until 1919 and performed very successfully for the Company.

The completion of the *Kootenay* in May enabled the Canadian Pacific to provide a daily service between Arrowhead and Trail beginning that month and using the new steamer and the *Nakusp*. The other vessels were available as required for relief, for handling freight (including construction materials for the rapidly growing network of railroads in the Kootenays), and for maintaining the route south of Trail to Northport.

While work on the *Kootenay* was nearing completion at the Nakusp yard, at Rosebery on Slocan Lake, construction was proceeding rapidly on the next new steamer. This sternwheeler was to serve the booming mining camps of the Slocan. She would connect with the Nakusp and Slocan Railway (a Cana-

The Kootenay *of 1897*

She was built at the Nakusp shipyards and was a fine tribute to the skills of Thomas Bulger and his men who built her. Like the *Nakusp*, she was large for a wooden-hulled sternwheeler. She measured 1,117 gross tons and until the construction of the *Bonnington* in 1911, she was the largest sternwheeler in tonnage terms, in the CPR fleet. Note the elaborate system of hog chains and cables required to strengthen her hull. The photos show the *Kootenay* above Pingston Creek near Arrowhead.
— VMM/PABC, 1506

The *Kootenay* had the second-hand engines from the sternwheeler *William Irving* and for her size was somewhat underpowered. However, she could still make an impressive sight when running under full steam.

— EARL MARSH COLLECTION

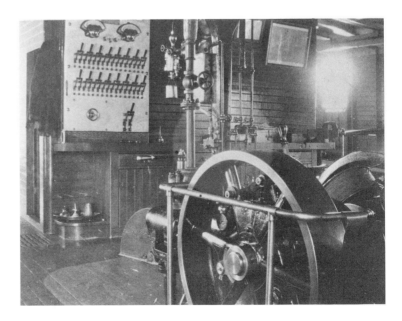

Photos of the engine rooms of the sternwheelers are unusual but fortunately a few have survived. This one shows the electrical panel in the *Kootenay* and the dynamo for generating electricity. The engineers took great pride in the condition of the machinery in their charge and the engine rooms were usually spotless.

— PABC, 1471

The dining saloon of the *Slocan* was nicely finished and was lit by electric lights and clerestory windows. The electric fixtures also included coal oil lamps just in case of trouble. — PABC, 1448

The completion of rail connections between Nakusp and Slocan Lake, and also between the southern end of Slocan Lake and the Columbia and Kootenay Railway, made it possible to bypass the troublesome narrows between Upper and Lower Arrow Lake. When water in the Columbia became too low for safe navigation or when ice built up above or below the narrows or other critical spots, through traffic could be maintained via the Slocan Lake route. The steamer *Slocan* was built at Rosebery in 1897 to provide a first-class service on the lake. She was a pleasingly designed sternwheeler and a dramatic improvement over the small, rather makeshift steamers previously on the lake. R. H. Trueman took these two lovely photographs of the *Slocan*. The upper view was taken from the wharf at New Denver while the lower scene is at Silverton. — PABC, 39128/VCA

dian Pacific subsidiary) at Rosebery in the north and with a branch line then under construction between the south end of Slocan Lake and South Slocan (then called Slocan Crossing) on the Columbia and Kootenay Railway.

The launch of the new vessel was a cause for celebration in the Slocan district and a large crowd was in attendance on Wednesday, May 12, 1897. Captain Troup was Master of Ceremonies and local civic dignitaries and Canadian Pacific officials, including James Bulger, the builder, were present. "At 4:35 p.m.," reported the *Slocan City News*, "the blocks were knocked away and the beautiful vessel slid into the water with the buoyancy of a duck. All present were pleased and expressions of delight were heard at every hand."

The newest steamer in the CPR fleet was christened *Slocan* and was an attractive vessel of 578 gross tons. She measured 156 feet (47.5 m) long by 25 feet (7.6 m) in breadth. In the *Slocan City News*, her length was reported at 171 feet (52 m), which may have been the measurement over the paddle-box. Loaded, she drew approximately three feet (one metre) of water.

By no means a large vessel, she was nonetheless impressive and well fitted out. Since she was designed for the short daylight service on Slocan Lake, there was no need for large numbers of staterooms and only two were incorporated into her passenger deck. She was licensed to carry 300 passengers. Her small size was not a limitation since she could always make an extra run on the lake if traffic warranted. In design, the *Slocan* was typical of the other sternwheelers of the period. Her engines, which were new, came from the B.C. Iron Works in Vancouver and were rated at 17 horsepower.

On May 22, 1897, the *Slocan* was ready for her maiden voyage, although not all of her passenger accommodations were as yet completed, and she steamed down the lake to Slocan City. The people of the bustling little community were delighted with the sternwheeler that would provide such an improvement in their communications with the rest of the world. "Her siren whistle sent a thrill of pleasure through each and every citizen," recorded the *Slocan City News* in a lead story. "She presents a very creditable appearance comparing very favourably with and even eclipsing either the *Kokanee* or the *International*, the crack steamers of Kootenay Lake. The *Slocan* was greeted with three hearty cheers from the throats of the several hundred persons who had gathered at the wharf to witness her first appearance and the response through the blood-curdling siren whistle will long be remembered."

She was ready for service on May 24 and was able to provide two round trips a day on the lake connecting with the train service to Nakusp over the Nakusp and Slocan Railway. When the line from the south reached the end of the lake, service to the Slocan from Spokane would improve to the point where a traveller could leave Spokane in the morning and be in Slocan by evening, saving a day and a half.

The third sternwheeler built by the CPR for its newly-acquired steamboat lines in the Kootenays was the *Rossland*. She was designed for express passenger and tourist service on the Arrow Lakes routes. The *Rossland* was the fastest steamer on the Upper Columbia and a beautifully-proportioned vessel as well. As she backed away from the wharf at Arrowhead, one cloudy day in the late 1890's, R. H. Trueman recorded this vignette. — MOYIE MUSEUM

In another view at Arrowhead, the tug *Columbia* is shown beside the *Rossland*. Late afternoon sunshine makes the gleaming white paint of the *Rossland* sparkle. — CPCA

Before the CPR built the *Slocan*, the largest vessel on Slocan Lake was the rather dumpy little steamer *William Hunter*. She was a useful vessel, even if lacking in aesthetics, and the CPR bought her to supplement their services and also purchased the small tug *Denver*. — PAC, PA-16047

The CPR also purchased two small vessels to supplement the *Slocan*'s service on the lake and more transfer barges. The boats were the small screw tug *Denver* and the ungainly little steamer *William Hunter*. This latter vessel had been built in 1892 by Fred Hume, who had started the C&KSN, William Hunter and a man named McKinnon. Their company, known as the Slocan Trading and Navigation Company, had held a steady business before the arrival of the CPR. The *Denver* had been built the previous year on the coast and assembled at Slocan City.

With the completion of the *Kootenay* and *Slocan*, Captain Troup and the Bulgers turned their attention to the third new vessel required for the growing services, an express passenger steamer. This vessel was to be a departure from the earlier sternwheelers on the Arrow Lakes route which had been designed to handle freight, passengers, and where necessary, to push barges. The new express steamer clearly reflected Captain Troup's flare and ability for designing fast, attractive passenger steamers. These talents were to be developed to the full in later years when he became superintendent of the Canadian Pacific's British Columbia Coast Steamship Service in 1901. Whereas the other steamers, like the *Kootenay*, had flat bottomed barge-like hulls, the new vessel was to have a deeper, more rounded hull with greater moulding and a more graceful bow. This hull pattern was typical of the lake boat design. Although not as well suited for operating in shallow water, it was faster and more efficient on the lakes where depth of water was normally not a serious problem. The deeper hulls also made the vessels less susceptible to being blown about by crosswinds and generally provided greater stability.

Troup planned to put particularly powerful engines into the new steamer, to make her the fastest sternwheeler on the lakes. These were supplied by the B.C. Iron Works in Vancouver and were rated at 32.2 horsepower, compared to the 21.6 horsepower engines in the *Kootenay* which, in tonnage terms, was considerably larger.

The new sternwheeler, at 183 feet, 6 inches (55.9 m), was almost exactly the same length as the *Kootenay*, but she was 3 feet, 6 inches (1.1 m) narrower. Due to her deeper hull form, her depth exceeded the *Kootenay*'s by nearly one foot (0.3 m). Her gross tonnage, however, was only 884 compared to the bulkier *Kootenay* at 1,117 tons.

Construction proceeded at a slower pace than on the previous two vessels. She was laid down in the summer and launched on November 18, 1897, amid the usual cheerful ceremony, at Nakusp. Named the *Rossland*, after the booming mining town, she was towed to the city wharf by the *Nakusp* for further fitting out. Soon after, while not yet ready for carrying passengers, she was put into service working the freight barges while the *Lytton* was given a needed overhaul. Consequently, it was early the following year before the beautiful *Rossland* began regular passenger service on the Columbia. She soon established a justified reputation for speed. When pushed she could pound down the Columbia at over 22 miles per hour (35 km/h). However, at this speed, her coal consumption was excessive, so economy dictated that she seldom operated this fast. No doubt, the firemen, who had to hand-fire the boiler, also were happier that way.

In the *Rossland*, Troup produced a particularly attractive boat. Perhaps one of the most pleasingly designed sternwheelers ever operated in the Kootenays, her overall lines were carried further in later additions to the fleet. Her saloon deck was extended right forward to the bow as had been done on the *Kokanee* on Kootenay Lake. This feature and her rounded pilothouse and trim lines contributed to a particularly elegant design. Her passenger accommodations were well laid out and spacious, although their design was traditional. Forward and aft were lounges, while the dining saloon occupied the centre portion of the saloon deck. On either side of the saloon were passenger staterooms. She was licensed to carry 300 passengers.

In the August 1896 issue of *The British Columbia Mining Record*, a trade journal published in Victoria, an unidentified correspondent described a voyage down the Columbia from Revelstoke to Trail. Later, in the April 1897 issue, the editor recounted his travels to the mining districts of Nelson and Kaslo, having sailed on several sternwheelers during a winter business trip. The two articles complement each other well and give many insights into both summer and winter travel at the time of the Canadian Pacific's purchase of the Columbia and Kootenay Steam Navigation Company's steamers. The narratives are noteworthy as well because they include coverage of the entire Columbia River route from Revelstoke to Trail just before railway construction ended scheduled navigation below Robson.

The correspondent began his story at Revelstoke, the branch line to Arrowhead having been closed by many washouts caused by the high water in the river that year.

"About five o'clock in the afternoon the CPR...ran a train down the spur track from their station to the boat, on reaching which a regular scramble among the passengers for berths ensued. The steamer *Nakusp* is a fine, large boat, well appointed in every way. There are two tiers of staterooms and passengers during the summer months will do well to secure a berth in the top row, as they will find it much more comfortable than below. The current in the river was very swift, and as the steamer swung off from the landing she began going down stream at a great pace. The scenery all around was superb, and as the evening was cool the trip commenced in the pleasantest way possible. Everybody seemed to be out on deck enjoying the air and the scenery as we passed rapidly down the river. About six o'clock a most enjoyable supper was served to the passengers. It was equal to the best meals served on the CPR.

Here at Robson, the *Rossland* is by the wharf with the Nelson passenger train along side. The *Lytton* is just arriving from Trail to the south and will pull in just ahead of the *Rossland*. The photo dates from late 1897 or 1898; the *Rossland* has not long been in service but the Columbia and Western Railway has not yet been completed between Trail and Robson West (West Robson). — PABC, 40376

Two Trips Down the Columbia

"After supper it was not long until the boat touched at Arrowhead, which is located on a narrow strip on the river bank with precipitous, almost over-hanging rocks hundreds of feet high immediately behind it . . .

"On leaving Arrowhead darkness came on and the two great searchlights of the steamer were brought into use. Without them it would be difficult to navigate the Columbia, especially at high water. With them it becomes as light as day ahead of the steamer. During the night Nakusp was passed [most likely the *Nakusp* made a brief stop while the author was asleep] and in the morning we stopped at a place called Deer Park near which several mineral discoveries have recently been made. Deer Park itself possesses a fine location for a town, being level, with rising ground at the back. Quite a number of buildings are already erected there and if the mines turn out as expected it will be quite a place.

"The boat was crowded with passengers and it was amusing to see them, note book in hand, comparing experiences with each other. All seemed to have but one idea — mining — and the number of samples of rock that were produced from side pockets, valises, etc., and passed around for inspection was amazing. Prospectors in their rough garbs, miners, speculators and tourists, all hobnobbed together and the subject was confined to one theme — mining. From the shore we were frequently hailed by prospectors on the tramp and on several occasions the boat stopped and took one or more of those hardy pioneers aboard.

"As we descended the river the current seemed to become swifter, and when Robson was reached it was running at a pretty rapid rate. Robson consists merely of a railway station, an hotel and one or two houses . . . The track was practically under water so that the cars alongside the steamer were even with the deck and made the transfer of freight comparatively easy. One express trunk, however, managed to tumble into the river and the man had hard work to fish it out.

"We remained at Robson an hour or so waiting for the train, but on its arrival lost no time in getting way. A short distance down the river we put into a place with a sign having 'Montgomery' on it and underneath the words 'Lillooet, Fraser River & Cariboo Gold Fields Ltd.' and in swinging round we managed to break one of the rudder cables. To repair the break took some time . . .

"On leaving Montgomery the boat passed into the grandest part of the river. The scenery along the bank was magnificent and the river seemed like one continuous chain of rapids, the water foaming, circling and breaking every now and then into long lines of crested waves and throwing spray high into the air. Meantime, the steamer flew past the banks at lightning speed . . . [and] in a short time Trail came in sight with its smelter high in the air on the hill overlooking the town . . .

"Hundreds of people were down to meet the boat and the scene on landing presented a busy sight. The railway track runs close to the boat [but] the passengers bound for Rossland . . . learned that the train would not leave for several hours.

"About seven in the evening the steamer *Lytton* arrived from Northport and soon after we started on a train of the Columbia & Western R.R. [*sic*] for Rossland. The trip over the switchback owing to the crowded state of the cars, was not an enjoyable one, and as we steamed into the station we were thankful that we were now at the end of our journey."

Summer travel was nearly always heavier on the steamer routes. It was, of course, a more pleasant time to travel and navigation was also generally safer and easier. In the next account of travel on the Columbia, the trip took place in late winter and the journey was probably typical of off-season travel. Rail service had been re-established south to Arrowhead, shortening the journey by sternwheeler and being more typical of travel on the route during this period. The editor of *The British Columbia Mining Record* travelled to Revelstoke over the main line of the CPR from Vancouver in preference to the Great Northern route through northern Washington.

"At Revelstoke quite a number of passengers disembarked and wandered about the station or through the town from 9 a.m. till 5 p.m., when the Arrowhead train left for the Columbia River. It was a long wait, and...I would suggest [that the company] make the station more attractive than it is at present to enable passengers to kill time more pleasantly while waiting.

"About 5 p.m. after the arrival and departure of the express from the East we made a start for Arrowhead, which we reached in about two hours, time. Here again we had another wait until a number of freight cars were shunted to allow the passenger coach to run alongside the steamer...In due time, however, we reached the steamer *Nakusp* and the air of comfort which her well-lighted saloons presented was a pleasant change from the dingy railway carriage. The *Nakusp* is really a most comfortable boat and her staterooms and general appointments excellent. She was packed full of freight when we boarded her, amongst which was a large blower for the Nelson smelter, and everything being ready for a start no time was lost in getting on the trip down the river. The air was sharp and there was a good deal of floating ice which, however, did not seem to interfere with the speed of the boat, but inside, the saloons were warm and comfortable.

"A tasty supper was served just after leaving Arrowhead which I certainly thoroughly relished, and then while enjoying a fragrant cigar I had time to look about me...The boat even at this early season of the year was crowded and I thought of what it would be when spring and summer came and travel to the mines really set in.

"About 11 p.m. I retired to bed and enjoyed a very comfortable night's rest, expecting to find myself near Robson in the morning. But on awakening I found that the steamer had run on a bar in the narrows about thirty miles [48 km] below Nakusp and there we were hard and fast, the gravelly bottom on which we rested and over which the water was rushing, being plainly visible from the deck of the steamer. With the aid of a small stern wheeler [probably the *Illecillewaet*] we managed to slide off the bar soon after daylight and made our way down a narrow channel cut through the ice. At the bow was a strongly built barge which we pushed ahead of us and thus kept the steamer from coming into contact with the ice. The ice we were encountering was lodged in the narrows between the upper and lower Arrow lakes, but when we passed through this channel it disappeared and we had open water all the way to Robson.

"About 4:30 p.m. we reached Robson and there the Trail passengers were transferred to a railway train which took them a short distance down the river where another of the company's

With the completion of the branch line from Revelstoke to Arrowhead in 1896, there was seldom any need for the sternwheelers to navigate the Columbia north of Arrowhead. However, if there was a lengthy closure of the branch line, the sternwheelers, in this case the *Kootenay*, steamed upriver to Revelstoke. — PABC, 23580

boats was waiting to carry them to their destination. This transfer is caused by the shallowness of the water at this season of the year just below Robson. When the Trail passengers had left, the Nelson train drew alongside the steamer and we who were bound for Kootenay Lake embarked thereon. It took us about two hours to reach Nelson . . . and about 7 p.m. we drew into the station of the central city of West Kootenay. It was too dark to see the splendid scenery along Kootenay River, but we heard the roar of the falls and the rapids as we passed along winding our way around the many curves of the road . . .

"I spent a quiet Sunday in Nelson, and on Monday took the steamer *International* to Kaslo. This is a new boat run by the International Navigation and Trading Company, and, I understand, the fastest on the lake. The saloon of this steamer is a gem for comfort and elegance combined, and one of the best features in it is the row of large plate glass windows on each side which permit of a splendid view of the lake as you skim along. Darkness overtook us quickly however, and I did not enjoy the view very long. The dinner served on board was excellent, and the extent and variety of the bill of fare a genuine surprise to me.

"The *International* now connects with the Spokane Falls and Northern R.R. [*sic*] at Five Mile Point, near Nelson and takes passengers . . . on to Kaslo and intermediate points. The *Kokanee* used to make this connection, but since the C.P.R. took over the boats of the C&KSN Co., the Spokane road made an arrangement with the International Navigation and Trading Company to do the service. The C&KSN Co. boats will hereafter be run purely in the interests of the CPR system.

"The *International* had a large number of passengers on board and fearing that there would be a scarcity of room in the hotels at Kaslo I telegraphed from Ainsworth to secure accommodation. To my utter disgust, however, the boat reached Kaslo before my telegram, and I was the only one of the passengers who could not get a room . . . The proprietor of the [Kaslo Hotel] secured me very comfortable quarters for the night in a neighbouring house . . .

"Kaslo is wonderfully improved, its streets are brilliantly lighted by electric lamps, it has a system of water works with force enough to control any fire. As one citizen remarked, if the water does not put the fire out it has force enough to knock the building into smithereens. Large sampling works, saw and planing mills, shipyards and several factories of various kinds are among the industries . . . Kaslo cannot fail to be a most important place, especially as it is the doorway to the great Slocan district.

"On the evening of the second day I went on board the steamer *Kokanee*, of the Canadian Pacific line, a very beautiful and fast boat. I took a berth in a roomy and most comfortable stateroom, and being tired, soon fell asleep. The steamer left the dock at Kaslo about seven in the morning for Nelson, so when I awoke we were well out on the Kootenay Lake. A tasty breakfast, followed by a pleasant smoke, was enjoyed, and soon afterwards I found myself once more in Nelson."

The author then travelled by train to Robson where a two hour wait was required before boarding the steamer for Trail. With little to do at Robson, the time passed slowly.

"The Columbia just below Robson at this season is not navigable for steamers, so the CPR have built a short spur to connect with one of their steamers about four miles [6.5 km] down... We now boarded the freight steamer *Trail*, and it looked as if we would have to go without dinner but a vigorous representation of our state of hunger brought the steward to time, and we were served with a good meal.

"The river all the way to Trail is at this season of the year one succession of shoals and rapids, and navigation is very difficult. The building of the railway from Trail to Robson is therefore an actual necessity... We stopped at Montgomery and Waterloo, two new towns which have sprung into existence during the past few months through the proximity of promising mines and several logging camps in the neighbourhood... We now sighted the railway track, on which construction is being carried... On the way down we had to stop at several points and discharge contractors' supplies, and this consumed so much time that it was almost dark when we stopped at the Trail landing."

Neither writer commented on his return trips up the lakes so it may be assumed that these were essentially repetitions of the downstream journeys. The Kootenays were booming at this time with mining, smelting and construction activity growing with no apparent end in sight. There was a constant flow of people into the area; businesses prospered. It was an auspicious time indeed for the CPR to have purchased the Columbia and Kootenay operations.

The beautifully situated city of Kaslo on Kootenay Lake was an important outlet for the mining wealth of the Slocan district. It was the eastern end of the Great Northern-controlled Kaslo and Slocan Railway and the home port for the steamers of the International Navigation and Trading Company which was also a GN operation. It is afternoon at Kaslo and the *International* is at the dock shown in the centre of the photo while the steamers *Argenta* and *Kaslo*, whose stories are described in the next chapter, are to the right. In the distance, at left, is the CPR wharf near the mouth of the bay. The photo dates from about 1900. — PABC, 9981

Loss of the Nakusp

Just two days before Christmas, on December 23, 1897, the *Nakusp* caught fire at Arrowhead and was a total loss. It was a sad end for a beautiful vessel that still should have had many years of useful life left in her. Fortunately, no one was injured. — PABC, 750

The Canadian Pacific had barely begun its expansion efforts when disaster struck one of its finest steamers on the Arrow Lakes. The brief life of the *Nakusp*, the second largest vessel in the fleet, had been marred already in the year 1897 when she had run hard aground on the Kootenay bar two miles (3.2 km) south of Robson while steaming upriver from Trail on September 8, 1897. At this point the Kootenay River flows into the Columbia with considerable force and the current had swept her aground. Efforts to refloat her were unsuccessful and the passengers were landed to make their way to Robson. On arriving at the scene, the *Kootenay*, which picked up the mails and the passengers, tried to pull the *Nakusp* free but once again the attempts were frustrated by falling water in the river. The efforts to refloat the steamer actually moved her 40 feet (12 m) along the bar. Tackles and other salvage equipment were sent down from Revelstoke, but it was not until November that she was refloated. The New Denver *Ledge* reported that the salvage cost $7,000.

Then, on December 23, while at the dock at Arrowhead, the two-year-old *Nakusp* caught fire. She was a total loss. The flames spread so fast that little could be saved although all on board escaped safely. Four carloads of freight, already loaded onto the vessel, were also lost in the fire. These included a carload of bran, one of oats, one of hay and one of general merchandise. The cause of the fire was undetermined, but the results were devastating.

So the year that began with such promise and which was marked by such excitement, ended on a sadder note. But the setback was only a temporary one and at least no one had been injured in the loss of the *Nakusp*. It is noteworthy that the *Nakusp* was the first and only passenger vessel in the Canadian Pacific's Lake and River Service fleet to be lost to fire but the freight boat *Trail* soon met the same fate and the *Rossland* narrowly escaped it. The sternwheelers were very vulnerable to fire as these disasters and the losses of the *Columbia* and *Spokane* had also demonstrated.

Despite the setbacks, the CPR was pleased with the first year's operations of its new steamboat fleet. In the Annual Report for 1897 it was noted that, "the results of the purchase of the C&K steamers as authorized by the shareholders a year ago, have been most gratifying. Additions have already been made and more boats are required." The report went on to announce the purchase of two steamships for the trade between Victoria and Vancouver and the Yukon and stated that, "Your directors have also caused to be put under contract eleven steamboats, costing approximately $350,000 for the lakes and rivers of Southern British Columbia mining districts and for river service in Canadian Yukon trade." This latter announcement was particularly interesting since it marked the beginning of the most ambitious venture in steamboat construction the CPR ever was to undertake in British Columbia and also the most disastrous.

The discovery of gold in the Yukon turned the attention of the
western world to the North. The name, Klondike, became a household
word as stories spread of the fabulous wealth of placer gold discovered
in the rivers of the Yukon. Transportation to the Yukon goldfields
became a key problem, prompting the Canadian Pacific Railway to
begin a most ambitious sternwheeler construction program. The new
vessels were to be part of an "All-Canadian" route to the Klondike via
the Stikine River. The *Ogilvie*, named for the noted Yukon explorer,
William Ogilvie, was the second CPR steamer completed for the
Stikine service and is shown during trials on Burrard Inlet near
Vancouver. — PABC, 722

CHAPTER III

STERNWHEELERS
FOR THE KLONDIKE

*An All-Canadian Route
to the Goldfields*

IN THE SUMMER of 1897, news of vast gold discoveries in the Yukon spread throughout North America and Europe, exciting and enticing thousands of fortune seekers to the Klondike to find the elusive placer gold. Even the Canadian Pacific Railway could not remain aloof from the madness — the "gold fever" — that gripped the western world. At this time, the Yukon, northwestern British Columbia and Alaska were still largely unexplored and poorly understood by politicians, businessmen, bureaucrats and the general public alike.

The distances were vast; the gold discoveries near the site of Dawson were nearly as far north of Victoria as the Mexican border was to the south and were approximately 3,000 miles (4,800 km) from Ottawa. Separating the major settlements in southern Canada from the goldfields were mile after mile of mountains, untracked forests, swamps and muskeg. It was enough to deter almost anyone from venturing north; almost anyone, that is, until the stories of the fabulous gold discoveries spread and were exaggerated each time with the retelling. The temptation to try to find a fortune in the Klondike became irresistible. However slim the chances, here was an opportunity to find riches and a new life. Thousands quit their jobs, and began the long, body-breaking and soul-testing journey to the Klondike goldfields. Optimism was boundless and it needed to be, for it carried the Klondikers farther than reality ever could have.

There were overland routes to the Klondike from Edmonton in northern Alberta and interior points in British Columbia along the Canadian Pacific Railway, but the most direct routes were by sea up the northwest coast from Seattle, Victoria and Vancouver to Skagway and Dyea in southern Alaska. From there the trails took the shortest overland routes to the Yukon River, but the treks were still arduous, and backbreaking. It was also possible to travel by sea to St. Michael near the mouth of the Yukon River and from there journey by riverboat upstream to the Klondike but the route was long, expensive and limited to summer travel.

So many people wanted to travel to the Yukon in hopes of finding gold that the existing shipping services were taxed to the limit. The Canadian Pacific Navigation Company, the major British Columbia coastal shipping firm, used its vessels to great advantage. Here the CPN's *Islander*, at left, and *Tees* are nearly ready to leave Victoria for the north. — CPCA

It was the route over White Pass, chosen by the White Pass & Yukon Route, that ultimately became the most important.

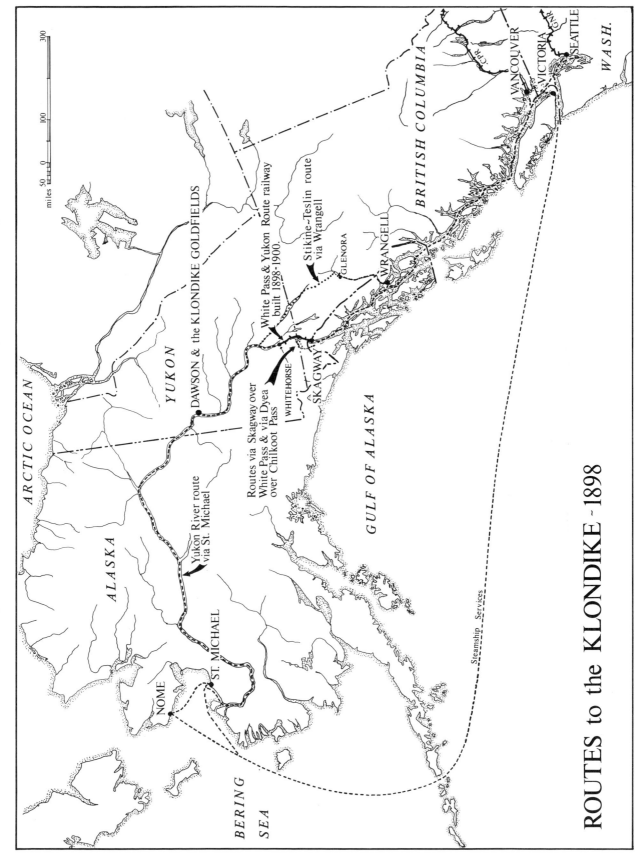

ROUTES to the KLONDIKE ~ 1898

The problem with most routes, particularly as far as Canadian businessmen and politicians were concerned, was that they were mostly through United States territory. From both a commercial and a nationalistic perspective, an all-Canadian route to the Klondike and its awaiting fortunes seemed highly desirable. The overland routes from southern British Columbia and northern Alberta were too long and difficult, and the most practical alternative seemed to lie in a route connecting with the Stikine River* which, while having its lower reaches in Alaska, was open to Canadian navigation as part of the international boundary treaty. The Stikine River route required the use of Wrangell, Alaska as a transshipment point from ocean steamers to riverboats, but aside from Wrangell's port facilities and brief stretches of American waters, the route was indeed "all-Canadian." From the head of navigation on the Stikine, it was possible to travel overland to Teslin Lake at the head of the Yukon River drainage system. On paper, and in preliminary surveys, the route looked promising. However, to be truly functional and competitive, a wagon road, and ultimately a railroad, was required to connect the Stikine with Teslin Lake.

The actual extent of CPR involvement in the railway schemes is difficult to determine. In late summer and throughout the fall of 1897, the newspapers clearly associated the Company with railway development from the Stikine to Teslin Lake. Following a meeting of the CPR's General Superintendent Marpole, Chief Engineer Cambie and Superintendent Duchesnay at Victoria early in September *The Daily Colonist* noted that, "the construction of a railway from Telegraph Creek, at the head of navigation on the Stikine River, to Teslin Lake, was the specific business they had in view, and tomorrow [September 13, 1897] Engineer Duchesnay leaves Vancouver on the *Princess Louise* with a party to make the preliminary survey for the road."

A report from Winnipeg on September 12, cited Robert Kerr, CPR traffic manager, as confirming that the Company "would establish a steamship service from Vancouver, connecting with the contemplated construction of a CPR line from a point on the Stikine River to Teslin Lake." However, the report was qualified by the comment that, "if decided upon, construction will start as soon as possible to have the line open for next year [i.e., 1899]." The newspapers of this era were quick to make optimistic statements about such projects even if uncertainty still existed. Rumours abounded as interest in the Klondike mounted.

The preliminary survey of E. J. Duchesnay began in September 1897 and was an important one for the future of CPR

* Spellings adopted in this chapter are based on present day usage. Often in early reports and newspapers differing spellings were used. Original spellings are retained in quoted material. Stikine was often spelled "Stikeen" and Wrangell as "Wrangel."

steamship services. His party reached Wrangell by steamer on September 18, 1897, and set out the next morning for the Stikine. They arrived at Telegraph Creek, British Columbia on the 30th, and continued overland to the head of Teslin Lake which they reached on October 13. In Duchesnay's opinion, the route presented no serious problems for the construction of a wagon road or narrow gauge railway. He was back at Wrangell on October 25. His recommendations called for a fleet of 12 sternwheelers, two coastal steamships (to cost, in total, $450,000) and 145 miles (about 235 km) of narrow gauge railway, fully equipped, costing about $1,680,000. Later, published estimates of the railway's costs went as high as $3,957,000.

During the winter of 1897-98 the scheme was pushed by both the governments of British Columbia and Canada. The federal government was prepared to offer a substantial land grant and monopoly provisions as incentives, and early in 1898, let a contract to Mackenzie and Mann, railway contractors, to begin construction on a wagon road and railway from Glenora, near the head of navigation on the Stikine River, to Teslin Lake.

During that winter thousands of men and women were preparing to head north, hoping to arrive in the Klondike in the spring of 1898 and to have a full season of prospecting before the bitter sub-Arctic winter set in. A number of companies were attracted by the promise of the Stikine route and in Vancouver and Victoria, many fine sternwheelers began taking shape at the shipyards. The work was rushed through as quickly as possible to have the vessels ready by early May for the opening of navigation on the Stikine.

There was a vast amount of misinformation circulated in the press and in books by would-be experts during the peak of the Klondike rush about the different routes to the goldfields. Some was best explained by ignorance while other statements reflected commercial interests and nationalism. The Stikine received a great deal of publicity as the best route, but it would appear that most people heading north saw the most direct routes — via Skagway and other ports on the Lynn Canal — as the best alternatives. Several thousand people did try the Stikine, arriving at Wrangell during the winter and making their way over the ice towards Glenora or simply waiting for navigation to open up. However, the vast majority of Klondikers went to Skagway, ignoring the politicians, the newspaper editorials and the planned railway scheme from Glenora. Nevertheless, during the winter of '97 and '98 the prospects of the Stikine route looked bright and the planned railway seemed very real.

While the CPR was prepared to initiate steamer operations on the Stikine, it did not commit itself to the railway, the most costly and risky aspect of the venture. In fact, on February 1, 1898, *The Daily Colonist* reported that, "Sir W. C. Van Horne being asked whether the Canadian Pacific was interested in the Teslin Lake Railway, said the Company had no interest in the new rail line apart from their very active general interest in having a Canadian Route." The CPR did not become involved in the construction of the line but may well have intended to acquire the railway by lease once construction was completed. Later events were to make the ultimate outcome of the CPR's interest in the rail line academic. In the end, the plans for the railway collapsed, leaving the CPR with a splendid fleet of vessels for which it had little or no use. But in the exciting, optimistic fall and winter months of 1897-98, the scheme seemed full of promise.

Work on the steamer service proceeded quickly. To be profitable, it had to be operational by the opening of navigation on the northern rivers the next spring when, it was believed, the real rush to the Klondike would begin.

The CPR purchased the ocean steamers *Tartar* and *Athenian*, shown at left, to provide a connecting service between Victoria and Vancouver and Wrangell. From there, the new sternwheelers were to operate up the Stikine River to Glenora where the proposed railway was to begin. The two ships had been built for service between Britain and South Africa and were large compared to the coastal steamships then operating to Alaska. After the collapse of the Stikine River service, the two ships were used as supplemental vessels in the Canadian Pacific's trans-Pacific steamship service and for a time were also used as transports, under charter, by the United States Army during the Spanish American War. — PABC, 71051

An additional consideration for the Canadian Pacific in establishing its own steamship service up the coast to Alaskan ports as well as to the Stikine, was a desire to draw traffic from the Great Northern and Northern Pacific lines which were funnelling great volumes of traffic through Seattle and Tacoma for the Klondike. The CPR's and Company President William C. Van Horne's rivalry with the Great Northern had been of long standing and was also being fought out in the Kootenays.

The Canadian Pacific's plans were ambitious and showed the Company's determination to capture a "lion's share" of the expected business to the Yukon. The CPR based its plans on the recommendations of the Duchesnay report. The Company intended to provide all of the steamers Duchesnay had recommended: two coastal liners and 12 riverboats.

The Canadian Pacific advertised the planned service extensively and published lengthy and detailed brochures on routes to the Klondike. The Stikine route was given prominence and praise in this advertising. Additionally, the CPR was anxious to encourage travel over its rail routes to the coast or other points such as Edmonton, Alberta, where the long trails to the Klondike began.

In a brochure, published early in 1898, details were provided outlining the Stikine route:

"Take the Canadian Pacific Railway to Vancouver or Victoria, B.C.; thence ocean steamer via the inland channel to Fort Wrangel; river steamer up the Stikine River to Glenora or Telegraph Creek; pack trail or waggon road to Teslin Lake, and river steamer down the Hootalinqua and Lewes rivers to Fort Selkirk and Dawson City and other points on the Yukon.

The approximate distances are:

Vancouver or Victoria to
Fort Wrangel .... (ocean) 700 miles [1,125 km]
Fort Wrangel to Glenora .... (river) 125 " [200 km]
Glenora to Lake Teslin .. (trail or waggon) 145 " [235 km]
Teslin to Fort Selkirk ...... (lake and river) 400 " [645 km]
Fort Selkirk to Stewart River .... (river) 105 " [170 km]
Stewart River to Dawson City .... (river) 67 " [108 km]
Total distance from Vancouver and Victoria to
Dawson City .... 1,542 miles [2,481 km]

... at Fort Wrangel [Alaska], baggage and freight will be transshipped in bond and passengers transferred from the ocean to river steamers. The Stikine is easily navigable for flatbottom river steamboats to Glenora, and when the water is high, they can reach Telegraph Creek, 12 miles further up stream. The Stikine has been regularly navigated for some years, but during the coming season there will be many additional steamers placed on this route, on each of which there will be good accommodation for 50 first-class and from 100 to 150 second-class passengers. The trip from Wrangel to Glenora occupies 36 hours. About 40 miles from the mouth of the Stikine, Canadian territory is entered, and the route thence to the Klondike lies entirely within Canada."

Rates were quoted in the earlier additions of the brochures, but were deleted or modified in later printings.

"Rates from interior points can be found by adding the current rates to Vancouver or Victoria via the Canadian Pacific Railway to the following:

Vancouver or Victoria
    To

	1st Class	2nd Class
Wrangel	$25.00	$13.00
Glenora	40.00	25.00
Juneau	32.00	17.00
Pyramid Harbor Landing	40.00	25.00
Haines' Mission	40.00	25.00
Dyea	40.00	25.00
Skagway	40.00	25.00
Sitka	40.00	22.00 [sic]

First-class rates include meals and berth on steamships, second-class rates meals and bunk on steamships, except that rates to Glenora do not include meals and berths beyond Wrangel. Berths (for first-class passengers only) are $3.00, and meals are 50 cents each, between Wrangel and Glenora.

Vancouver or Victoria to Dawson City via St. Michael's Island	1st Class $300.00	2nd Class 250.00"*

The detailed brochures that provided these fare schedules also outlined the supply requirements for the miners, suggested departure dates, steamship schedules and extracts from mining regulations for the Yukon. But much was still unknown about the vast, remote interior of Alaska and the Yukon and few reading the optimistic literature might have guessed the hardships and toil that awaited many who set out to find fortunes in the Klondike.

The Stikine Fleet

While promotional activities continued for the routes to the Klondike, the CPR began acquiring the necessary vessels. The ocean steamships, to be the largest vessels in the Alaska trade, were purchased in England and were former Union Line steamships designed for the trade to South Africa. These were the *Athenian*, of 3,877 gross tons, and the slightly larger *Tartar*, of 4,339 gross tons. Both were capable of carrying large volumes of cargo and several hundred passengers. The two liners were purchased in December 1897, for a total cost of $529,249.62.

The *Tartar* was the first of the two to reach the Pacific Coast, arriving in Vancouver on April 1, 1898, after a voyage

* From the brochure "Klondike and Yukon Gold Fields via Canadian Pacific Railway." Spellings of place names have been left in the form originally published.

Glenora was to be the beginning of the railway to Teslin Lake. The town was situated on a low river flat on a sweeping bend of the Stikine River. But the railway was never built and the town was doomed to obscurity as a small, remote settlement. Although the CPR steamers were withdrawn from the Stikine in the summer of 1898, other sternwheelers continued a summer service up the Stikine until 1916. In this photograph by F. W. Carlson, a sternwheeler, probably the Hudson's Bay Company's *Strathcona* or *Caledonia*, nears Glenora.

— ALASKA HISTORICAL LIBRARY

The *Constantine* was one of the four sternwheelers built at Port Blakely, Washington for the Canadian Pacific. She was the only CPR sternwheeler to have two funnels and was designed primarily as a freighter.

— WILLIAMSON COLLECTION, PSMHS

of nearly two months from Southampton. The *Athenian* followed and arrived on April 12.* Part of the *Tartar*'s cargo had been a submarine cable and this was laid to Vancouver Island soon after her arrival. Then, ready to make her first trip north, she sailed on April 28, while the *Athenian* was scheduled to follow one week later.

While the vessels for the coastal route to the Stikine could be purchased ready for service, the sternwheelers had to be built in local yards. So dramatic was the boom in coastal shipping at this time that all available vessels, including some unbelievable old hulks that had been hurriedly patched up, were pressed into gold rush service.

The required sternwheelers represented a major shipbuilding program for the CPR. Of the 12 vessels, nine were entirely of wooden construction while three were to have composite hulls. Four of the wooden vessels were constructed at Port Blakely, Washington in 1898. These were the *Constantine*, *Dalton*, *Schwatka* and *Walsh*; all were registered in the United States to give further flexibility of operation in American waters and, no doubt, to help ease any concern by Americans about a Canadian fleet operating out of Wrangell. Supervising the work was Captain James Troup from the Company's Lake and River Service and Thomas Bulger, the experienced master builder from the Canadian Pacific's recently acquired operations in the Kootenays. For both men, who had supervised three new vessels under construction in the Kootenays during 1897, it must have been a busy and stressful time indeed. Fortunately, both were experienced and the designs of the recently-built Kootenay boats provided a sound starting point for the new Stikine fleet.

The planned fleet was to comprise the following vessels: ocean steamships — *Athenian* and *Tartar*; and river steamers — *Constantine*, *Dalton*, *Duchesnay*, *G. M. Dawson*, *Hamlin*, *McConnell*, *Minto*, *Moyie*, *Ogilvie*, *Schwatka*, *Tyrrell* and *Walsh*. There were considerable differences among the vessels. The *Ogilvie* and *McConnell*, near sister ships, were designed primarily as passenger vessels, whereas the *Hamlin*, *Schwatka*, *Duchesnay* and *Constantine* were intended principally for freight. The freight boats owed much in design to the *Trail*, recently built for service on the Columbia. The *Tyrrell*, *Minto* and *Moyie*, with composite hulls, differed in detail and tonnage from the *Ogilvie* and *McConnell* but were essentially the same in overall design and layout. The configuration of the *G. M. Dawson* is uncertain, although she may have been like the freight steamers in general design.

The four Port Blakely-built vessels were built to two designs. In appearance, the *Constantine* was the most unique among the four, having two funnels. She was the only CPR

* For further details of the voyages to the Pacific by the *Tartar* and *Athenian*, and their subsequent service on the Canadian Pacific's trans-Pacific steamship routes, see *The Pacific Empresses* (1981).

sternwheeler so equipped and this unusual feature was probably a result of her being fitted with the machinery from the Ohio River steamer *Mary Morton*. Aside from her twin funnels, she was essentially a sister ship to the *Schwatka* and had limited passenger accommodations. The other two steamers, *Dalton* and *Walsh*, were very similiar in appearance to the *Ogilvie*, *McConnell* and the three composite hulled vessels, although differing in dimensions.

The steel components for the first of the three composite hulled steamers were ordered from the Polson Iron Works in Toronto, while the contract for the other two was awarded to the Bertram Iron Works of Toronto. The intention was to ship the prefabricated components for the hulls by rail to the coast to speed construction and presumably to provide more durable vessels for winter operations. The hulls for the three sternwheelers had steel frames and steel plating for the sides of the hull. While their bottoms were to be planked in wood, the steel sides and bows made them much stronger and less susceptible to damage from ice. The upper works were typical in their construction and all of the cabins were to be constructed at the assembly yards on the coast. Only one of the three steamers, the *Tyrrell*, was assembled in Vancouver. She was launched on June 6, 1898.

The two other vessels, the *Minto* and the *Moyie*, were shipped to the coast and some preliminary work may have begun on them. However, before any advanced work had been done on the hulls, prospects for the all-Canadian route to the Klondike were looking bleak, and on the verge of collapse. The vessels were diverted to the Kootenays, one going to Nakusp and the other to Nelson for assembly. They were to serve the Kootenays well into the 1950's, long after the Stikine River route to the Klondike had been all but forgotten.

However, in the spring of 1898, work on the fleet for the Stikine service was still being pushed forward enthusiastically and the new vessels completed in orderly fashion. At the False Creek yards in Vancouver, the first four vessels were completed in rapid succession. The first was the *Hamlin*, launched on April 21, 1898 in a pelting rain which kept away any crowds of visitors for the launch. Vancouver's *Daily World* noted that, "while it was a prosy affair and with not even a bottle of wine to christen her, the launching of the *Hamlin* was very successful." Later, once steam had been raised, she ran brief trials around False Creek.

The *Hamlin* was essentially a freight boat. She measured 146.2 x 30.8 x 4.6 feet (44.6 x 9.4 x 1.4 metres) and she was designed to draw only 19 inches (48 cm) of water when fully loaded. She was capable of 14 miles per hour (22.5 km/h); it was anticipated that she could make two round trips a week between Wrangell and Glenora. She was licensed to carry 100 passengers.

The speed with which the False Creek yards completed the first vessels was amazing. On April 23, 1898, the day after the

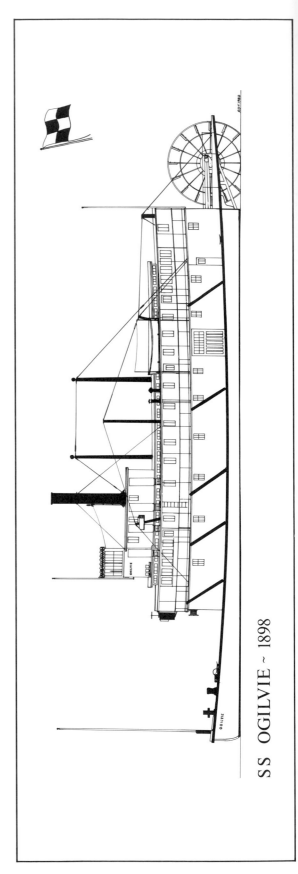

SS OGILVIE ~ 1898

Proudly flying the CPR's red and white chequerboard house flag, the *Ogilvie*, the first passenger steamer for the Company's Stikine River service, steams across Vancouver Harbour on her trials. The *Hamlin*, a freight steamer, was the first of the fleet to be completed.
— THOMPSON PHOTO, PABC, 721a

Hamlin's launch, two more were ready for launching: the *Ogilvie* in the morning and the *McConnell* in the afternoon. On the heels of the other three, the *Duchesnay* followed on the 24th. In the end, these four were the only CPR sternwheelers to see service on the Stikine.

The great burst of shipbuilding activity in Vancouver was followed with particular interest by the press and, following the launch of the *Hamlin*, *The Vancouver Daily World* noted that, "for nearly three months the shipyard has been one of the busiest places in Vancouver." The newspaper went on to comment that James Troup was "a practical ship-builder of ability and has handled the business part of the matter to the satisfaction of everybody, especially the individual workmen."

A complication in the building program was the location of the shipyard which, although fronting on False Creek, was on the inland side of the Granville Street bridge which carried streetcar traffic as well as pedestrians and horse-drawn vehicles. No provisions had been made for the passage of vessels the size of the sternwheelers so a section of the bridge wide enough for the steamers to be eased through had to be removed temporarily.

To minimize the disruption of traffic to and from Vancouver, work on removing the section of bridge did not begin until late Saturday night after the last streetcar had passed over. Then, under the direction of the CPR's Chief Engineer Cambie, two trestle bents on the south side of the bridge were removed. With the waterway open it was then possible to begin moving the vessels. The *Hamlin*, the only vessel fully ready, was used to tow the other three sternwheelers around to the Canadian Pacific wharf on Burrard Inlet. Captain E. C. Bridgeman, the Company's coast pilot for the *Athenian*, brought the new steamers around under the watchful supervision of Captain Troup.

The Vancouver Daily World reported that by 7:30, Tuesday morning, although there had been quite a strong ebb tide running by the time the narrows was reached, all four sternwheelers had been moved through and had all arrived at the CPR wharf by 10:00 a.m. "It was quite a sight," the reporter commented, "to see four such fine river steamers all . . . [at] the wharf fast together with their flags flying and there was quite a crowd of people down on the wharf to see them come in."

The *Hamlin*, her towing duties over, was then readied to sail for the Stikine, while the *Ogilvie*, the next steamer, was being given the finishing touches preparatory to her trials. On April 30, she made her debut by taking dignitaries and invited guests on a cruise of Burrard Inlet, steaming to Port Moody and then to Rainy Ranch 16 miles (25.8 km) away. During the course of the cruise, the steamer was put through full trials of her machinery, running full ahead, full astern, turning and carrying out emergency stops. She steamed the distance between Port Moody and Rainy Ranch in just over one hour.

The design for the freight steamers for the Stikine service was based on the sternwheeler *Trail*, built in 1896 at Nakusp for the Columbia River service. The *Hamlin* was the first of the CPR's new fleet to be completed and inaugurated CPR service on the Stikine River.
— PABC, 38510

The *Dalton*, built at Port Blakely, was intended for both passengers and freight. Interestingly, James Troup was recorded as the owner, for U.S. Customs purposes, of the four Port Blakely-built vessels but he was clearly acting as the CPR's agent since the cost of the vessels was carried in CPR accounts.
— WILLIAMSON COLLECTION, PSMHS

The *Schwatka* was a fine, well-built freight
vessel, and despite being finished too late to
operate on the Stikine for the CPR, eventually
operated on the Yukon River. Her similarity to
the *Trail*, illustrated in Chapter One, is obvious.
— WILLIAMSON COLLECTION, PSMHS

Although completed in June 1898, the
Constantine was not needed by the Canadian
Pacific and was sold to the British American
Corporation for service on the Yukon. However,
while under tow to Alaska, she foundered on
July 4, 1898. With the exception of her
funnels, she was a twin to the *Schwatka*.
— WILLIAMSON COLLECTION, PSMHS

The Port Blakely-built *Walsh* was never placed in service by the CPR and was sold in 1902. The unfortunate steamer was destroyed by fire in 1903. — WILLIAMSON COLLECTION, PSMHS

Launched in Vancouver on June 6, 1898, the *Tyrrell* was one of three composite hull sternwheelers ordered for the CPR's Stikine River service. Her hull was prefabricated by the Polson Iron Works of Ontario and was assembled at the CPR's shipyard at False Creek. Her steel-framed hull would have been a real advantage on the Stikine but it served her well in any case on the Yukon after her sale in July 1898. Eventually, she was laid up at Dawson and, along with the decaying remains of other sternwheelers, survives as one of the last reminders of the CPR's Klondike ventures.

— VOGEE COLLECTION, YUKON ARCHIVES

Operations on the Stikine

She was described in the Vancouver *Daily News-Advertiser* as being "beautifully appointed and replete in every detail." The paper went on to comment that, "the *Ogilvie* and her sisters should prove an inducement to travel on the northern rivers."

The *Ogilvie* was licensed to carry 200 passengers and measured 146.8 feet (44.7 m) long by 30 feet (9.1 m) in breadth. Her depth was 4.6 feet (1.4 m) and she drew approximately two feet (0.6 m) of water. Her gross tonnage was 741.9, making her the largest of the vessels built in Vancouver by the Canadian Pacific. Her accommodations were in keeping with the high standard the CPR maintained in its other passenger services. "The saloon passengers," noted *The Daily News-Advertiser*, "are provided with comfortable cabins, replete with every comfort for the journey and the smoking room, saloon, and ladies cabin are handsomely appointed, particularly the latter." On completing her trial trip, the *Ogilvie* was prepared for the voyage north to the Stikine River. Not a day was wasted and the new steamer sailed for the north on May 2, 1898 to begin what was to be her short-lived career on the Stikine.

The *Ogilvie* soon was followed to the Stikine by the *McConnell* and *Duchesnay* while construction work continued on the rest of the fleet. Meanwhile, at Wrangell, work crews were busy building the necessary wharves, offices and warehouses. Since Wrangell was to be the major transshipment point between the deep-sea vessels and the riverboats, a substantial facility was required to handle the steady arrivals and departures of the steamers and the transfer of their cargo. The main wharf, called the "Troup" wharf, was impressive. It was fully 495 feet (151 m) long and 40 feet (12.2 m) wide. The "T" at the end of the wharf was 70 feet (21 m) long by 300 feet (91.4 m) wide. Four slips, each 100 feet (30.5 m) long, were provided for the sternwheelers along the wharf. A warehouse, measuring 250 x 50 feet (76.2 x 15.2 m) was constructed at the end of the wharf to handle the expected heavy burden of cargo. At wharfside, the depth of water was an ample 27 feet (8.2 m). Built in only six weeks, it was described as the finest wharf in Alaska.

By May, the CPR at last was ready for the great, hoped-for boom in traffic on the Stikine. Wharf facilities were complete, four sternwheeler steamers were in operation, several others were nearing completion, and the *Tartar* and *Athenian* had proven themselves equal or superior to any vessels in the Alaska trade. Considering the time taken, this was a considerable accomplishment.

By the end of April 1898, the Stikine was clear of ice and within a week, melting snow had raised the water sufficiently for sternwheeler navigation over the river shallows. The *Tartar* arrived at Wrangell on Sunday, May 1, 1898 with a number of passengers, discharged her cargo and sailed on north making possible the first direct connection via CPR ship from the southern coast to the Stikine sternwheelers. However, other riverboats were to beat the CPR boats upriver. The first vessel to sail was the *Ramona*, which on May 2, 1898, steamed away from the CPR dock at Wrangell amid the cheers of a large crowd. She took on railway construction cargo at Cottonwood Island at the mouth of the Stikine and proceeded up the river. She was followed on the 4th by the *Monte Cristo* and the *Courser* and on the 5th by the *Hamlin*, the first of the CPR fleet in service in the north. The *Hamlin* was under the command of Captain A. Insley and, like the other steamers, loaded cargo at Cottonwood Island for the Mackenzie and Mann railway work.

Captain Troup sailed north on the *Ogilvie*, and arrived at Wrangell on the morning of May 8, 1898. At 3:15 a.m. on Wednesday, May 11, the sternwheeler steamed towards the mouth of the Stikine on her first run up the river. In a style that must have pleased Captain Troup, she quickly established herself as the fastest boat then on the river. Previously, the best time to Glenora had been four days, established by the *Ramona*. In fine form, the *Ogilvie* steamed upstream in only 26 hours and made the downstream run in a smart time of only nine hours for a total distance of 309 miles (497 km).

On the return trip, she even took time to pull the *Ramona* off a bar on which the unfortunate vessel had grounded. Competition did not extend to passing by another vessel in trouble. Not only was helping out another vessel in the traditions of seamanship, but it made good pragmatic sense, for who knew what sandbars or snags awaited an unlucky captain around the next river bend?

A passenger on board the *Ogilvie* on her first voyage, H. B. Carter, described the round trip in *The Stikeen River Journal* published at Wrangell:

"Leaving Wrangel, the steamer skirts along the northern shore of Wrangel island, and across the channel 7½ miles [12.1 km] to Cottonwood island, which divides the mouth of the Stikeen river in two parts. The steamer takes the left channel, winding in and out among the foothills of the Coast range, which rise gradually while the snow-capped peaks appear in the distance.

"Thirty miles [48 km] from the mouth of the river the Canadian boundary is reached which is a police and custom's port under Inspector Primrose.

"Twelve miles [19 km] from the boundary is Great Glacier... extending 7½ miles along the river bank and back as far as the eye can reach... Passing on through every variety of mountain and river scenery combined with the Big Canyon, about 80 miles [130 km] from the mouth of the river, is the finest part of the whole trip. Here, for a mile and a quarter [2 km], the water rushes through the narrow gorge, a mountain torrent, and on both sides the rocky cliffs rise straight from the water's edge 60 to 70 feet [18 to 21 m]. The real power of this is not realized until the down trip is made, when the steamer rushes through with the current at a rate of 20 miles per hour [32 km/h]."

— *Glenora News*, June 17, 1898

84

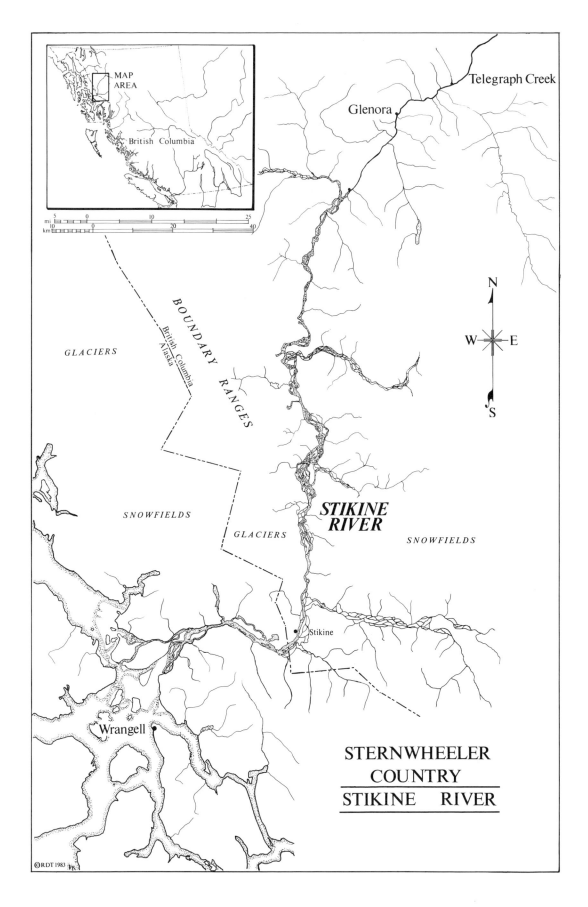

Telegraph Creek

Glenora

British Columbia

MAP AREA

mi
km

BOUNDARY RANGES

GLACIERS

British Columbia
Alaska

SNOWFIELDS

GLACIERS

N
W   E
S

STIKINE RIVER

SNOWFIELDS

Stikine

Wrangell

STERNWHEELER
COUNTRY
STIKINE   RIVER

©RDT 1983

"Here the Canadian government are establishing a semaphore at each end to be worked on the block system, the operators having telephone connections [see: Notice to Mariners, reproduced in this chapter].

"Just above this is another smaller passage, called Klootchman canyon. Twelve miles further are the Grand rapids, another piece of difficult navigation, which can be accomplished only by the most powerful steamers.

"Thirty-five miles [56 km] more and Glenora is reached, the head of navigation except in high water, when a steamer can make Telegraph Creek, twelve miles further. Glenora is at present a small settlement with a bright future, at the gateway to the Cassiar, Lake Teslin and Yukon country.

"The return trip is made in about nine hours, with the current, which averages six to eight miles an hour [9.5 to 13 km/h], there being a fall of 750 feet [228 m] from Telegraph Creek to the tide water. And this trip on a bright day combines more varied and wonderful river scenery than any I have ever seen.

"The *Ogilvie* on this record trip was commanded by Captain Sanborn and C. A. Moore, Master; with Pilot Rabe, while the genial purser, F. D. Moore, looked after the comfort of the passengers . . . "

The *Ogilvie*'s second voyage up the Stikine, basically a repetition of her first, commenced on May 18 and took just 53½ hours. It differed in that she tied up for the night two miles below the canyon and made the run through early the next morning. En route she passed five other sternwheelers all competing for what cargo and few passengers there were. However, to avoid the cut-throat competition that characterized steamboat operations on other rivers in the past, all but one of the operators agreed, in order to keep the prices up, to the following rates:

"Freight, measurement or weight
at the option of the steamer

per ton	$ 40.00
Horses, mules, burros and cattle	25.00
Dogs, sheep and goats, per head	5.00
Passengers	20.00
Berths	2.50
Meals	.75

In addition, 150 pounds [68 kg] of wearing apparel will be transported free, and the minimum rate for any package will be five dollars."

(from: *The Stikeen River Journal*, May 14, 1898)

It was clear that the companies were not about to let competition interfere with profits, if indeed there were any profits at all to be made.

By this time, a number of companies were operating on the Stikine. The growing fleet of steamers included the *Ramona, Monte Cristo, Mono, Courser, Louise, Elwood* and the CPR's own *Hamlin* and *Ogilvie*, and many more were on the way.

Excerpt from *Notice to Mariners*

"Rules for the Navigation of the Stikeen River"

"The Department of Marine and Fisheries of Canada has made arrangements for a system of signalling at Little Canyon, on the Stikeen river, to prevent collisions therein. Immediately after the opening of navigation a station will be established at each end of the canyon, at which signals will be displayed for the guidance of vessels.

A white ball, or disc, hoisted to the top of a mast will denote that the channel is clear, and that a vessel may enter the canyon from the end at which the ball is displayed.

A black drum or square will denote that the channel is not clear, and a vessel must not enter the canyon on any consideration when the drum is displayed.

The drum and ball shown together will be a signal between the two stations for information of the signalman, and no vessel may enter the canyon when this signal is shown.

In the event of vessels approaching the canyon from both ends simultaneously, the upward bound vessel will be held below the canyon until the descending vessel has run the canyon.

One prolonged blast of a steamer's whistle will be a request to the signalman to show the all clear signal.

In any other part of the river within Canadian territory, if a vessel is warping* up, a downward vessel must keep clear of her and her warping lines, stopping and tying up if necessary to prevent collision.

In the event of two vessels simultaneously approaching a place where warping is required, the upward bound vessel must allow the downbound vessel to pass before running out her warping line. Two long blasts followed by two short blasts of a steamer's whistle will be a signal that she is actually engaged in warping . . . "

Wrangel, Alaska, 19th April 1898

— *The Stikeen River Journal*

* Warping was a process of using lines, from the boat's capstan to the shore, for pulling the vessel upstream.

— The Stikeen River Journal

In addition, the Canadian government sternwheeled snagboat *Samson* was working to keep the main channels free of hull-ripping snags. A report in Vancouver's *Daily Province* of June 6, 1898 noted that the " . . . river is in splendid shape for navigation . . . the *Ogilvie* practically running on railroad time, making the round trip in three days."

By mid-June the *McConnell* and *Duchesnay* had arrived from Vancouver and were running up to Glenora, but traffic did not boom as expected. It barely trickled. Wisely, the CPR did not dispatch any more of the new boats north and by the end of the month, the *Constantine* had already been sold. Unfortunately, few records survive to provide many details of the operations of the four Canadian Pacific vessels that did reach the Stikine. Those that do, indicate that the vessels were well liked.

As far as can be determined, the most serious accident on the Stikine at this time involved a collision between the *Hamlin* and the *McConnell* on July 22, 1898 that resulted in an insurance settlement of $2,341 for the CPR. The *Hamlin* had been tied up below the canyon of the Stikine waiting for the *McConnell* to clear running downstream. However, something had apparently gone wrong in the *McConnell*'s engine room, or perhaps a steering failure, and she came sweeping out of the canyon on a collision course with the *Hamlin*. Both steamers were carried downstream by the force of the collision and the current. Damage was heavy and it is probable that neither boat operated again for the CPR on the Stikine. By this time too, the *Tartar* and *Athenian* had been withdrawn; there simply had not been enough business to keep them running. Any reservations for passage on the coastal steamers subsequently were handled by the Canadian Pacific Navigation Company.

By early July, the situation on the trail from Glenora had become disastrous. When frozen, the ground had been quite passable as long as the snow had not been too deep but as spring wore on and early summer came, the narrow trail deteriorated, becoming muddy. Not wide enough for wagons, its capacity was limited. The pack trail was not the easy route the promoters had touted and the wagon road which might have made the route tolerable was barely started. There was a shortage of pack animals and along the route there was little forage. Packing rates were $750.00 per ton [$827 per tonne]. The *Glenora News*, long a staunch supporter on the route, on July 1 condemned the trail in despair:

"Those who cannot wait another year for the road had best sell or give away their supplies and start on foot if they can't buy packhorses or pay $.35 a pound [$.77 per kg] for packing or else go back home for the winter. Much to our sorrow the *News* is no longer justified in leading Klondikers to hope for cheap or easy access to Teslin over the All-Canadian route . . . If you cannot bring the necessary horses to pack your supplies for you, or cannot pay at least $750 per ton freight to Teslin, you are crazy as a loon to try to make the trip via Glenora."

The narrow trail through the interior to Teslin forced the Klondikers to manufacture a variety of types of one-wheeled vehicles and wheelbarrows and to use dogs to pack their supplies over the rough, insect-plagued route. Some made it all the way, but many turned back in frustration.

Sternwheeler service was established on Teslin Lake that year, as had been required in Mackenzie & Mann's contract with the government. Machinery and equipment for the steamer, named the *Anglian*, was hauled over the trail and the 161-ton vessel was built on the lakeshore. The 85-foot (26-m) craft was operated by the Teslin Lake Transportation Company, a subsidiary of Mackenzie & Mann. This vessel was later incorporated into the White Pass & Yukon Route's fleet.

In late July 1898, the Canadian Pacific announced its intentions to withdraw the fleet from the Stikine, and the service was ended by early August, after just over three months of operation. Reports from early August 1898 indicated that, of the four CPR vessels, only the *Ogilvie* was still in service, making weekly trips to Glenora. She was pulled off the run, apparently having completed 13 voyages up the Stikine. Records for the summer's operations are incomplete but show the *McConnell* having made seven trips, the *Hamlin* eight and the *Duchesnay* "several." Financial reports for the one brief season indicate total earnings from these voyages as being only $2,416. The *Tartar* and *Athenian* had made only six voyages each and had not attracted sufficient traffic to be profitable. They too were removed from the service to the North.

By the time the *Ogilvie* had completed her last voyage, disposal of the fleet had already begun. Four sternwheelers of the planned fleet of 12 had been sold or diverted to other uses and work had been stopped on a fifth.

In its Annual Report for the year, published early in 1899, Canadian Pacific noted:

"your Company expended a considerable amount about the beginning of the year in ocean and river steamers for the expected large movement towards the Yukon (Klondyke) country, but, unfortunately, the steamers could not be got ready in time to take full advantage of such trade as there was; it is expected that the present season [1899] will afford them profitable employment."

However, despite the optimistic projection for the 1899 season, the dream of the all-Canadian route to the Klondike had vanished in the summer of 1898 when the bill to ratify the contract with Mackenzie & Mann, and to charter the railway from Glenora to the head of Teslin Lake, failed to win support in the Canadian Senate. As a result, the whole railway scheme had collapsed.

There were both practical and political reasons for the failure. The route was an impractical one compared with the other options for travel and transport to the Yukon. The

The Collapse of the Stikine Service

Dreams in ruin. All four of the CPR's sternwheelers that served on the Stikine during the spring and summer of 1898 rest quietly, their stacks capped and fires out. For the *McConnell* and *Ogilvie*, the future holds only scrapping for parts to be used in two new sternwheelers to be built for the White Pass and Yukon Route. The *Hamlin*, at left, and the *Duchesnay*, at right in the distance, will see many years of service under new owners but it will be far from the Stikine. — YUKON ARCHIVES

navigation season on the Stikine was short and the route difficult. Moreover, any cargo had to be reloaded at three points en route to the Klondike — namely Wrangell, Glenora and Teslin — which was inefficient and basically not very reliable. Compared to the much more direct route for a railroad then being developed over White Pass from Skagway to the Interior, the Stikine did not make much sense.

Development of the railway over White Pass to the Klondike began in 1897 when three companies were formed to gain the necessary charters. Since the route passed through Alaska, British Columbia and the Yukon, three charters were required. Consequently, the route's backers formed the British Columbia Yukon Railway Company (to operate in British Columbia), the British Yukon Railway Company (for operation in the federally administered Yukon Territory), and the Pacific & Arctic Railway & Navigation Company (a West Virginia company, to operate in the Alaska Territory of the United States). These companies were brought under the operational control of the White Pass & Yukon Company Limited, of London, England. Small wonder that the entire railway became popularly known as the "White Pass & Yukon Route," or simply, the "White Pass."

Unlike so many proposed railway schemes, the White Pass actually went ahead, despite facing some of the most awesome topography and winter weather on the continent. Moreover, it was built without benefit of a government subsidy or land grant. Construction was underway by the end of May 1898, up the Skagway River valley towards the towering Coast Mountains. At that time, on the Stikine, the CPR's sternwheelers had made less than half a dozen voyages upriver and the railway was still being debated. Through the summer and fall the crews toiled along the mountain faces, blasting their way to White Pass, dooming the ill-fated Stikine route with each foot gained.

On February 16, 1899, the railway reached White Pass summit and on July 6 of that year, the tracks were completed to the shore of Lake Bennett. The worst barriers — the mountain passes — had been breached and the route to the Klondike was secured. Any further schemes of an all-Canadian route via the Stikine were little more than impractical dreams. Just over a year later, the White Pass & Yukon Route was completed at Caribou Crossing (Carcross) and the line opened to Whitehorse, just downstream from one of the worst rapids on the Yukon River. From there navigation was comparatively easy all the way to Dawson City approximately 450 miles (725 km) further downstream.

By the spring of 1898, the political climate for the Stikine River-Teslin Lake route had changed. While the details of this aspect of the scheme go beyond the scope of this chapter, there had been a change of government in British Columbia, and in Ottawa questions were being raised in the House of Commons about Mackenzie and Mann's contract, which had been awarded without tenders being solicited. Moreover, the size of the land grant for the route was seen by opposition members as being excessive, a "give away." With the White Pass & Yukon route already under construction, the odds against the economic success of the Stikine route had grown, as had the political gamble involved. Like so many other schemes for railways, the all-Canadian route was soon forgotten.

The contractors, Mackenzie and Mann, were eventually awarded a settlement of $328,508.30 by the Exchequer Court for their preliminary work on the line and court costs but the CPR had no such recourse. All it could do was to dispose of its fleet of steamers. For the Klondikers who had made it through, there might have been some satisfaction, but for those — the majority — who turned back there was only frustration and financial loss. For the small businesses which had established at Glenora and counted on the route for their success, there was, instead, almost inevitable bankruptcy. The federal government expressed its obligation to the contractors by paying the settlement, but its sympathy, at least in financial terms, did not extend to anyone else.

The financial failure of the Stikine enterprise certainly was not attributable to the quality of the vessels used or to the skill of their crews. Considering the difficulty of navigation on the Stikine, the safety record of the vessels was good and they were handy, popular steamers. A man named MacKay, "down from the north" was quoted in Vancouver's *Daily World* as saying that the *Ogilvie* was the best boat on the river and that, "the other CPR boats, having very strong machinery, get along very well." MacKay went on to note that the river presented many obstacles to the steamboats. "There is a great jam of drift wood, and because of this and the swift current, the majority of the steamers are penned up," Mackay noted. However, by the time of his report, business had fallen off to such an extent that there would have been little reason for most of the boats to be running anyway.

Disposal of the Stikine River Fleet

By late spring, it was evident that traffic was not developing on the Stikine as quickly as had been hoped and there was little incentive to rush completion of the vessels still under construction. In fact, although the *Constantine, Dalton, Walsh, Schwatka* and *Tyrrell* had all been completed, there had been no reason to send them north. Work had continued at the False Creek yards, and by the time the end of the service was announced only the *G. M. Dawson* remained incomplete. By early August, with the whole scheme now a shambles, the Canadian Pacific found itself in the unfortunate position of having a fleet to dispose of. Realization of the failure of the project had not just come overnight so that two vessels, *Constantine* and *Tyrrell*, had been sold late in the spring and the two incomplete composite-hulled vessels were diverted to the CPR's Kootenay operations.

The *Constantine* was sold to the British American Corporation for service on the Yukon River and on June 22, 1898 set out for the north under tow by the steamer *South Portland*. Unfortunately, the two vessels ran into bad weather in the Gulf of Alaska and the comparatively frail, shallow-draught sternwheeler foundered on July 4, 1898, and was a total loss. Her owners recovered $32,000 in insurance for the vessel. The other Port Blakely-built CPR vessels were not sold immediately and were laid up on the lower Fraser River.

Unfortunately, it was not practical to dismantle any of the completed vessels and rebuild them for service in the Kootenays. The only alternative was sale, and the Company began to sell off the remaining nine vessels as fast as possible. Unfortunately, there were other operators in the same position so the market for sternwheelers on the coast was not an easy one.

The *Tyrrell*, which had a prefabricated composite hull, was the fifth of the False Creek-built vessels to be finished. She was launched on June 6, 1898 and successfully ran her trials. She steamed at a comfortable 15 miles per hour (24 km/h), but there was no reason it appears, to send her to the Stikine. She had the distinction of being the first vessel in the province to have her boiler protected with mica instead of the more traditional asbestos. She was licensed to carry 150 passengers and was a fine, if somewhat utilitarian-looking steamer.

Despite being too late for the Stikine, the *Tyrrell* was still a valuable vessel and she was sold in July 1898 for $40,000, for service on the Yukon River. She sailed north for St. Michael at the mouth of the Yukon and was in service that summer. However, the steamer had not been working long before she struck a rock and was badly damaged. Fortunately, her sturdy hull saved her and she was repaired and remained on the Yukon until the early 1920's. The *G. M. Dawson* was not completed and lay on the ways at False Creek until 1901 when she, too, was sold.

For a time, the remaining steamers were laid up pending sale. The *Dalton*, *Walsh* and *Schwatka*, the three surviving Port Blakely vessels, were registered in Portland and could not be sold to Canadian buyers without customs duty being paid. As a result, buyers for these vessels had to be found in the United States if at all possible.

In 1901, the *Dalton* was apparently acquired along with four of the other Stikine service boats by the White Pass through its subsidiary, the British Yukon Navigation Company, but she was resold that same year. Like her sister ship *Walsh*, the *Dalton* had spent several years laid up on the Fraser. The S. Willey Navigation Company purchased her and renamed her the *Capital City*. In October 1902, she suffered a near-fatal collision with the freighter *Trader* off Dash Point near Tacoma. With his steamer flooding rapidly,

The *Duchesnay* was sold by the Canadian Pacific in 1899 and was acquired later by the United States Army Quartermaster Corps for use as a work boat on the Yukon River. She was renamed the *General Jeff C. Davis* and is shown here during winter layup next to the *General J. W. Jacobs.* — ALASKA RAILWAY COLLECTION, ALASKA HISTORICAL LIBRARY

The White Pass & Yukon's sternwheeler *Dawson* was built at Whitehorse in 1901 using the engines from the CPR's never-completed steamer *G. M. Dawson* (sometimes also simply *Dawson*). — H. C. BARLEY COLLECTION, YUKON ARCHIVES

Captain Michael Edwards turned at full speed for the shore. His first mate, waist deep in water, kept the engines running until the steamer was safely aground.

The *Walsh* was not sold until 1902 when she, too, was purchased for service on Puget Sound, to operate between Seattle and Bremerton. However, she was gutted by fire at Bremerton in July 1903 and was lost. The *Schwatka* was luckier, although she remained unsold until August 1904. Her sale to Charles W. Thebo realized only $12,000. Like so many other sternwheelers built in the south, she was destined for the Yukon River and after wintering at Dutch Harbor entered service the next year on the Yukon. Eventually she became part of the White Pass & Yukon's subsidiary Northern Navigation Company fleet, which operated on the lower Yukon River. Of all the steamers built for the Stikine service, it was the *Schwatka* and *Tyrrell* (if the *Moyie* is excluded) that survived the longest. Both were beached across the Yukon River from Dawson City and gradually were stripped of useful parts. As derelict hulks, they remain along with several other sternwheelers, sad, crumbling reminders of the Klondike madness that gripped the world and the CPR.

The *Duchesnay*, the smallest of the fleet at only 276 gross tons, and licensed to carry only 40 passengers, was sold in June 1899 to E. J. Rathbone for $10,000. Later acquired by the United States Army Quartermaster Corps and renamed *General Jeff C. Davis*, she too saw extended service on the Yukon. The Army used the tough little steamer as a work boat and in the mid-1920's, she was transferred to the Alaska Railroad.

The *Ogilvie*, *McConnell*, *Hamlin*, *Dalton* and the *G. M. Dawson** were sold in January 1901 to the British Yukon Navigation Company, the steamer operation arm of the White Pass & Yukon Route in the Yukon. The *Hamlin* and *Dalton* were soon resold while the others were towed to Skagway to be dismantled. The *G. M. Dawson* had to be completed to a point where she could make the voyage north and was launched at False Creek on March 7, 1901.

The *Dawson*, as she was called following her launch for the White Pass & Yukon, was towed north by the tug *Peerless*, which then returned to Wrangell, where she took the *McConnell* and *Ogilvie* in tow for Skagway. There the three nearly-new steamers were stripped of parts, engines, boilers and major movable components. These were moved by rail to Whitehorse to be incorporated into three new sternwheelers being built there at the shipyards. The name *Dawson* was

---

* The naming of this vessel is somewhat uncertain as she was not launched until after her sale. Advertisements showed the name *G. M. Dawson*, as does the builder's half-hull model preserved at the Vancouver Maritime Museum. However, CPR Annual Reports note her as the *Dawson*, and under White Pass ownership she appears to have been named simply *Dawson*. The new steamer built at Whitehorse in 1901 using components from the CPR vessels also was named *Dawson*.

The hulls of the *McConnell*, *Ogilvie* and *G. M. Dawson* were still sound after all components useful to the White Pass & Yukon Route were removed for incorporation into the steamers *White Horse*, *Selkirk* and *Dawson* respectively. Eventually, the hull from the *G. M. Dawson*, which was actually launched as the *Dawson*, was used as a houseboat at Ikeda Bay in the Queen Charlotte Islands. This photo is from 1907.
— PABC, 95578

retained for one of the new vessels and the other two were named *White Horse* and *Selkirk*. The frames for the three steamers were constructed in Victoria and shipped north for assembly early in March 1901.

The construction of the three sternwheelers at Whitehorse was carried out at a frenzied pace; all three were ready for service within 45 days of the keels being laid. With the short navigation season on the Yukon, there was little point in having the vessels too late for profitable operations. This haste to put the boats in service may explain why the White Pass chose to scrap the three former Canadian Pacific vessels in favour of new construction. The long voyage to St. Michael was avoided in this way as was the possibility of further delay waiting for the lower Yukon to open for navigation in late June or early July. Additionally, by building essentially new vessels, the White Pass had steamers more ideally suited to its needs on the Yukon River route between Whitehorse and Dawson.

The story of the *Dawson, McConnell* and *Ogilvie* was not quite over, however, as the hulls were still sound and useful. The Vancouver *Daily Province* noted on August 15, 1901 that the tug *Pilot* had towed in three scows from Skagway. These were the stripped hulls of the three former CPR sternwheelers. They had been sold to a man named Campbell who planned to fit them out as freight scows and tow them to St. Michael, Alaska. A further report, on August 27, noted that two [unidentified] hulls, purchased at Skagway by a Mr. Adair were towed to False Creek to be converted to barges. "Some 15 hulls of former Stikine River sternwheelers are being fitted out at False Creek as scows or barges," the report noted. It was a sad end for many fine vessels. The ultimate end of the hulls is uncertain but the *Dawson*'s, at least, was used as the basis for a floating bunkhouse for a mining camp on the Queen Charlotte Islands.

The fate of the *Hamlin* was somewhat different from that of the other vessels. She was sold by the White Pass in January 1903 to John Banser, William McCallum and David Reider who in turn sold her to Thomas Kickham. Seven years later, in 1910, Kickham sold her to Edward Coyle, a steamship agent, who sold her in 1911 to a company known as the Hamlin Tug Boat Company of Victoria. At this time, apparently, she was operating on the Fraser River. In December 1913 her title passed to James Green and in 1917 she was acquired by the Defiance Packing Company of Vancouver. She remained on the register of shipping into the mid-1920's.

As a final comment on these unusual events in the story of the Canadian Pacific's sternwheeler service, it is interesting that of the 10 sternwheelers built on the coast for the Stikine to provide a transportation link to the Yukon, seven eventually were sold for operation in the Yukon or Alaska. While the scheme was certainly misguided, the vessels were sound and well thought out. In the end, the CPR had to write off

The Canadian Pacific's Stikine service sternwheelers were built
to provide transportation to the Yukon and it was in the Yukon,
fittingly, that several of the steamers, or at least components of
them, found useful employment. Here, in a 1903 photograph
from the Yukon, the *Tyrrell* and the three White Pass & Yukon
Route boats built from the *Ogilvie*, *McConnell* and *G. M.
Dawson* are all under steam. — VPL

$171,579 as a loss from the construction and sale of the vessels — certainly not a large amount for a corporation the size of the CPR, but neither was it insignificant. For the Canadian Pacific, the most enduring and beneficial result of the entire Stikine venture was the construction of the sternwheelers *Minto* and *Moyie* in the Kootenays following their diversion from the coast. It is to these vessels that the story of the Lake and River Service now turns.

Ghosts from the past. Eighty-four years after the shipwrights at Port Blakely put the finishing touches on the CPR sternwheeler *Schwatka*, her hull and cabins still withstood the trials of time and the weather. Across the Yukon River from Dawson City the *Schwatka*, at left, and the sternwheeler *Seattle No. 3* slowly succumb to decay. A short distance downstream are the remains of the *Tyrrell*. The wind whistles through their long-empty and now twisted and distorted cabins and shrubs grow up through their hulls but the fact that they survived at all into the 1980's was a tribute to the care that went into their construction.
— ROBERT D. TURNER

Whatever the setbacks were from the failure of the Stikine River service, the Kootenays were prospering and traffic on the Lake and River Service steamers was growing rapidly. A clear benefit to the Kootenay services was the return of experienced officers and crew members who had been transferred to the Stikine boats. A second benefit was the diversion of the steamers *Minto* and *Moyie*, originally intended for the Stikine, to the Kootenays. The *Minto* was assembled at Nakusp and made a fine addition to the service on the Columbia. Here, she is at Arrowhead, in the company of the nearly new *Rossland* and the *Trail*. — R. H. TRUEMAN, PABC, 1264

CHAPTER  IV

YEARS OF GROWTH
AND YEARS OF CHANGE

The Moyie, *the* Minto
and the Crowsnest Line

THE AMBITIOUS SCHEME for a steamship and sternwheeler service to the Klondike was in shambles, but at least the Canadian Pacific was able to redirect two of the prefabricated steel sternwheeler hulls to the Kootenays where the vessels could be put to profitable use. It was decided to assemble one vessel at Nelson and the other at Nakusp, in this way adding a new steamer to each of the two important lake routes. The vessel for the Arrow Lakes service was to replace the *Nakusp*, recently destroyed by fire, while the one for Kootenay Lake was to provide a badly needed addition to the overtaxed *Nelson* and *Kokanee*. With the planned completion of the CPR's Crowsnest Pass railway line to Kootenay Lake by the end of 1898, traffic was expected to increase significantly.

For service in the Kootenays, it was decided to lengthen the hulls by 20 feet (6.1 m) and during the summer and autumn of 1898 work progressed smoothly. The two new steamers were of the riverboat pattern, with wide, flat-bottomed hulls. As the vessels neared launching their overall utilitarian lines became evident. Neither new sternwheeler was to be as elegant or graceful as the speedy *Rossland* or *Kokanee* but in the end such aesthetic considerations would prove insignificant to the careers of the two sternwheelers; they would outlive all of their running mates by many years.

They were not large vessels. Their length was 161.7 feet (49.3 m) and their breadth 30.1 feet (9.2 m). The depth of the hulls was 5.1 feet (1.6 m). Minor differences were made in the vessels for the individual requirements of the services, so that the *Moyie*'s gross tonnage was 835 while the *Minto*'s was 829. In later years more modifications were made to the vessels and the *Minto* was considerably altered by the addition of extra cabin accommodations.

The prefabricated components for the first vessel, the *Moyie*, arrived at Nelson late in June 1898 and a crew of riveters began assembling the frames and steel plating. Their work took about one month and on July 26, the riveters left Nelson for Nakusp to begin work on the *Minto*. Reportedly,

99

there were 1,000 pieces to each of the steel hulls. With the hulls assembled, the work then fell to the carpenters, pipe-fitters and painters to complete the steamers.

The *Moyie* was launched at the CPR shipyard at Nelson on Saturday, October 22, 1898. She was christened by Mrs. Troup, who was presented with a cake basket by Chief Engineer Sproat on behalf of the shipyard workers. As usual it was an exciting time for the whole city and a large crowd was present for the launch. The *Kokanee* left the city wharf for the shipyard with a full load of spectators and several hundred walked to the yards. Even the train from Slocan pulled up opposite the shipyard so that the passengers could witness the celebration.

Mrs. Troup broke the traditional bottle of champagne over the bows, " . . . the ropes were cut, [and] the newly christened *Moyie* slid rapidly down the ways . . . She was floating gracefully on the water," continued *The Miner*, " . . . with her steam up and everything ready for her trial trip . . . Captain Troup was at the wheel and after circling around, the *Moyie* returned to the shore accompanied by the *Kokanee* . . . " One hour later the *Moyie* made a trial run to Five Mile Point to test her machinery. Reportedly, she steamed at 16 knots, not as fast as the *Kokanee*, it was noted by *The Miner*, but " . . . she gave every satisfaction to those in charge."

While she was sufficiently complete for a trial trip, the *Moyie* was still not ready for service because considerable work remained to be done on her passenger accommodations. The Company planned to have her first run coincide with a special excursion marking the opening of the Crowsnest Pass line to Kootenay Landing. This was scheduled for December 6, 1898, and the *Moyie* was ready for the event.

Invited guests from Rossland, Kaslo and Nelson boarded the *Moyie* at 8:00 a.m. on December 6 and, half an hour later, the steamer pulled away from the Nelson dock on her first passenger trip. The run down the lake was uneventful, and on arrival at Kootenay Landing, the dignitaries were served lunch on board. From there, they proceeded by special train to Cranbrook where they spent the night and a banquet was held. The next day, the party travelled on to Fernie, the coal mining centre of the Crowsnest. Later in the day they returned west for a banquet and reception by the Fort Steele Board of Trade. The festivities carried on until 2:00 a.m. The next afternoon, the special train left Cranbrook and reached Kootenay Landing at 8:00 p.m. for dinner on board the *Moyie* and the cruise back to Nelson. It was a festive initiation for the *Moyie* and somewhat in contrast to what would become her routine duties on Kootenay Lake.

On entering regular service, the *Moyie* took over from the *Nelson* on the run from Nelson eastwards. Initially, the route was to Kuskonook and way points but with the opening of the Crowsnest line to passenger service soon after the special excursion, the terminal changed to Kootenay Landing. The

Interior decorations in the *Moyie*.
— ROBERT D. TURNER

The *Moyie* was assembled at the CPR's shipyard at Nelson. In this photograph, much work remains to be done to her cabins and her sternwheel. The smaller vessel under construction in the foreground is probably the tug *Ymir*, which was launched in 1899. — PABC, 90338

A newly completed *Moyie*. With the benefits of a composite hull and a utilitarian design, she was destined to outlast all other CPR sternwheelers and finally to be preserved at Kaslo. — PABC, 724

Moyie remained the regular boat on this key service, linking the Canadian Pacific's main east-west rail route through southeastern British Columbia, until she was replaced by the larger *Kuskanook* in 1906.

Nelson had become the major transportation centre of the West Kootenays by the time the *Moyie* was built and was served directly by rail lines and steamships of both the CPR and the Canadian subsidiaries of the Great Northern Railway. Some idea of the activity that was developing around Nelson can be gained from the following schedule of passenger services available in late December 1898:

"Trains and Steamers Arriving and Departing From Nelson

6:20 a.m. Train leaves N&FS station for Rossland, Spokane and way points daily.

7:00 a.m. S.S. *Moyie* leaves for Kuskonook and way points Monday, Wednesday and Friday.

7:15 a.m. S.S. *International* arrives from Kaslo and way points daily except Sunday.

7:30 a.m. S.S. *Alberta* leaves for Kaslo and way points on Tuesday, Thursday and Saturday.

9:00 a.m. Train leaves CPR station for Slocan City daily except Sunday.

11:00 a.m. S.S. *Kokanee* arrives from Kaslo and way points daily except Sunday.

2:20 p.m. Train leaves CPR station for Slocan City and way points daily except Sunday.

4:00 p.m. S.S. *Kokanee* leaves for Kaslo and way points daily except Sunday.

4:30 p.m. S.S. *International* leaves for Kaslo and way points daily except Sunday.

5:35 p.m. Train arrives N&FS station from Spokane, Rossland and way points Monday, Wednesday and Friday.

6:30 p.m. S.S. *Moyie* arrives from Kuskonook and all way points Monday, Wednesday and Friday.

6:30 p.m. S.S. *Alberta* arrives from Kuskonook and way points Tuesday, Thursday and Saturday.

6:40 p.m. Train leaves CPR station for Robson, Rossland and all main line points daily.

10:30 p.m. Train arrives CPR station from all main line points, Rossland and Robson daily.

Steam tugs *Kaslo, Angerona, Red Star, Hercules, Surprise* and others ply Kootenay Lake to and from Nelson but have no regular times of arrival and departure."

(*Nelson Daily Miner*, December 23, 1898)

Meanwhile, at Nakusp, the *Minto* had joined the Arrow Lakes fleet. She was launched from the busy Nakusp shipyard on November 19, 1898, and was ready for service one month

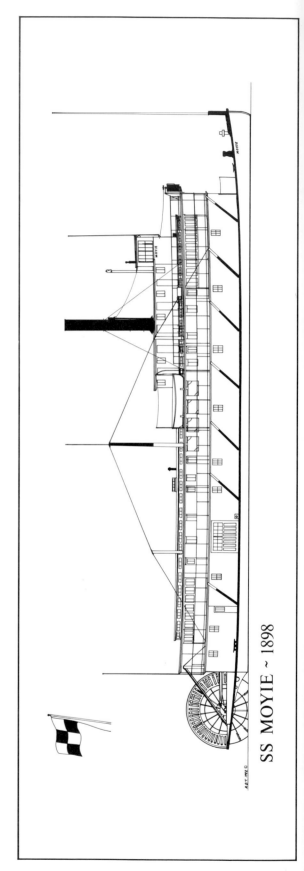

SS MOYIE ~ 1898

The completion of the *Moyie* coincided closely with the opening of the CPR's Crowsnest Pass railway through to the southern end of Kootenay Lake. The *Moyie* provided an important link between Nelson and the end of the railway at Kootenay Landing. — CPCA

At Nelson, the *Moyie* rests at the city wharf between runs to Kootenay Landing. Behind her is the Great Northern's steamer *Kaslo* which was built in 1900 and is discussed later in this chapter. — J. D. SPURWAY COLLECTION

The official invitation to the opening excursion on the new Crowsnest Pass railway which included a cruise on the new *Moyie*.
— GERRY WELLBURN COLLECTION

The steel sheeting and frames of the *Minto*'s composite hull gave her extra strength to battle ice but even with these advantages, the normal procedure was to push an ice-breaking barge ahead of the steamer to clear a channel.
— OMER LAVALLEE COLLECTION

It is a beautiful, crisp spring day at Nakusp as the *Kootenay* approaches the steamer wharf. A light dusting of snow, melted from the docks and buildings, still covers the ground. To the left, the new *Minto* is docked beside the transfer slip for the railway car barges. — CPCA

Some of the crew of the *Minto* on her maiden
voyage in December 1898.
FRONT ROW, LEFT TO RIGHT: Jack Young, second
engineer; Jack Fife, chief engineer; Captain
John C. Gore; Jim Taylor, purser; and
William Kirby, mate.
BACK ROW, LEFT TO RIGHT: Walter Wright,
watchman; Harry Cook, expressman; the freight
clerk; steward; and William Thomson, bartender.
Captain Gore later succeeded Captain Troup as
manager of the Lake and River Service. Walter
Wright later became a captain of the *Minto*.
Photo taken aboard *Rossland*.
— MRS. RAY KOSIANCIC COLLECTION

The passenger tug *Sandon*, built in 1898 at
Rosebery for the Slocan Lake route. She was
used to supplement the sternwheeler *Slocan* and
was particularly useful moving railway car
barges. — EARL MARSH COLLECTION

The tug *Valhalla* was launched amid ice and snow early in 1901 at the Nelson shipyard as a small crowd looked on. After the completion of the *Moyie*, the greatest need was for tugs and barges to move railway cars between Nelson (after January 1901, Procter) and Kootenay Landing. The shipyard, as illustrated above, was located at the west end of the CPR yards at Nelson and was too crowded for the growing needs of an expanding service. In 1903, new property was purchased at Fairview to the northeast, past the site of Nelson's present day highway bridge spanning the West Arm of Kootenay Lake. In 1904 and 1905 the yard was developed so that by the time the *Kuskanook* was built in 1906, a large, modern facility was in operation. The *Valhalla* was the last boat constructed at the old shipyard. — PABC, 741

later. She provided a fine and sturdy replacement for the *Nakusp* and, because of her steel-framed hull, was better able to operate in the winter months when ice could become a problem. The completion of the *Minto*, together with the new *Rossland* and *Kootenay*, gave a total of three modern sternwheelers on the Arrow Lakes as well as the *Trail* and the older *Lytton*. The *Illecillewaet*, the little self-propelled barge, was also still available for service and was used along with the *Trail* to haul rail and other construction materials for the extension of the Columbia and Western Railway to the Boundary district. Additionally, the Company had the steam tug *Columbia*, which was employed on the barge service between Arrowhead and Nakusp. Built in 1896, she was still in good condition and was an important, if not especially dramatic, unit of the fleet. Consequently, through a combination of hard work and, indirectly, the collapse of the Stikine service, the Lake and River Service had replaced all of the major sternwheelers, except for the *Lytton* on the Arrow Lakes service. The older vessels — the *Lytton* and *Illecillewaet* — were retired in the next few years, and the *Trail* was lost to fire. Thereafter, the fleet remained unchanged until 1909, when a new tug was added.

The fleet on Kootenay Lake comprised the new *Moyie*, the *Nelson*, and the speedy *Kokanee*. However, with the completion of the important Crowsnest rail link, the need for tugs to move railway car barges between Kootenay Landing and Nelson became critical. Consequently, work at the shipyard shifted from sternwheeler construction to the building of tugs and barges. On February 27, 1899, the first of the Canadian Pacific's tugs for Kootenay Lake was launched at the Nelson shipyards and named *Ymir*. She was a sturdy, wooden-hulled, screw-driven vessel of 90 gross tons. She measured 77.7 feet (23.7 m) long by 16.7 (5.1 m) in breadth. Her depth of hull was 6.5 feet (2 m) and her compound engines were rated at 27.3 nominal horsepower.

The *Ymir* was followed the next year by the *Procter*, a 65-foot (19.8-m) screw tug of 43 gross tons, and in 1901 by the larger and more powerful tug *Valhalla*. At that time, the *Valhalla* was the largest tug on Kootenay Lake, measuring 102.5 x 20.8 x 9.0 feet (31.2 x 6.3 x 2.7 m). At 153 gross tons, she was powered by a two-cylinder compound engine rated at 36.5 nominal horsepower, produced by the Polson Iron Works of Toronto.

The final addition to the Canadian Pacific's Lake and River Service during the 1890's was for Slocan Lake. In October 1898, the tug *Sandon*, was launched and placed in service at Rosebery to act as a relief vessel for the *Slocan* and to tow railway barges up and down the lake. The *Sandon* was a wooden-hulled vessel with a tall, raked funnel that gave her a distinctive appearance. She measured 76.0 feet (23.2 m) in length and 16.9 feet (5.2 m) in breadth at 97.2 gross tons.

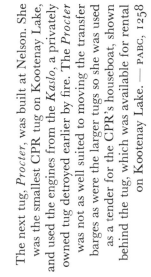

The *Ymir* was the first tug built for the CPR
barge service on Kootenay Lake. She was
similar in design to the *Columbia*, built for the
C&KSN in 1896. — PABC, 740

The next tug, *Procter*, was built at Nelson. She
was the smallest CPR tug on Kootenay Lake,
and used the engines from the *Kaslo*, a privately
owned tug detroyed earlier by fire. The *Procter*
was not as well suited to moving the transfer
barges as were the larger tugs so she was used
as a tender for the CPR's houseboat, shown
behind the tug, which was available for rental
on Kootenay Lake. — PABC, 1258

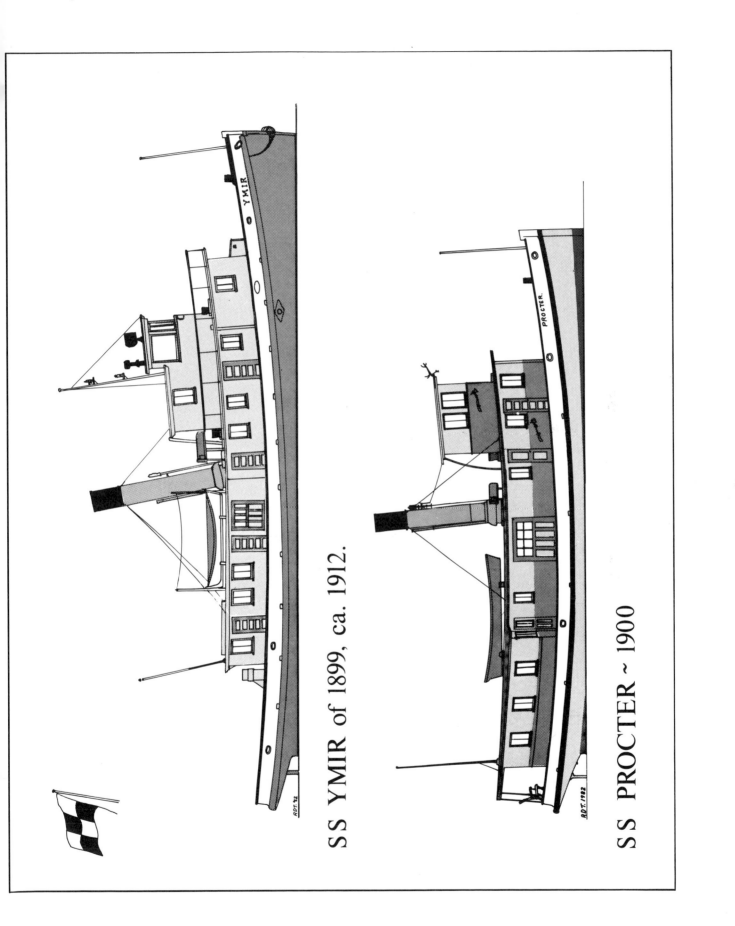

SS YMIR of 1899, ca. 1912.

SS PROCTER ~ 1900

When a new sternwheeler arrived on the scene, races were irresistible. Racing neck and neck, the *International* and the *Moyie* steam down the West Arm of Kootenay Lake. Who won is uncertain but the competition was spirited.
— PABC, 2013

The *International* was a racer and her crew tested her against several of the CPR's sternwheelers. In the lower far left photo, she appears to have fallen behind her rival. Unfortunately, which steamer she is racing is not known but quite possibly it is the *Moyie*. The photo on the near left shows the *International* racing once again, but later in her career after deck railings were added in front of her pilot house. Here, she is racing along the West Arm with fury, but did she win? If she were racing the *Kuskanook* in 1908, as shown on page 133, then her chances were slim and she was destined to be defeated.
— PABC, 1509, 1462

No new vessels were added to the Okanagan Lake service at this time; the *Aberdeen* was still the only Canadian Pacific vessel in the Okanagan.

Canadian Pacific Railway construction to replace or supplement the steamer services during this period was restricted to extending the tracks along the shore of the West Arm of Kootenay Lake from Nelson to Procter. The purpose of this line was to bypass the West Arm of the lake, which was prone to freezing over in the winter. It also reduced the length of the freight runs for the tugs and barges and brought the planned rail line along Kootenay Lake to Kootenay Landing a small step closer to completion. The branch line was opened for service on December 6, 1900, and the barge slip for transferring the railway cars was completed on January 20, 1901. In bad weather, the sternwheelers were able to terminate their runs at Procter, with a connection to Nelson being provided on the railway.

Overall, the Lake and River Service was in an excellent position by the turn of the century to handle the trade from developing mining, lumbering and agricultural communities of southeastern British Columbia. The next decade would see many changes in the service but the basic pattern of operations was established and would remain more or less the same for another quarter century.

The Great Northern's Finest: the *Kaslo*

While the Canadian Pacific had been building its fleet and extending its railway system in the Kootenays, the Great Northern had not been idle. Its most important move, in terms of sternwheeler operations, was to build a branch line north from Bonners Ferry, Idaho, to Kuskonook on Kootenay Lake. The line bypassed the slow and difficult-to-navigate section of river between the two points and was designed to facilitate moving passengers, freight and ore from the Kaslo-Slocan district to the Great Northern's main line at Bonners Ferry.

The American end of the branch line was built using the charter of the Kootenai Valley Railway Company, whereas the Canadian portion was incorporated as the Bedlington and Nelson Railway. In an apparently rare mood of co-operation, the Great Northern and the Canadian Pacific agreed to an exchange of running rights over their trackage. The CPR secured running privileges between the outskirts of Nelson and Troup Junction (Five Mile Point) on the Nelson and Fort Sheppard Railway to facilitate the construction of the branch to Procter noted in the previous section. In exchange, the GN was able to operate over the CPR between Sirdar and Creston, just below the south end of Kootenay Lake. Such pragmatic exchanges of running rights saved both lines a great deal of money and inconvenience without endangering either's competitive position.

For the Great Northern, the new line provided a more direct route for traffic from the Slocan mining district to Spokane and enabled it to direct traffic away from the steeper, more mountainous route of the Nelson and Fort Sheppard.

Politically, the Great Northern, as an American railroad, had experienced difficulty building under its own name into British Columbia and had operated through subsidiaries to minimize the image of the large foreign railroad drawing off traffic to the south. In the Kootenays, during the 1890's, GN had acquired control of Daniel Corbin's Spokane Falls and Northern-Nelson and Fort Sheppard lines, and also his extension to Rossland. Additionally, the GN had backed, and in fact controlled, the Kaslo and Slocan Railway operating between Kaslo and Sandon in the heart of the Slocan mining district. In 1898, to further improve its competitive position for the trade on Kootenay Lake, GN backed the incorporation of the Kootenay Railway and Navigation Company (KR&N).

The purpose of this company was to take over the operations of the Kaslo and Slocan Railway and the International Navigation and Trading Company. Shortly afterwards, the KR&N also gained control of the operations of the Bedlington and Nelson Railway and the Kaslo and Lardo-Duncan Railway. The latter was a projected line from the head of Kootenay Lake up the Lardeau River which was planned to tap new mining discoveries in the area. The GN-backed line was never completed, although some grading was done, but a CPR branch line was completed in 1902 from Lardeau to Gerrard at the southern end of Trout Lake.

The KR&N was formed following a meeting between James J. Hill and Henry W. Forster, M.P., and was capitalized at 500,000 pounds. Forster, however, was never able to raise as much British capital as he promised Hill, and the Great Northern was forced to put more and more money into the venture to maintain its influence in the area. The KR&N was financed through the issue of both common stock and debenture stock. The common stock was issued to the original owners of the companies consolidated into the KR&N, including the International Navigation and Trading Co. The debentures were publicly subscribed and most of these were eventually acquired by the Great Northern. The KR&N was not a financial success and only made a profit in one year — 1902. In 1910-11, the Company was forced into liquidation, having lost almost half a million dollars in the preceding 10 years. By this time GN, which had acquired all of the common stock of the Company, ended its unprofitable bid for the traffic of the Slocan.

Although the KR&N was doomed to financial failure and eventual liquidation, nonetheless its small fleet of sternwheelers provided worthy competition to the CPR's steamers. The KR&N boats may have lost money, but at least they did it "with class." They were fine examples of turn-of-the-century sternwheelers and their presence certainly kept the Lake and River Service on a keener competitive edge.

The river steamer *Argenta* was built by the Kootenay Railway and Navigation Company in 1900 to run from Kaslo across Kootenay Lake to the Duncan River and from there upstream in connection with the proposed Kaslo and Lardo-Duncan Railway. — MOYIE MUSEUM

The magnificent sternwheeler *Kaslo* was the finest vessel in the Kootenay Railway and Navigation Company's fleet. She was fully comparable to any of the CPR's steamers and well built. Launched at Mirror Lake on September 17, 1900, she began service on a new route between Kaslo and the town of Kuskanook at the southern end of Kootenay Lake at the end of the Great Northern-controlled Bedlington and Nelson Railway. — MOYIE MUSEUM

Steamer excursions were always popular and the new *Kaslo* was used for her share. She was a fast and comfortable boat and certainly made a most appealing sight as she steamed down Kootenay Lake. — PABC, 1742

The *Kaslo* has just been launched from the Mirror Lake shipyard near Kaslo and is a splendid sight for the guests of the KR&N, local residents, and the families of the shipyard workers. Here, a large crowd boards the *Alberta* for the return to Kaslo after the ceremonies have been completed. — MOYIE MUSEUM

At the time of its formation, the KR&N owned the sternwheelers *International* and *Alberta*. The *Alberta* was beginning to show signs of age and two new vessels were promptly ordered. The first of these was the small sternwheeler *Argenta*, completed at the Mirror Lake shipyard in August 1900, especially for service up the Duncan River from Kaslo. At only 206 gross tons and measuring a modest 92 x 20 feet (28 x 6.1 m), she was approximately the size of the ill-fated *City of Ainsworth*, and was smaller than any of the CPR vessels on Kootenay Lake.

Far more impressive was the next vessel launched at the Mirror Lake shipyard — the magnificent steamer *Kaslo*, a boat pretty enough and fast enough to make even James Troup take careful notice. In many ways she looked like an enlarged version of the *Kokanee* but with a rounded, more elegant pilothouse. She had a deep lakeboat hull, large paddlewheel, enclosed in a paddle box, and fine lines. She measured 173.5 x 27.0 x 7.4 feet (53 x 8.2 x 2.3 m) and her gross tonnage was 765. She was longer and narrower than the *Moyie*, largest sternwheeler on the Lake in 1900, but somewhat smaller in tonnage. It did not take a naval architect to see that she was built for speed and it was clear that the *Kokanee* was to be eclipsed as the "speed queen" of Kootenay Lake.

On September 17, 1900, the *Kaslo* was launched and was christened by Miss Maggie Bell. A holiday had been declared in Kaslo and most of the town's population was in attendance. The *Alberta* provided a free excursion from Kaslo, and the steamers *Marion* and *Vixen* also carried parties to the launching. The launch was flawless and Kaslo waited expectantly for the completion of the new steamer.

Robert Elliott, shipwright and foreman of the yard, was the designer. T. M. Macdougall was construction engineer, while the interior details, estimates and stores had been supervised by James Waugh. The boiler and engines were supplied by the Polson Iron Works and she was fitted throughout with electric lights.

The KR&N had spared little expense in furnishing the *Kaslo*. All staterooms were fitted with basins and taps, a feature not included in CPR vessels built 10 years later. The dining saloon was arranged as an alcove with large outside windows, affording passengers, *The Kootenaian* noted, " . . . a perfect view of the passing scenery while at the table." The interior of the boat featured carved mahogany and mirrors while the transoms were in ground glass, " . . . relieved with photographic transparencies or choice local scenes." A large smoking room was located forward and aft was the ladies' cabin, carpeted and upholstered in tapestries.

The *Kaslo* was placed in service between the railhead at Kuskonook, Pilot Bay and Kaslo, while the *International* provided a connecting service between Pilot Bay and Nelson. A chronic problem with the GN service from the Slocan mines was the Kaslo and Slocan Railway. Because the railway was

Smelters were particularly important to the developing hard-rock
mining industry of the West Kootenays. At the smelters, the ores
were processed to remove a high percentage of waste rock. The
resulting concentrates could then be shipped to refineries for
further purification. Several smelters were built in the West
Kootenays during the 1890's, including the large facility shown
above at Pilot Bay on Kootenay Lake. Other smelters were built
at Revelstoke and Nelson but the largest and most important
smelter in the district was the famous one at Trail which the
CPR acquired in 1898. The sternwheeler at the dock is the
CPR's *Nelson*. — PABC, 38413

narrow gauge, it was not possible to transfer cars by barge directly to Kuskonook for movement south. Consequently, any freight or ore had to be unloaded from the rail cars at Kaslo and moved onto the steamer for movement down Kootenay Lake. At Kuskonook, the cargo had to be transferred again back to the railway. This was a time-consuming, labour intensive, and therefore costly, operation.

By early October, the *Kaslo* was close enough to completion to carry a party of Great Northern officials, including James J. Hill's son, J. N. Hill, and his two daughters, from Kuskonook to Kaslo and then to Five Mile Point and south over the N&FS. Their private car had been transferred from one railhead to the other by barge. However, the *Kaslo*, was not actually ready for regular passenger service until November 29, 1900. She soon showed her capacity for speed, beating the rival *Kokanee* on several occasions early in December.

Despite the Great Northern's efforts to develop the route via Kuskonook, traffic did not materialize as expected. KR&N expenses ran well ahead of revenues. For example, in December 1900, the month after the *Kaslo* entered service, expenses were $7,517.08 whereas revenue was only $4,782.60. The picture did not improve and by the end of 1901, the *Kaslo* was withdrawn from this route to operate instead on the more heavily travelled route between Kaslo and Nelson. The *International*, *Alberta* and *Argenta* continued in service as business demanded, but the route to the south via Kuskonook had proved to be an unfortunate venture.

Interlude: 1900 to 1905

While the Great Northern was making its final determined effort to win the trade on Kootenay Lake, three of the sternwheelers from the Columbia and Kootenay Steam Navigation fleet had finally reached the ends of their careers. It was less than a decade since the first of them, the *Lytton*, had been built, but newer and bigger boats had come and the life of the wooden-hulled sternwheelers was short. Their hulls soon became waterlogged and needed rebuilding usually after seven or eight years. The *Lytton* and *Illecillewaet* spent their last productive period working in connection with the extension of the Columbia and Kootenay Railway westward from Castlegar towards Grand Forks and Midway. They were used for bringing in rail and other cargo and then, until a railway bridge was completed across the Columbia, a ferry service had to be maintained. The *Lytton* was used in this capacity until March 1902, when the bridge was completed. After that she was taken to Nakusp and stripped of usable components. The *Illecillewaet* was sold at this time for $500, and the cedar planking from her cabins found its way into a number of homes in the vicinity of Burton City.

The *Trail* escaped the inglorious end of the other two former C&KSN sternwheelers when she caught fire at West Robson in June 1900, and her entire superstructure was de-

The *Trail* met an unfortunate end when she caught fire at Robson West in June 1900.
— PABC, 40372

Before the completion of the large railway bridge across the Columbia at Castlegar, a barge service was operated to connect the Columbia and Western Railway with the Columbia and Kootenay. Both were CPR lines and the sternwheelers provided the vital connection until July 1902. Here, the *Illecillewaet* is using her best efforts to keep the river channel open from ice while in the distance the *Lytton* is moving a transfer barge towards the Robson West wharf.
— PABC, 1415

The small screw-driven steamer *York* of 1902 was originally intended for Trout Lake service but was diverted instead to the Okanagan to provide a relief vessel for the *Aberdeen*. The two steamers are shown together at Kelowna in 1906.
— KELOWNA MUSEUM

stroyed. All that remained of her was a charred hull with the boiler intact and the funnel standing, incongruously tall, above the deck.

In terms of human fatalities, at least, the safety record of the sternwheelers was good, although many of the vessels themselves seemed destined to short lives, abbreviated by fires or groundings. Still, the story of the Lake and River Service focuses for the most part on the happy times — the launchings, excursions, steamboat races — and on the daily, generally unexciting routine of service to the communities along the routes. However, there were always risks and lives were lost.

On April 8, 1901, the *Valhalla* with barge No. 15 was steaming towards Procter from Kootenay Landing in calm weather when, without warning, the barge gave a sudden lurch, throwing five coal cars into the lake. Immediately, it lurched in the other direction and dumped three more cars into the lake at which point Captain Taylor of the *Valhalla* cut the lines to the barge. No sooner had the tug been cut free than a man was seen struggling in the water, crying for help. He managed to scramble up onto the barge which had by then settled onto an even keel. The tug crew took the barge in hand again and eased it to the shore. On questioning the man who had been rescued they found that he and two others had hidden aboard the train at Fernie. The other two, he said, had also been on the barge, but no trace of them was ever found.

That fall, the *Kokanee*, when approaching Pilot Bay, was the scene of another personal tragedy. A deckhand, George Young, slipped and fell overboard. He must have lost his footing while preparing the heavy gangplank, and have been injured. Immediately, other crew members threw two life buoys, one right to him where he surfaced, but he sank immediately. A lifeboat was lowered, but the man was gone. He was survived by a wife and four children.

Overall, there were few other fatal accidents on the Lake and River Service boats. Probably the worst occurred on the sternwheeler *Kuskanook* in 1925, when a water trap in the main steam pipe leading from the boiler aft to the engine room gave way, shooting high pressure steam all over the engine room. Three crew members, J. E. Parker, R. A. Davis and H. Forbes, could not escape in time and were scalded to death.

*　　*　　*

In 1901, the Canadian Pacific purchased the coastal steamship operations of the Canadian Pacific Navigation Company (CPN), headquartered at Victoria. This fleet served a number of important routes between Victoria and the British Columbia mainland as well as coastal routes which extended all the way to Skagway, Alaska. By the time of the CPR purchase, the CPN fleet was in need of modernization and overall improvement. To oversee this work, Captain Troup was appointed manager of the CPR's new venture, and Captain John C. Gore succeeded him as superintendent of the Lake and River Service at Nelson.

For James Troup, the new British Columbia Coast Steamship Service was to be an all-consuming challenge for the remainder of his working life. He put his talents as a naval architect and his persuasive abilities to work immediately and convinced Canadian Pacific's management to build some of the finest coastal liners ever seen on the Pacific Coast. The first was the outstanding *Princess Victoria* and others, such as the *Princess Charlotte*, *Princess Marguerite* and *Princess Kathleen*, were to follow before his retirement in 1927.[†]

Included in the purchase of the CPN were three sternwheelers used primarily on the lower Fraser River. These were the *Transfer* of 1893, the *Beaver* of 1898 and the old *R. P. Rithet* of 1882. While these vessels were not included in the British Columbia Lake and River Service, a brief note on their careers is appropriate to complete the story of the CPR's sternwheelers.

The *R. P. Rithet*, a wooden-hulled steamer of 817 tons, was the largest, and was used on the Fraser and also, during the summer months, in service to Vancouver Island. She had been built in 1882 for John Irving's Pioneer Line and the following year was incorporated into the CPN fleet when Irving merged his fleet with the coastal vessels of the Hudson's Bay Company. The *Transfer* was a smaller steamer of only 264 tons and her route was between New Westminster and points downstream on the Fraser, such as Ladner and Steveston. The *Beaver*, a modern, steel-hulled boat, had been built in 1898 for service on the Stikine but had been diverted instead to the Fraser. She had the distinction of being the first steel-hulled vessel built in British Columbia. She was built by the Albion Iron Works of Victoria. The *Beaver*'s run was from New Westminster upstream to Chilliwack and way points. These sternwheelers served as an important link from the Coast to the small agricultural communities developing in the Fraser Valley but they were particularly vulnerable to competition from automobiles and the electric interurban railway system being built in the area. The *Transfer* and the *R. P. Rithet* were both sold in 1909, the latter becoming the *Baramba* for the Terminal Steam Navigation Company, and ultimately being stripped to a barge in 1917. The *Beaver* operated for the CPR until 1913 when she was retired following the completion of the B.C. Electric's interurban line to Chilliwack. Five years later, she was sold to the government of British Columbia and was rebuilt as a ferry to cross the Fraser between Ladner and Steveston. She was replaced by a new vessel in 1930.

*　　*　　*

† For a detailed account of the Canadian Pacific's British Columbia Coast Steamship Service, see *The Pacific Princesses* (1977).

Trout Lake City about 1900. — VPL, 101

Trout Lake, north of Kootenay Lake, was the scene of further mining activity and the CPR expanded its interests into the area by building a branch line from Lardeau to Gerrard at the southern end of Trout Lake. The Company bought the steamer *Victoria* to operate on Trout Lake. She is shown at Trout Lake City as ore is being tallied on a barge. — VPL, 115

Page from June 7, 1903 timetable, Columbia and Kootenay Steamers. — BCPM

Time Table No. 3, June 7th, 1903.
COLUMBIA AND KOOTENAY STEAMERS

COLUMBIA RIVER ROUTE—Steamers "Rossland," "Kootenay" and "Minto"

SOUTHBOUND		NORTHBOUND	
l DAILY		*a* DAILY	
10.15	.... Arrowhead	14.50	
11.15	...... HALCYON HOT SPRINGS	13.50	
{ 13.00	.... Nakusp	11.50 ⌐	
{ 13.10		10.50 ⌐	
20.00	.... Robson	22.00	
a DAILY		*l* DAILY	

SLOCAN LAKE ROUTE—Steamer "Slocan"

l DAILY Ex. Sunday	*l* DAILY Ex. Sunday		*a* DAILY Ex. Sunday	*a* DAILY Ex. Sunday
15.30	10.00	.... Rosebery	9.00	14.40
16.00	10.20	.... New Denver	8.15	14.10
16.40	10.50	.... Silverton	7.30	13.40
17.20	11.20	.... Enterprise	6.45	13.10
18.20	12.00	.... Slocan City	6.00	12.40
a DAILY Ex. Sunday	*a* DAILY Ex. Sunday		*l* DAILY Ex. Sunday	*l* DAILY Ex. Sunday

KASLO ROUTE—Steamer "Kokanee"

l DAILY Ex. Sunday		*a* DAILY Ex. Sunday	
7.30	.... Kaslo	18.10	
8.30	.... Ainsworth	17.05	
9.00	.... Pilot Bay	16.30	
9.15	.... Balfour	16.15	
11.00	.... Nelson	14.30	
a DAILY Ex. Sunday		*l* DAILY Ex. Sunday	

LARDO ROUTE—Steamer "Kokanee"

l Monday Wednesday & Friday		*a* Monday Wednesday & Friday	
20.30	.... Lardo	20.00	
22.00	.... Kaslo	18.30	
a Mon Wed & Fri.		*l* Mon. Wed & Fri.	

CROW'S NEST ROUTE—Steamer "Moyie"

l DAILY		*a* DAILY	
5.00	.... Nelson	17.00	
10.00	.... Kuskanook	11.50	
10.30	.... Kootenay Landing	11.30	
a DAILY		*l* DAILY	

OKANAGAN LAKE ROUTE—Steamer "Aberdeen"

l Mon. Wed. & Fri.		*a* Tues. Thr. & Sat.	
10.30	...... Okanagan Landing	13.00	
14.00	.... Kelowna	9.30	
15.30	.... Peachland	8.00	
17.30	.... Penticton	6.00	
a Mon Wed & Fri.		*l* Tues. Thur. & Sat.	

TROUT LAKE ROUTE—Steamer "Victoria"

l Mon. Wed. & Fri.		*a* Mon Wed & Fri.	
15.00	.... Trout Lake City	24.00	
17.00	.... Gerrard	22.00	
a Mon Wed & Fri.		*l* Mon Wed & Fri.	

The country to the north of Revelstoke on the Columbia, known as the Big Bend, was served irregularly by the *Lytton* and other steamers but no vessel of any consequence was built specially for this demanding service until 1902. Then, the Revelstoke Navigation Company had the 309-ton sternwheeler *Revelstoke* built at the CPR's Nakusp shipyard. She was a tough, rugged boat, well suited to the white water conditions of the Big Bend and licensed to carry 10 passengers. — PABC, 40387

In 1905, the *Slocan*, after nine years of demanding service, was rebuilt with a new hull at the Rosebery shipyard. The original cabins and machinery were retained and visually there were few differences except for the arrangements of the hog posts. — EARL MARSH COLLECTION

Many farms were located on the benchlands along the Arrow and Kootenay lakes and harvest time was busy for the sternwheelers. The deck hands would more than earn their wages loading the produce. — W. TRIGGS

The CPR maintained three houseboats — one on Kootenay Lake, one on Okanagan Lake and the third on Shuswap Lake — which were available on a rental basis. They could be towed to scenic locations for a fee and it was possible to have the services of a steward. This is the Kootenay Lake boat. — PABC, 69002

Excursions were popular on all the routes during the summer months. On Kootenay Lake, the Outlet Hotel at Procter was a common destination for picnic parties. — PABC, 39537

The *Moyie* with a typical picnic party disembarking at one of the many sandy beaches on Kootenay Lake. — PABC, 69010

The Lake and River Service in the Kootenays continued to develop and was expanded to some of the more remote parts of the region. In 1900, one of the more unusual steamers to join the fleet was purchased. This was the hastily-built stern-wheeler *Victoria*, bought from Captain N. P. Roman, who had built her for service on Trout Lake. The 107-ton boat was really a self-propelled barge, much like the *Illecillewaet* but probably not as sturdily built. She had been fitted with new engines and boilers built at Trail.

Trout Lake was situated in a valley that ran from the head of Kootenay Lake at Lardeau to the northwest towards the head of Upper Arrow Lake. This area, like so many others in the Kootenays, flourished briefly when some promising mineral deposits were uncovered. Moreover, it was another area of contention between the Canadian Pacific and the Great Northern, with both companies planning to build rail lines up the valley from Lardeau. In the end, only the CPR line was built and it lasted only until 1942, when traffic no longer justified its maintenance.

The Canadian Pacific purchased the little steamer, the *Victoria*, in 1900 when its plans for the railway from Lardeau looked most promising. However, she was never very successful and the CPR replaced her with the tug *Procter* from the Kootenay Lake fleet and used the *Victoria* as a wharf at Trout Lake City.

In the Okanagan, the *Aberdeen* had been busily providing the backbone of water transportation since 1893, running on a busy schedule without a reliable relief vessel. By 1902, she was badly in need of a major refit which would include rebuilding her hull over a period of probably two months. Since no replacement was available, the Canadian Pacific diverted to the Okanagan a small steamer that had originally been intended to replace the *Victoria* on Trout Lake. The vessel was the *York*, a prefabricated steel-hulled twin-screw-driven steamer, built by the Bertram Iron Works of Toronto. She was a modest little vessel of only 134 gross tons and measured just 88 x 16 feet (27 x 4.9 m). However, she was a useful addition to the hard-pressed *Aberdeen* and remained in service in the Okanagan until 1932 when she was sold.

The constant maintenance of the wooden-hulled vessels kept the shipwrights busy, and by 1905, the *Slocan*, the only sternwheeler on the short, but important, Slocan Lake route, was in need of major work on her hull. As would later be done with the *Rossland*, an entirely new hull was built and the cabins and machinery were moved from the old, rotted hull to the new one. While this work was in progress, the tug *Sandon* maintained the service.

Increasingly, the CPR directed traffic over the Slocan route in preference to the Columbia River route to avoid the longer steamer run. Bypassing the narrows on the Columbia was a decided advantage and, particularly during the winter, facilitated traffic movement when the river could be closed to navi-

Slocan Lake Service

Between Revelstoke and Robson the navigation season varied but usually for several winter months the steamers would experience difficulty in the narrows due to low water or at other locations due to ice build-up. The completion of the railway between Nakusp and Slocan Lake and the rail connection between the south end of Slocan Lake and the Columbia and Kootenay Railway provided an alternate route avoiding the most troublesome parts of the Columbia. Slocan Lake seldom had severe winter freeze-ups.

Until the completion of the Kettle Valley Railway, the Slocan Lake service remained an important link in the Canadian Pacific's transportation system to the West Kootenays. However, with the expansion of the rail system, it was no longer necessary to route through traffic via the Slocan Valley. The Slocan Lake steamer service remained important for local traffic and as a rail route to Nakusp. In this form it outlived all other Lake and River Service operations.

Rosebery was the northern terminus of the steamer service on Slocan Lake. There, the passenger trains to and from Nakusp met the vessels and exchanged travellers, mail and express. At right, the *Slocan* awaits the arrival of the train from Nakusp which is just rounding the curve across the bay. The passenger cars were backed down onto the wharf, as shown above in 1913, to make the transfer to the steamer as convenient as possible. Both photos show the effects of forest fires on the surrounding mountains. — Top, BENEDICT PHOTO, B.C. FOREST SERVICE; Bottom, PABC, 1460

New Denver, on Slocan Lake, is a small community which had its
beginnings in the mining boom of the 1890's. It survived, after many
of the other camps had disappeared, as a town whose economy was
based on local farming, lumbering and the remaining mining in the
district. During World War II many Canadians of Japanese descent
were interned at New Denver; some remained there, making the
valley their home. Long after the boom years, the *Slocan* and the tugs
provided New Denver and the nearby town of Silverton with their
main link with the world. — PABC, 53413

On a calm, clear morning in 1919, the *Slocan* swings smartly in towards the wharf at New Denver. — B.C. FOREST SERVICE

The role of tug often fell to the *Slocan* since she was quite capable of handling two barges. The barges were not towed. Instead, they were tied together at the front and the sternwheeler eased in between them from astern, keeping her paddlewheel and rudders clear of the after end of the barges. The weather is beautiful and a few passengers are enjoying the sunshine on deck in this scene from 1911. — PABC, 1372

Slocan City, at the southern end of Slocan Lake, was the end of the run from Rosebery for the *Slocan* and the tugs. Trains met the steamers at the wharf for the connection to South Slocan and points east or west. — PABC, 40382

The *Sandon* was a useful steamer for handling the barges and supplementing or relieving the *Slocan*. She had a small passenger lounge aft but her passenger accommodations could not be compared favourably with the *Slocan*'s. — CPCA

gation. In 1905, it was suggested that through service on the Columbia could be eliminated altogether. However this did not come about.

The Kuskanook, the Okanagan and the Rossland

By 1906 traffic had grown enough on both the Kootenay Lake "Crow boat" route, between Nelson and Kootenay Landing, and in the Okanagan, to justify larger vessels. Moreover, no new sternwheelers had been built for the Kootenay Lake service since the *Moyie* of 1898 and nothing had been added to the Okanagan service since the *Aberdeen* was built in 1893, except the small steamer *York*. New vessels were clearly required here and on the Arrow Lakes, particularly when the increasing age of the other available steamers was considered.

Plans were developed for two sister ships that were to become perhaps the most attractively designed sternwheelers yet to operate in southern British Columbia. The design was based on that of the earlier, successful *Rossland*, but the new vessels were considerably larger. The first of the pair, which was to be named *Kuskanook*, was 1,008 gross tons and just under 200 feet (61 m) long. Her breadth was 30.9 feet (9.4 m) and her depth of hull was 7.0 feet (2.1 m). The hull form was the deep, fast, lakeboat pattern. The *Kuskanook*'s sister ship, to be the *Okanagan*, was essentially similar.

The boats were typical in general arrangements, with two decks devoted to passenger accommodations above the freight and machinery deck. The wheelhouse was placed just forward of the funnel and was stepped back attractively from the front of the cabins below. The net effect was a particularly pleasing design: graceful without the top-heavy or boxy quality of some steamers; elegant and fast.

The *Kuskanook* was ready for launching on May 5, 1906, and the usual celebration ensued. A half-day holiday was declared for the event and all of Nelson, it seemed, turned out to see the newest sternwheeler take to the water. Even the rival Great Northern could not resist participating by offering a free trip on the *Kaslo* from the city wharf to the shipyard. This was of course good business since it focused attention on the *Kaslo*, but it was also part of the public-spirited interest nearly everyone in the interior communities took in the launch of a new vessel.

The launch proceeded flawlessly except that the gangplank was removed before the Mayor and a clergyman who were to ride her down the ways could board her. They were forced to climb up the staging as best they could with undoubtedly some minor loss in dignity. Miss Hazel Gore, daughter of Captain Gore, christened the steamer saying, "Good luck to the *Kuskanook*," as she swung the champagne but the bottle refused to break. Finally, Captain Gore provided some assistance, and the deed was done in customary fashion. For her sponsorship, Miss Gore was presented with the traditional gift from the shipyard staff. Dave Bulger gave the young lady a gold and

May 5, 1906 and the *Kuskanook* is launched at Nelson amid appropriate celebrations.
— OMER LAVALLEE COLLECTION

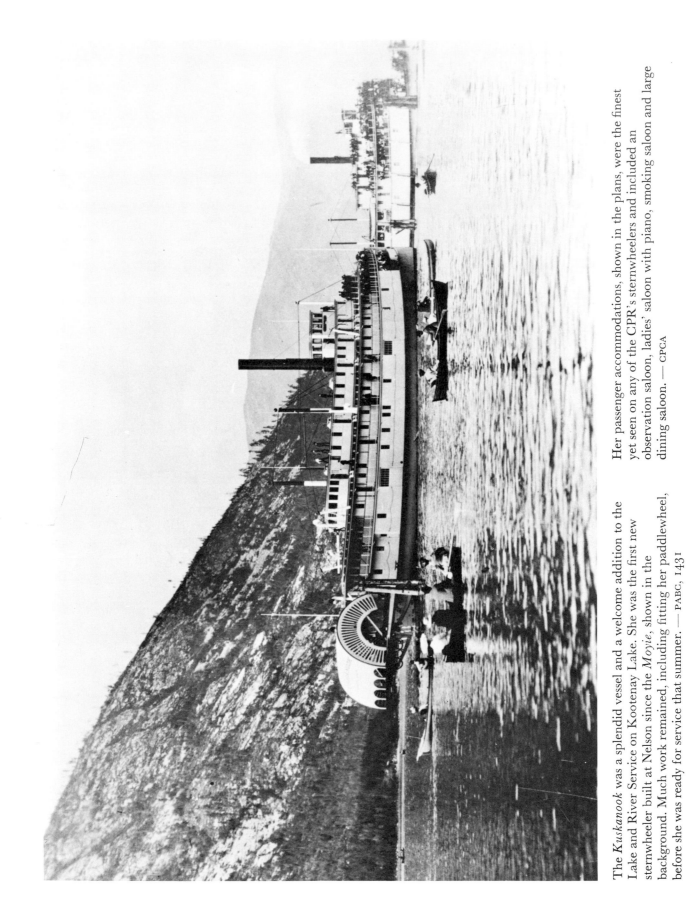

The *Kuskanook* was a splendid vessel and a welcome addition to the Lake and River Service on Kootenay Lake. She was the first new sternwheeler built at Nelson since the *Moyie*, shown in the background. Much work remained, including fitting her paddlewheel, before she was ready for service that summer. — PABC, 1431

Her passenger accommodations, shown in the plans, were the finest yet seen on any of the CPR's sternwheelers and included an observation saloon, ladies' saloon with piano, smoking saloon and large dining saloon. — CPCA

S.S. KUSKANOOK

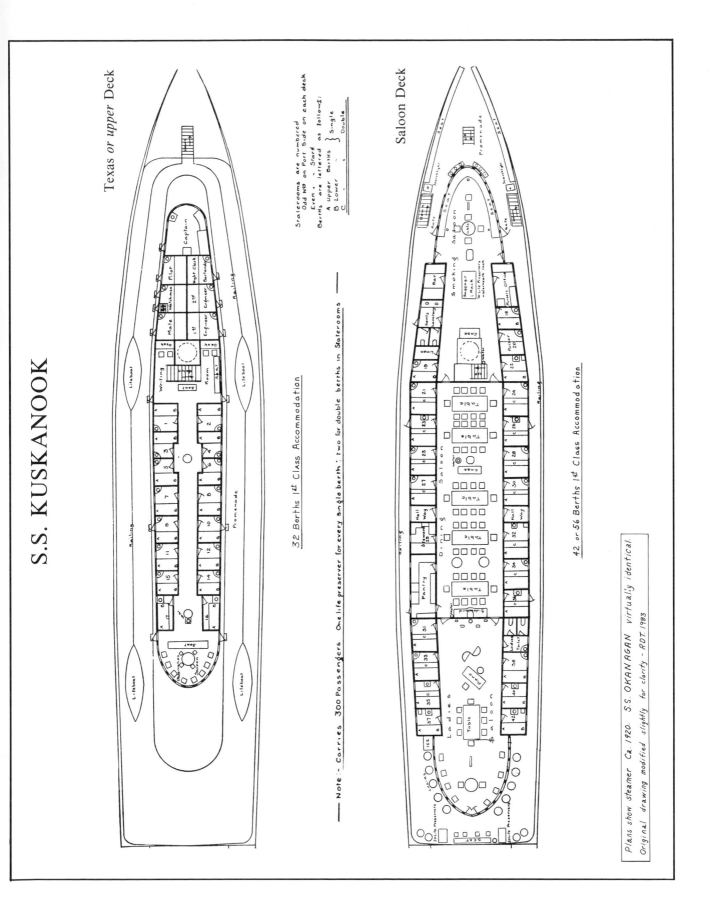

Texas or upper Deck

Captain

Pilot
Watchman
Mate

Night Clerk
2nd
1st   Engineer Bartender

Writing   Engineer
Room

Lifeboat

Lifeboat

Railing

Promenade

Railing

Lifeboat

Lifeboat

32 Berths 1st Class Accommodation

Staterooms are numbered
Odd N⁰ on Port side on each deck
Even - Starb'd
Berths are lettered as follows:
A Upper Berths } Single
B Lower "   }
C "   "   } Double

—— Note:- Carries 300 Passengers. One life preserver for every single berth : two for double berths in Staterooms ——

Saloon Deck

Promenade
Seat

Searchlight

Searchlight

Smoking Saloon

Bar

Baggage Rack
Life Preservers underneath rack

Purser's Office

Dining Saloon

Table

Table

Table

Table

Pantry

Ladies Saloon

Table

Piano

Railing

42 or 56 Berths 1st Class Accommodation

Plans show steamer Ca. 1920 S.S. OKANAGAN virtually identical.
Original drawing modified slightly for clarity - R.D.T. 1983

131

pearl bracelet. As *The Daily News* noted, "the *Moyie* was the last steamer launched here and that is some nine years ago now. We do not have a launching every day in this city but when one comes along the most is made of it."

The *Kuskanook* was built under the watchful eye of James M. Bulger who worked on the construction of nearly every other vessel in the fleet. His brother Dave, David Stephens and George Kemp were other key employees in the skilled team. Costing about $80,000 to construct and a further $10,000 for fittings, the *Kuskanook* was the most expensive steamer yet. Unlike the *Moyie*, which had run preliminary trials immediately after launching, the *Kuskanook* was not steamed up for runs that day. She was taken in tow by the *Moyie*, which brought her in to the docks for final fitting out. She ran preliminary trials in June and by early July was ready to enter service. However, she was delayed because crockery and other furnishings, on order from England since the winter, had not yet arrived to complete her passenger accommodations.

During June and early July, it appears, rumours had spread around Nelson that there might be troubles with the new steamer's machinery and that she would not be as fast as the *Kaslo*. All such concerns were permanently laid to rest when the *Kuskanook*, still not ready for scheduled passenger service, raced the *Kaslo*.

The Daily News of July 5, 1906, noted that word had been sent to Kaslo that the *Kuskanook* was taking a cargo of oats to Lardeau and that " . . . she would like the *Kaslo*'s company part of the way and that the *Kuskanook* would be in racing trim and meant business . . . It is said that the *Kaslo* prepared for trouble and met it bravely." The report captured the spirit of the race:

"When [the *Kaslo*] reached Procter on Tuesday, the *Kuskanook* was waiting for her. Both boats went over to Pilot Bay, the *Kaslo* leading out. The new steamer held back while the *Kaslo* unloaded and gave her the right of way up the lake, the *Kaslo* getting a good start. Then the *Kuskanook* started out to disprove stories about her make up. She started a little slowly but soon got going and was quickly just behind the *Kaslo*. Those on the leading steamer had been watching the new boat through their glasses very closely and as she came flying along, they had to give in that she had the heels of the older boat. The *Kuskanook* rang out her signal for the right to pass, just two whistles. The *Kaslo*'s a perfect lady, and she promptly answered the call and gracefully made way for her latest rival, who danced along and passed her in fine shape. Those who claim to know say the *Kuskanook* can beat the *Kaslo* a mile in every six and it is semi-officially declared that the new boat can make 22 miles per hour when she is asked to do it."

The *Kuskanook*'s sister ship *Okanagan*, long needed to supplement the services of the *Aberdeen* and *York* on Okanagan Lake, was built the following year at the Okanagan Landing shipyard. She was essentially identical to the *Kuskanook*,

The *Kuskanook* was built for the express service between Nelson and Kootenay Landing. At Kootenay Landing, the passenger trains to and from the east, travelling over the Crowsnest Pass route, met the steamers. — GLENBOW ARCHIVES

Establishing herself as the fastest sternwheeler on Kootenay Lake, the *Kuskanook* defeated both the *International* and the *Kaslo* in spirited races and outpaced all the other CPR vessels in service. F. A. Buchholz captured this enduring portrait, which he titled "On Kootenay Lake," about 1908. While the steamer the *Kuskanook* is overtaking is not identified, the location of cabin windows behind the pilot house, the width of the paddlewheel and the location of hog posts identify her as the KR&N's *International*. — DAVID WEBSTER COLLECTION

The *Kuskanook* was a particularly attractive steamer, well balanced and nicely proportioned. In the stillness of the morning, Kootenay Lake could be perfectly calm and mirrorlike. — GLENBOW ARCHIVES

A good-sized crowd turned out to meet the new *Okanagan* on her maiden voyage to Penticton in 1907. — HUDSON PHOTO, VERNON BOARD OF MUSEUM AND ARCHIVES

The *Okanagan* was a virtually identical sister ship to the *Kuskanook* and was completed at the Okanagan Landing shipyard in 1907. She was a welcome addition to the CPR's small fleet on Okanagan Lake and brought a significant improvement in the quality of the service.
— VERNON BOARD OF MUSEUM AND ARCHIVES

The *Okanagan*, shown above right steaming by Kelowna, was nearly twice the tonnage of the *Aberdeen* illustrated below. Her passenger accommodations were more spacious and considerably improved. With the *Okanagan* available for express passenger service, the *Aberdeen* was useful for calling at the way points and with the growing agriculture in the valley both were busy during fruit season. — VERNON BOARD OF MUSEUM AND ARCHIVES/PAC, PA-20958

With the completion of the *Kuskanook*, the *Moyie* was relegated
to calling at the smaller landings to ease the schedule on the
main line route. The *Kokanee* was used on the Kaslo service and
the *Nelson* was available for freighting and relief. The boats were
shifted around as conditions and repairs required. To provide
the most direct connection possible for passengers from Kaslo
and other points, the Kaslo boat met the Crowsnest boat and
exchanged passengers, mail and freight. This was normally done
at Procter but if the schedule were tight and the weather
co-operative sometimes the steamers would meet out on the lake.
Here, the *Kuskanook*, at left, meets the *Moyie* from Kaslo. The
GN's *Kaslo* was also on hand. — J. D. SPURWAY COLLECTION

An annotated CPR timetable from 1910 showing
the service from Revelstoke, via the Slocan
Valley, through to the Crowsnest Pass. — BCPM

Crowsnest Pass Route

Through Arrow and Kootenay Lakes and Crowsnest Pass.

Miles from Revelstoke	Eastbound Train	STATIONS—Descriptive Notes	Westbound Train	Miles from Koote'y Land'g
0	Leave 8.25 Daily PACIFIC TIME	**Revelstoke** –Alt. 1,475 ft.—The shortest and quickest route to the mining regions of West and East Kootenay from the west is provided by the combined water and rail service furnished by the Canadian Pacific Railway Co., which also gives an alternate way through the mountains of south-eastern British Columbia to the Canadian North-West, where close connection is made with the trans-continental trains which run on the main line.	Arrive 16.55 Daily PACIFIC TIME	212
28	a 9.45 l 10.00 Arrow Lakes	**Arrowhead** — From Revelstoke, the Arrow Lake branch of the Canadian Pacific Railway follows the eastern bank of the Columbia River, 28 miles, to *Arrowhead*, at the head of Upper Arrow Lake—an expansion of the Columbia—where one of the fine steamers of the Company is boarded. It is a most delightful sail through the lakes and river, the scenery having that picturesqueness and charm characteristic of mountain waters. On either side crag and cliff alternate with wooded ravine, their beauty accentuated by many little rills and cascades dropping over the overhanging banks	l 15.25 a 14.30 Scenic wealth Daily	185
41		**Halcyon Hot Sps.**	The first port of call is *Halcyon Hot Springs*, whose waters		172
64	a 12.50 l 13.15 Mon. Wed. Fri. To mining regions	**Nakusp** possess those qualities which make the place a popular health resort. A fine hotel is erected here, and there are several cottages for the use of visitors. Twenty-three miles further down the lake is *Nakusp*, the starting point by rail over the Nakusp-Slocan branch of the Canadian Pacific Railway to Rosebery and Sandon, the latter being the centre of the silver-lead mining district, one of the richest on the continent.	l 11.30 a 11.00 Mon. Wed. Fri.	149
92	a 15.20 l 8.55 Daily ex. Sun.	**Rosebery** — Nakusp is 89 miles from West Robson, just below which the Columbia River is bridged. Trains run in one direction to Trail, the great smelter centre, and Rossland, the	l 8.45 a 15.35	121

l Refreshment Stations.

(60

Miles from Revelstoke	Eastbound Train	STATIONS—Descriptive Notes	Westbound Train	Miles from Koote'y Land'g
	Arrive Daily ex. Sun.	progressive mining town of the Trail Creek district, where are located Le Roy and other wealth-producing mines, and through the Boundary District to Midway (alt. 1,770 ft.), on	Leave Daily ex. Sun.	
117	a 11.35 l 14.00 Daily ex. Sun.	**Slocan City** the international boundary, passing en route the mining towns of Grand Forks (alt. 1,583 ft.) and Greenwood (alt. 2,298 ft.), where immense smelters are in active operation. The wealth of the Boundary District is yearly becoming more apparent, and the construction by the railway company of short spurs to different camps is materially aiding in the work of development. From West Robson, the Columbia & Kootenay branch of the Canadian Pacific parallels on the north bank the Lower Kootenay, which flows in turbulent rapids from Kootenay Lake to the Columbia, which it enters just below Robson. The Kootenay is a magnificent trout stream, and yearly	l 12.50 a 10.55 New mining regions Daily ex. Sun.	96
149	a 16.05 l 16.10	**Slocan Junction** attracts large numbers of anglers. *Bonnington Falls*, near Slocan Junction, is a grand waterfall, whose power has been harnessed by an electric company which supplies both light and power to the mines of Rossland and elsewhere. Thirteen miles east of Slocan Junction is the	l 8.45 a 8.40 Daily ex. Sun.	64
160	a 16.50 l 6.00 Daily Fishing	**Nelson** Alt. 1,671 ft. picturesque and prosperous city of *Nelson*, one of the best residential towns of British Columbia, and the judicial centre of the district. Nelson (population 7,000), has an electric street car system, fine hotels, churches, schools and several public buildings, and is rapidly progressing. Its commerce is steadily expanding. The Hall Mines' Smelter is here, and the company's mines are on Toad Mountain, four miles away, and connected by aerial tramway for carriage of ore. Nelson is situated on an arm of Kootenay Lake, and in the locality excellent shooting and fishing are to be had. The Canadian Pacific Railway has a houseboat, which can be chartered by parties for an outing. From Nelson all parts of the lake are reached by the splendid steamer of the Canadian Pacific Railway — Pilot Bay, Ainsworth, Kaslo,	l 8.00 a 19.00 Daily PACIFIC TIME	52
212	a 10.00 Daily	**Kootenay Landing** Lardo, Argenta, Kootenay Landing etc, *Kootenay Landing* is the western terminus of the Crowsnest Pass Route—the intervening distance between Nelson and this place affording a most enjoyable water trip.	l 15.45 Kootenay Lake Daily	0

137

although slightly larger. Her launching on April 16, 1907, was witnessed by the largest crowd yet assembled at Okanagan Landing. Vernon had declared a half-day holiday for the event and extra coaches had been required on the special train run to the Landing. Mrs. Gore christened the boat and was presented with a bouquet of roses and a silver water dish by Misses Annie Milligan and Kate Smith on behalf of the shipyard employees. The Vernon fire brigade band was in attendance and that evening Captain and Mrs. Gore hosted a ball at the Strand Hotel.

The beautiful new steamer made a fine sight as she slid down the ways into Okanagan Lake. The shipyard workers and the crowd had every right to be proud of the *Okanagan*, and her impact on the service offered to the communities along the lake would be immense. Following her completion and inspection, it was planned to use the *Okanagan* in freight service for "running in" before beginning a daily express passenger service on June 6, 1907, calling at Kelowna, Peachland, Summerland and Penticton. The *Aberdeen*, meanwhile, made three trips a week to handle freight and call at smaller communities along the lake. The population and agricultural development of the Okanagan Valley were growing rapidly and the CPR sternwheelers were kept busy carrying the produce of the valley to the railhead at Okanagan Landing.

With new vessels in service on both Kootenay and Okanagan Lakes, attention now shifted to upgrading the boats on the Arrow Lakes route. Additional accommodations were required to handle the increasing tourist traffic on the route and during the 1908-09 winter lay-up period, the Texas deck of the *Rossland* was extended aft to provide more staterooms. Similar work was carried out on the *Kootenay* at that time, and the following winter, on the *Minto*. The renovations cost a modest $2,290 for the *Rossland*, $3,159 for the *Kootenay* and $2,953 for the *Minto*.

The work on the *Rossland*'s cabins had been quite successful, but her hull was in need of extensive work. Rather than rebuild it, James Bulger decided to replace it entirely during the 1909-10 off season. The steamer was pulled out of the water onto the slipways and the superstructure and machinery were jacked up onto timbers. The old hull was then launched to clear the ways and a new hull constructed. When the work on the rejuvenated vessel was sufficiently complete, she was launched and then made ready for service. It was an efficient and economical process that was almost equivalent to building an entirely new boat. At this time as well, a further small addition was made to the *Rossland*'s Texas deck to provide a few more staterooms.

Two new additions to the tug fleet were made at this time, when the *Hosmer* of 154 gross tons was built for the Kootenay Lake barge service and the *Whatshan* of 106 gross tons was completed at Nakusp for the Arrow Lakes route. The barge service from Arrowhead to Nakusp remained a vital link in

By the end of the 1909 summer season, the *Rossland* had been in service 12 years and her waterlogged hull was no longer useful. Since her cabins and engines were still in excellent condition she was fitted with a new hull at Nakusp. The photograph at right shows her being launched following the reconstruction with the old hull in the foreground. — VPL, 16702

The tug *Whatshan* joined the Columbia River fleet in 1909 for the barge service from Arrowhead. With the completion of the Kettle Valley Railway through to the coast, the barge service on the Arrow Lakes was soon phased out. The *Whatshan* was then modified with the addition of a small passenger cabin on her after deck to make her more suitable for winter service on Lower Arrow Lake between Robson and Needles. Through service was suspended during the winters and the *Minto* worked only as far south as Burton. — PABC, 1743

For the Kootenay Lake barge service, the Nelson shipyard crew built the tug *Hosmer* in 1909. Proud men posed beneath the bow of the tug they have just completed.
— QUEEN STUDIO, BILL CURRAN COLLECTION

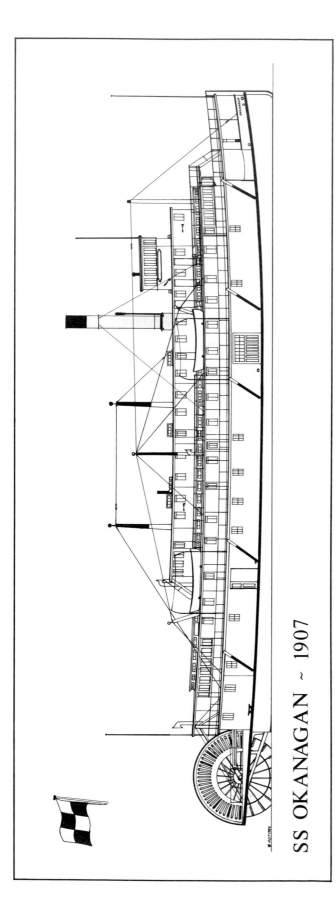

SS OKANAGAN ~ 1907

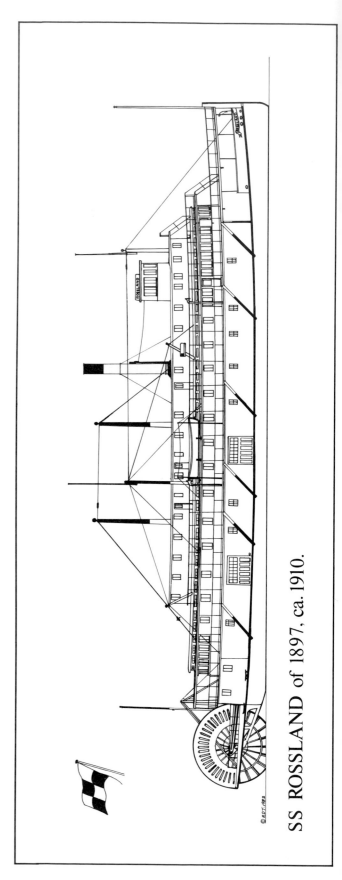

SS ROSSLAND of 1897, ca. 1910.

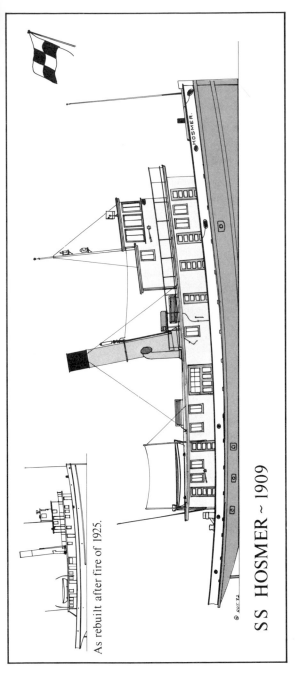

As rebuilt after fire of 1925.

SS HOSMER ~ 1909

The tug *Whatshan*, pushing two barges towards Arrowhead, steams by either the *Minto* or *Kootenay* on Upper Arrow Lake in 1913.
— BENEDICT PHOTO,
B.C. FOREST SERVICE

The
Rossland

The prettiest steamer on the Arrow Lakes was undoubtedly the *Rossland* and the modifications to her cabins did nothing to detract from her appearance. She was fast and powerful and could make 22 miles per hour (35 km/h), although such speed was uneconomical. She is shown above battling rough water and at left at Arrow Park, while at right she is pulling into the dock at Arrowhead. — PABC 31753, 31755/ ARCHIVES OF THE CANADIAN ROCKIES

The *Rossland* was normally used from spring through fall when traffic was most plentiful and then was relieved during the off season by the *Minto*. Spring high water finds the *Rossland* at Edgewood where the long steamer dock is nearly submerged. Even the small shelter, which was moved up and down the dock as required, was partly underwater. — MOYIE MUSEUM

It is a tranquil day on Upper Arrow Lake as the *Rossland* approaches. This photo shows her before the additions, evident in the photo above, were made to her cabins. — PABC, 77615

The small steamer *Kaleden* was built at Okanagan Landing, using the engines from the retired *Victoria*, for an unsuccessful service between Penticton and Okanagan Falls. Subsequently, she was used as an extra boat on Okanagan Lake. Note the shallow water.
— KELOWNA MUSEUM

the rail system to the Kootenays until the completion of the Kettle Valley Railway during World War I.

Moreover, two further additions were made to the Okanagan Lake service: the small sternwheeler *Kaleden*, built in 1910, and the tug *Castlegar*, of 1911, both built at Okanagan Landing. The *Kaleden* was intended to operate on Skaha Lake, a few miles south of Penticton. However, the service was not a success and she was used as an extra vessel, particularly during the busy fruit season, on Okanagan Lake. The *Castlegar* was built to handle railway car barges on the lake and was a significant improvement over existing vessels in the Okanagan for the service. Moreover, construction was beginning on the Kettle Valley Railway, to connect with the western extension of the Canadian Pacific's Columbia and Western at Midway. Such a large construction project brought increased passenger and freight traffic to the Okanagan Lake route and the line's completion was to have very significant effects on the future of the Okanagan Lake service as well.

Overall, a great deal had been accomplished to improve the CP fleet, but even the completion of the new sternwheelers and the renovations to the older boats did not fully solve the problems of increasing traffic or provide for the potential of summer tourist travel on the routes. Before long, more new vessels would be required.

The Great Northern Bows Out

Despite its substantial investments and the construction of a fleet of fine, well-planned vessels, the Great Northern, operating under its Kootenay Railway and Navigation Company, had made a profit from its lake and river operations only in 1902. In 1906, the *International* had been given a very thorough rebuilding at Mirror Lake but after that, it appears that little maintenance was done on any GN boats except the *Kaslo*.

The *Alberta*, her hull rotten, sprang a leak and sank on March 1, 1905. She was raised on April 7, and stripped of machinery and any usable equipment. Her engines and other machinery were sold to Ernest M. Merck of Seattle for $1,700 and her hull, the following year, to Gustave B. Matthews for use as a houseboat. In 1909, the *International*'s boiler gave out; it was removed in 1910 and sold but no attempt was made to acquire a replacement and put the steamer back in service.

The end came in 1910 when, on May 27, the *Kaslo* was driven against the wharf at Ainsworth and seriously damaged. Superintendent P. H. Walsh, in his report, described the incident:

"As the steamer was coming in abreast of the dock a gale struck her stern and swung the steamer hard against the dock, the guard of the steamer going over the edge, which left the hull exposed, and one of the fender piles tore a hole in the side. As it was

simply a mail landing, the steamer immediately backed out and turned round to proceed North, when it was noticed that water was pouring in rapidly and the steamer settling at an alarming rate.... there was not time to lose, and Captain Moore, who was at the wheel [Mate Samuel Matheson had been at the time of the impact], turned and drove the steamer hard on the beach where she settled down in 20 minutes.

"... Captain Moore dispatched a launch to Procter, a distance of eight miles [13 km], with a message to me at Kaslo asking for help. The Str. *Hercules* was down Kootenay River near Port Hill and I promptly wired Capt. Gore for a tug. All their tugs were away in the direction of Kootenay Landing and Capt. Gore wired Procter to send the first tug available to the scene to render all possible assistance. The tug *Hosmer* finally reached Procter with a barge from Kootenay Landing. They immediately dropped the barge and ran full speed to Ainsworth, arriving there about 5:30 p.m., but all was over...There was no freight damaged and no injuries to passengers or employees.

"As you know, the Str. *International* has been lying here over a year in good condition with the exception of a boiler, and as no progress has been made toward getting a boiler we are out of business as far as traffic on Kootenay Lake is concerned, with the exception of zinc ore which is handled by tug and barges...The mail will be turned over to the *Kokanee* of the CPR's line at once."

The beautiful *Kaslo*, once the finest steamer on Kootenay Lake, was raised and towed to the Mirror Lake shipyard but she was not repaired. In 1911, when the KR&N ceased all operations, the *Kaslo*, *International* and *Argenta* were all beached at Mirror Lake. Later, the *International* was sold and ended her days as a rotting hulk at Galena Bay. The *Kaslo* and the *Argenta* were eventually scrapped at Mirror Lake. They had been owned by the Great Northern, and used by the KR&N under lease.

The demise of the KR&N steamboats and also the K&S Railway as a Great Northern operation was a blow to Kaslo, but it had been inevitable since soon after the completion of the *Kaslo*. The routes had not produced enough revenue to cover their costs, let alone make a reasonable return on investment. The K&S Railway had closed following a disastrous fire in 1910 which destroyed much of the line. It had then been acquired by a group of local residents who eventually sold their interests to the CPR which, with the aid of a subsidy, rebuilt the line to standard gauge and thus made a through route all the way from Kaslo to Nakusp. A barge slip was built at Kaslo and a regular rail car service to and from Procter was established as part of the CPR operation.

Without the fast, attractive sternwheelers of the KR&N, there really was no effective competition for the CPR boats on Kootenay Lake and the rivalry that had produced the spirited races was a part of the past.

The dreams for the Kootenay Railway and Navigation Company's fine steamers never materialized and the deficit-ridden operations ceased in 1911. The steamers were based at Kaslo where the *International*, *Kaslo* and, partly visible, the *Alberta*, were photographed at the ore sampler which was just across the bay from the city. By this time the *Alberta* was probably out of service, but the other steamers were still operational. — PABC, 1579

The *Alberta*, sold by the KR&N for use as a bunkhouse, ended her days as a beached, stripped-out hulk at Galena Bay, a curiosity for picnickers. — MOYIE MUSEUM

The launching of the *Bonnington* on April 24, 1911 was a cause for real celebration in Nakusp. The sternwheeler was the largest ever seen in British Columbia and the first of three very similar vessels the Canadian Pacific was to build for the Lake and River Service. At 1,700 gross tons and 202.5 feet (61.7 m) long she was dramatically bigger than any of her predecessors. With a steel hull, powerful engines and a finely crafted superstructure, the *Bonnington* was indeed a steamer for the CPR and the men who built her to be proud of. A CPR business car which brought Captain Gore and other officials from Nelson is visible ahead of the steamer. — PABC, 74349

CHAPTER

FROM HEYDAY
TO DECLINE

The Bonnington
Enters Service, 1911

THE YEARS IMMEDIATELY preceding World War I were busy ones for the Lake and River Service. Immigration, settlement and industry were booming in southern British Columbia and there seemed a bright future for the steamboats. Overall, the building program between 1905 and 1910 had left the fleet in good condition, but still short of tonnage to meet the expected increases in traffic. The *Minto* and *Moyie* were still excellent vessels and with their composite hulls would be good for many more years, but the older *Aberdeen, Nelson, Kokanee* and *Kootenay* were nearing the end of their useful lives and soon would have to be withdrawn. It was clear that new and larger vessels were warranted on the three main lake routes. Consequently, plans were developed for three nearly identical sternwheelers that would overshadow any vessels yet seen on the lakes and rivers of southern British Columbia. These new boats were to be the Canadian Pacific's last major effort to expand its Lake and River Service and marked the real zenith of the sternwheeler fleet.

As already mentioned, the main limitation of all of the sternwheelers in the fleet except the *Minto* and the *Moyie*, was their wooden hulls. These required constant maintenance and even with good care and attention they quickly became weak and waterlogged. To overcome this problem, it was decided to use steel hulls on the new steamers although the cabins would be built of wood. Beyond this significant advance over earlier vessels, the new boats would have much larger and better passenger accommodations, a large freight capacity and new machinery of an advanced design.

As the plans developed, the most striking visual difference between the new design and those of the other boats in the fleet was the high, towering superstructure. Whereas vessels like the *Kuskanook* had three decks and a pilothouse, the new plans called for vessels with four decks to provide additional passenger accommodations. This way, with only a modest increase in length and breadth, a significantly larger vessel

A great deal of work remained to be done on the *Bonnington* before she could be placed in service between Arrowhead and Robson when this photograph was taken of her on the Nakusp ways prior to her launch. Many cabin windows and doors had to be finished and extensive interior work was required. — KELOWNA MUSEUM

Finally the work was completed and the *Bonnington* was ready for service. Normally, she was used in the summer months with the *Rossland* when water levels were high and traffic volumes sufficient to justify her use. In winter, the *Minto* and *Kootenay* took over.
— PABC, 42367

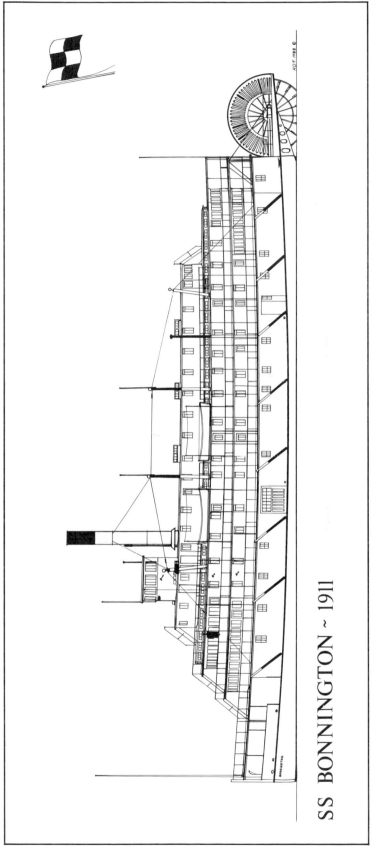

SS BONNINGTON ~ 1911

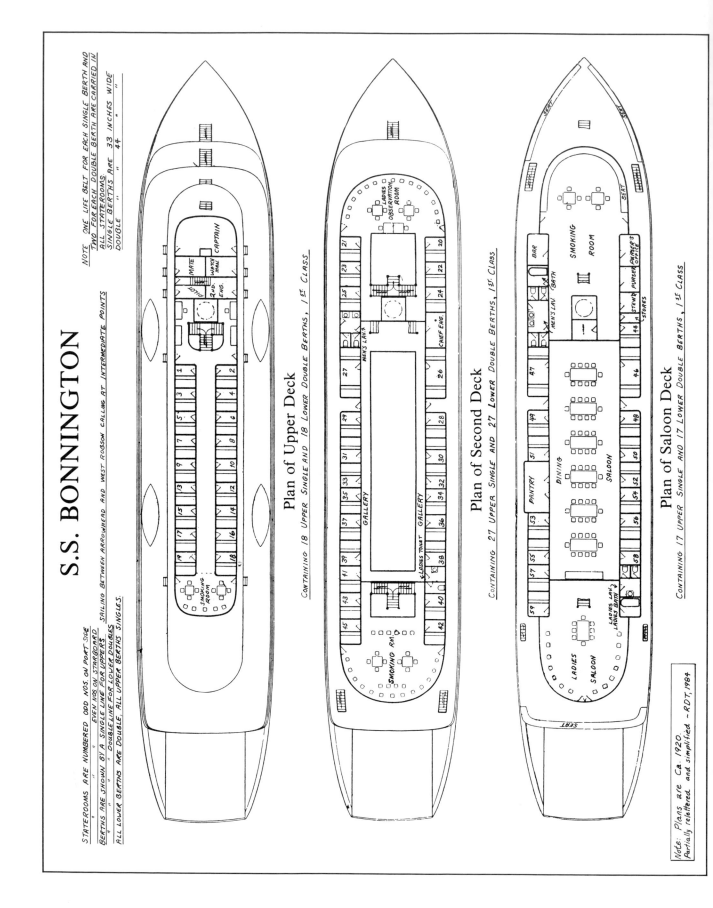

S.S. BONNINGTON

STATEROOMS ARE NUMBERED ODD NOS. ON PORT SIDE
EVEN NOS. ON STARBOARD

BERTHS ARE SHOWN BY A SINGLE LINE FOR UPPERS
A DOUBLE LINE FOR LOWER DOUBLES

ALL LOWER BERTHS ARE DOUBLE. ALL UPPER BERTHS SINGLES.

SAILING BETWEEN ARROWHEAD AND WEST ROBSON CALLING AT INTERMEDIATE POINTS

NOTE ONE LIFE BELT FOR EACH SINGLE BERTH AND
TWO FOR EACH DOUBLE BERTH ARE CARRIED IN
ALL STATEROOMS
SINGLE BERTHS ARE 33 INCHES WIDE
DOUBLE " 44 " "

Plan of Upper Deck

CONTAINING 18 UPPER SINGLE AND 18 LOWER DOUBLE BERTHS, 1ST CLASS

Plan of Second Deck

CONTAINING 27 UPPER SINGLE AND 27 LOWER DOUBLE BERTHS, 1ST CLASS

Plan of Saloon Deck

CONTAINING 17 UPPER SINGLE AND 17 LOWER DOUBLE BERTHS, 1ST CLASS

Note: Plans are Ca. 1920.
Partially relettered and simplified ~ RDT, 1984

152

The dining saloon on the *Bonnington* seated 60 people and was centrally located on the saloon deck. On the deck above, a gallery overlooked the saloon. Clerestory windows and electric lights provided ample illumination for the tables below. — PABC, 51326

could be built that would have the required capacity to meet the anticipated demands for travel in the years ahead.

Because of the length of the run on the Arrow Lakes and the rapid growth in traffic to and from the CPR main line at Revelstoke, it was decided to begin work on the first of these new sternwheelers at the Nakusp yards. The vessel was to enter service in time for the summer season in 1911. The Lake and River Service shipyards were not equipped to fabricate steel components of the size and complexity needed in a large vessel's hull, so a contract was let to the Polson Iron Works of Toronto to construct a prefabricated hull for the new sternwheeler. The hull was first assembled at the Polson yards, then taken apart and shipped by rail to Nakusp for reassembly by a Polson crew on the ways at the CPR shipyard. The shipment consisted of 19 carloads. The steel hull was subdivided into 20 watertight compartments and to secure a particularly shallow draft, the bottom of the hull was almost perfectly flat. It measured 202.5 feet (61.7 m) long, 39.6 feet (12 m) in breadth and 7.5 feet (2.3 m) in depth. This was only 7 feet (2.1 m) longer than the *Kuskanook*, but 7 feet (2.1 m) wider. The extra width was most significant for with the added deck, noted earlier, it meant that the new steamer could have an increase in gross tonnage over that of the *Kuskanook* of nearly 70 percent (from 1,008 to 1,700 gross tons).

Engines for the new sternwheeler were to have compound cylinders. The steam exhausted from a high-pressure cylinder was used a second time in a cylinder of larger diameter, operating at lower pressure. This system resulted in greater fuel economy and though used extensively in most coastal and deep-sea steamships, had not been used before in sternwheelers in British Columbia. The new steamer's engines were to have a high-pressure cylinder measuring 16 inches (41 cm) in diameter, while the low-pressure cylinder would measure 35 inches (89 cm). The stroke of the engines would be 96 inches (244 cm). As planned, the boiler to supply steam to the engines was located in the traditional position forward in a well, was 7.5 feet (2.3 m) in diameter and was equipped with a forced draft. Operating pressure would be 200 pounds per square inch (1,380 kp). The sternwheel would have a diameter of 25 feet (7.6 m) and be fitted with 20 buckets. Four rudders were located just forward of the paddlewheel. It was anticipated that the engines would develop a little over 1,000 horsepower when operating at 25 revolutions per minute. The nominal horsepower rating for the engines was 96.7.

The keel for the new steamer, which was to be named *Bonnington*, was laid in November 1910, and work went ahead rapidly at the Nakusp shipyards during the winter of 1910-11 under the supervision of D. T. Bulger, foreman of the shipyards. In April 1911, the striking new steamer was ready for a gala launching. The excitement in a small community like Nakusp at the launch of one of the sternwheelers can be readily understood, reflecting both civic pride in the new

CANADIAN PACIFIC RAILWAY COMPANY
B.C. LAKE AND RIVER SERVICE.

Luncheon

Canapes aux Sardines	Ripe Olives
Consomme Julienne	Puree of Beans, aux Crouton

Fried Halibut Steak, Tartare Sauce

Pickled Beets	Radishes
Baked Ham, Champagne Sauce	Jelly Omelet
Supreme of Chicken, with Dumplings	Roast Ribs of

Cold

Roast Beef   Mutton   Ham   Pork   Ox Tong

Baked, French Fried and Mashed Potatoes
Vegetables in Season

Orange Custard Pudding

Boston Cream Pie	Apple Pie

Baked Apple and Cream

Cheese	Fruit	Assorted Past
Tea	Coffee	

SS. "BONN

The Canadian Pacific prided itself on the quality of both service and cuisine on its steamships and trains. The luncheon and dinner menus shown on these pages reflect the range of foods served on the steamers and the quality was excellent. The prices were reasonable too. During and immediately after World War I, shortages made it difficult to maintain the diversity and quality, but every effort was made to do so.
— L. S. MORRISON COLLECTION

The dining saloon came under the supervision of the chief steward. He directed the stewards and cooks in serving the passengers. Normally, the crews were all men, although during World War I, women were hired as waitresses. After the war this practice, apparently, was discontinued although in later years, women were employed again. — L. S. MORRISON COLLECTION

Wartime menus included the following admonition: "The Food Controller requests that all persons ordering food consider the needs of Great Britain and her Allies and their Armies, in the matter of wheat, beef and bacon, and that the public do everything in its power to add to the available supply of these articles for export by eating as little as possible of them, making use of substitutes and avoiding waste."

vessel's contribution to trade and commerce, and pride in local workmanship in her construction. Moreover, life in the relatively isolated communities of British Columbia's interior could become routine and a launching was a good opportunity for a change of pace and some festivities. For Nakusp, the afternoon of April 24, 1911 was declared a civic holiday and banks, stores and the school was closed for the festivities.

By 2:00 p.m. virtually everyone from Nakusp and the surrounding district had gathered for the launching. Captain Gore had travelled up from Nelson with his family in a CPR business car for the event. Crowds lined the shore, watched from railway car barges tied up next to the slipways, and crowded the decks of the *Rossland*, *Minto* and *Whatshan*, while some excited people stood on the decks of the new steamer herself.

The steamer was decorated in the usual launching tradition with flags and bunting and Miss Hazel Gore, daughter of Captain Gore, broke the ceremonial bottle of champagne over the steamer's bow with the words: "I christen thee *Bonnington*: success!" At that moment, David Bulger unfurled the Union Jack and the steamer slid gracefully onto the lake amidst cheers from the crowds and the whistles of all the steamers and small craft waiting offshore.

From the *Minto*, which had paused to watch the launch before pulling in to the wharf to pick up passengers and mail for Nelson, came the report that the *Bonnington* drew three and one half feet of water aft. This was particularly pleasing as it meant that the new vessel actually drew less water than the much smaller vessels in the fleet.

Katherine Bulger presented Hazel Gore with a silver cake basket, a gift of the shipyard workers, and a round of congratulations followed. Miss Bulger and two assistants, Miss Taylor and Miss Fyfe, served claret to the ladies on the forward saloon deck and, in the words of Nelson's *Daily News*, "... numerous kegs of beer were broached in order that the shipyard employees and the general public might drink the health of the new steamer."

The official party included: W. D. Miller, divisional superintendent, and J. H. Taylor, port steward, and their families from Nelson; Captain L. H. Fraser of the *Kootenay*, who was to assume command of the *Bonnington*; G. H. Keys, foreman joiner from Nelson, who had supervised the wooden construction work for the cabins; J. Fyfe, chief engineer of the Nakusp yards, who had been responsible for installing the steamer's machinery; and James McPhee, who oversaw the electrical systems. Nelson's James Bulger, general shipyard foreman, was in charge of the launch. Unfortunately, David Stephens, who had designed both the machinery and the hull, was unable to attend the festivities.

Following the launch, a soccer game was arranged between the shipyard employees and the town citizens, with the yard crew winning two to zero. In the evening, a ball was held in

Nakusp

The centre for sternwheeler traffic on the Arrow Lakes was Nakusp. Here a shipyard, transfer slip and a passenger wharf were built. The steamers connected with the Nakusp and Slocan Railway at Nakusp and operated between Arrowhead to the north and Robson to the south.

The Nakusp station with the Lealand and Grand hotels in the background. — COMINCO, COURTESY PAT HIND

Wintertime at Nakusp, 1913. — R. E. BENEDICT, B.C. FOREST SERVICE

The *Minto*, at left, being overhauled at the shipyard. The *Bonnington* at right. — CHARLES F. TURNER

The *Kootenay* during high water. — CPA

The *Kootenay*, left, *Rossland* and *Bonnington*. — PABC, 1465

Rebuilding the *Rossland*, 1910. — SPILLER COLLECTION

Rails at dockside, *ca.* 1905. — PABC, 68372

157

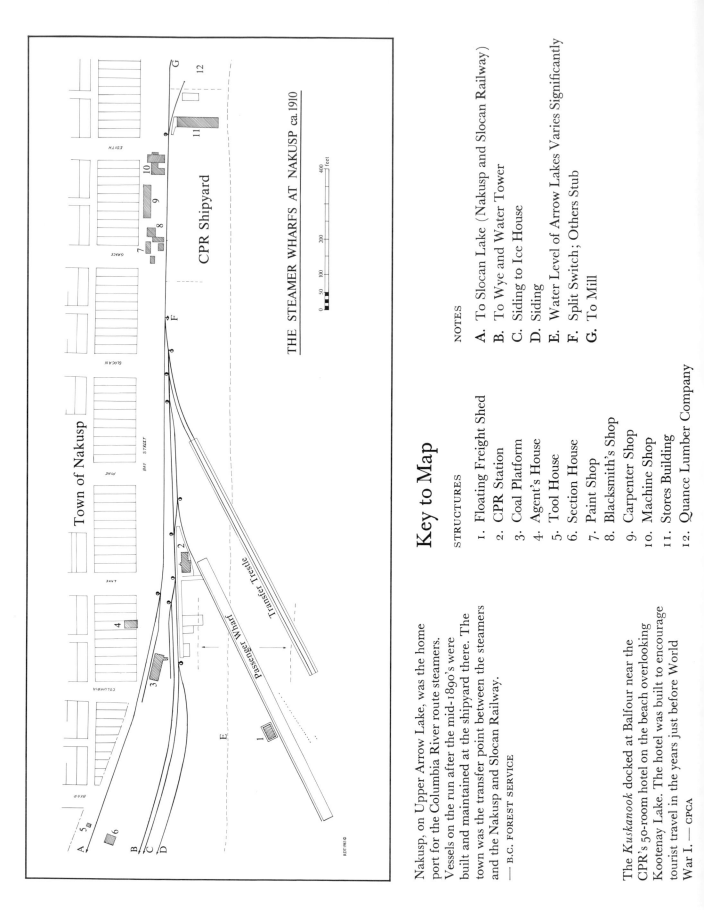

Town of Nakusp

BEAR
COLUMBIA
LAKE
PINE
BAY STREET
SLOCAN
GRACE
EDITH

CPR Shipyard

RDT 1981 O

THE STEAMER WHARFS AT NAKUSP ca. 1910

0 50 100 200 400 feet

Key to Map

STRUCTURES

1. Floating Freight Shed
2. CPR Station
3. Coal Platform
4. Agent's House
5. Tool House
6. Section House
7. Paint Shop
8. Blacksmith's Shop
9. Carpenter Shop
10. Machine Shop
11. Stores Building
12. Quance Lumber Company

NOTES

A. To Slocan Lake (Nakusp and Slocan Railway)
B. To Wye and Water Tower
C. Siding to Ice House
D. Siding
E. Water Level of Arrow Lakes Varies Significantly
F. Split Switch; Others Stub
G. To Mill

Nakusp, on Upper Arrow Lake, was the home port for the Columbia River route steamers. Vessels on the run after the mid-1890's were built and maintained at the shipyard there. The town was the transfer point between the steamers and the Nakusp and Slocan Railway.
— B.C. FOREST SERVICE

The *Kuskanook* docked at Balfour near the CPR's 50-room hotel on the beach overlooking Kootenay Lake. The hotel was built to encourage tourist travel in the years just before World War I. — CPCA

Nakusp's new opera house, sponsored by the Nakusp Quadrille Club.

The *Bonnington*'s accommodations were viewed by the press and spectators with particular pride and delight. Her cabins were framed with coast fir while the finishing work was done in cedar. There was far greater space in the steamer devoted to lounges than in the other lake steamers and the 60-seat dining room was particularly spacious. Located midships on the main saloon deck, the dining saloon measured 71 feet, 10 inches (21.9 m) long by 21 feet, 6 inches (6.6 m) wide and was two decks high. The furnishings were of golden oak and Australian mahogany. At the forward end of the saloon deck was the men's smoking room. Aft was the ladies' observation room, which featured Wilton carpet, leather and Morris chairs and mahogany armchairs. On either side of the dining saloon were staterooms. The gallery deck above also featured two observation rooms, the forward one furnished with wicker plush furniture, centre tables and writing desks, while the after lounge was decorated in what *The Daily News* described as an "early English" style. On the Texas deck was yet another lounge, staterooms and officers' quarters.

In total, the *Bonnington* had 62 staterooms on the three upper decks. Two were suites with baths and four others were designed for family accommodations. All were provided with steam heat, electric lights and electric bells. Strangely, no provision was made for running water in the staterooms although the Great Northern's *Kaslo* had featured this in 1900. However, this standard of accommodation was a vast improvement over the "bare boards" standards of the first steamers on the lakes of only two decades earlier. Overall, the *Bonnington* was estimated to have cost the Canadian Pacific between $130,000 and $135,000.

When work on the *Bonnington* was finished the next month and her trials of May 10 successfully completed, the attention of the officials and builders could be turned to the construction of the second of the new sternwheelers. This vessel, to be named the *Nasookin*, was to be built at the Nelson shipyards for the Kootenay Lake service and was essentially identical to the *Bonnington*. The new sternwheelers were certainly handsome vessels, but they were not to capture the speed records of the *Rossland* or *Kuskanook*. The new boats could work up to a respectable speed but their boilers could not supply sufficient steam to keep up the pace. The *Rossland*, newly refitted, had no difficulty leaving the *Bonnington* trailing in her wake.

One of the major concerns in the design of the *Bonnington* and her sister ships was the developing tourist trade in the Kootenays and the Okanagan. Complementing the addition of these vessels to the fleet was a new hotel built at Balfour, overlooking Kootenay Lake from a high bench above the lake. The Hotel Kootenay Lake had 50 rooms providing accommodations for a total of 100 guests. It was an impressive, wooden-framed structure 205 x 150 feet (62.5 x 46 m). Situated across

Halcyon Hot Springs on Upper Arrow Lake was a popular spa and an important stop for the steamers. A substantial hotel and resort was developed there which contributed to the growing tourist trade on the Columbia River route before World War I. The sternwheeler is the *Kootenay*. — PABC, 1443

The Canadian Pacific's Hotel Kootenay Lake, more commonly known as the Balfour Hotel, opened in 1911 as the CPR expanded its tourist-oriented facilities in the Kootenays. World War I forced the closure of the hotel but it was used as a convalescent home for wounded soldiers and, as such, was visited by the Prince of Wales in 1919. — PABC, 90346

from Procter with broad, sweeping views of the surrounding mountains and the lake, it was an ideal setting for a vacation hotel. It opened for business in the summer of 1911 but unfortunately World War I was to force its premature closure.

The Nasookin and the Sicamous

Throughout the fall of 1912 and the winter months of 1913, work on the *Nasookin* progressed rapidly at the CPR's Fairview shipyards at Nelson. She was to be the largest steamer ever to operate on Kootenay Lake and certainly the most luxurious. Like the *Bonnington*, completed the year before for the Arrow Lakes route, the *Nasookin* was designed to handle both increasing local traffic and to improve accommodation for the tourist trade which the CPR was actively developing. It was intended that at least during the busy summer months the new steamer would replace the *Kuskanook* on the run between Procter and Kootenay Landing, providing the essential link along Kootenay Lake between the ends of the railway on the CPR's east-west route across southern British Columbia.

The *Nasookin* was essentially identical to the *Bonnington* although minor modifications had been made to better suit her to the Kootenay Lake service. Her engines were slightly more powerful and it was anticipated that she would be about two miles per hour (3 km/h) faster than the *Bonnington*. There were slight differences in the hull form and whereas the *Bonnington* had a wooden deck, the *Nasookin*'s was of steel.

Like the *Bonnington*, the *Nasookin* had a steel hull, prefabricated and shipped to British Columbia for assembly. The *Nasookin*'s was built by the Northwestern Shipbuilding and Dry Dock Company at Port Arthur, Ontario. Her work was supervised by David Stephens, chief engineer of the Company's Lake and River Service under the direction of James M. Bulger, master builder, and J. French, yard foreman. All of the upper works, including the passenger accommodations, were built locally and provided a minor boom for local suppliers. Joinery work and cabinet making were supervised by George H. Keys, joiner for the Company, and the elaborate electrical lighting system was installed under the care of James McPhee. The Nelson shipyard was well-equipped for the work at hand and construction of the steamer proceeded smoothly.

On April 30, 1913, all was ready and a crowd estimated at 2,000 gathered for the launching. All of Nelson was proud of the *Nasookin* and a festive atmosphere brightened the entire city. The new steamer was decorated in flags and bunting and Miss Bertha Bulger, daughter of the master builder, christened the sternwheeler *Nasookin*. The name was said to be derived from the Kootenay Indian language and to translate as "The Supreme Chief," which seemed appropriate for the largest vessel yet seen on the inland lakes.

Crowds surrounded the vessel and barges had been placed on either side of the steamer to provide more vantage points for watching the launch. In addition the tug *Ymir* and the

Captains and Chief Engineers of Lake and River Service Steamers, 1913:

	CAPTAINS	CHIEF ENGINEERS
Aberdeen	J. Weeks	S. Collacott
Castlegar	J. Fitzsimmons	G. Smith
Hosmer	F. Orr	M. McKinnon
Kokanee	L. McKinnon	A. McLeod
Kootenay	G. Robertson	A. Thompson
Kuskanook	W. Seaman	J. Cameron
Minto	A. Forslund	F. Swanson
Moyie	W. Wright	D. Betts
Okanagan	G. Estabrooks	O. Estabrooks
Rossland	O. Alfsmo	J. Thompson
Sandon	G. Graham	D. Morrison
Slocan	W. Kirby	A. McDonald
Valhalla	J. Ferguson	W. Johnson
Whatshan	J. Dougal	D. Campbell
York	M. Reid	A. McLena

From *Canadian Railway and Marine World*, May 1913. Presumably, the *Bonnington* was out of service for the winter season while the *Nasookin* was as yet incomplete when the summary was prepared.

Underway on Kootenay Lake on the important run between Nelson and Kootenay Landing, the *Nasookin* was an impressive sight. — VPL, 13258

The *Nasookin* was an almost identical sistership to the *Bonnington* and was built at the Nelson shipyards. She was launched on April 30, 1913. In the photo, upper left, all is ready for the christening as the huge sternwheeler sets on the sliding cradles on the slipways. Moments later, as shown at left, she was afloat and, with one of the tugs standing by, ready for final fitting out before entering service.

— PABC, 51348/GEORGE DONALDSON COLLECTION

sternwheeler *Nelson* were on hand for more spectators. Small private craft also stood by off the lakeshore. To the delight of the cheering crowds, the launch was flawless and it was estimated that the *Nasookin* would be ready for trial trips in about one week since much of the finishing work had been completed on the vessel before she was launched.

In fact, she was ready for a preliminary trial on May 4, 1913, and under the command of Captain McKinnon, with Dave Stephens serving as chief engineer, the *Nasookin* steamed up the West Arm as far as Procter and then out into the main lake. She made "a splendid impression," noted Nelson's *Daily News* the next day " . . . although no records were broken, the time was said to have been good." Captain Gore, superintendent of the Lake and River Service and W. D. Miller, superintendent of the Nelson Division of the railway, both of whom were on board for the trials, were undoubtedly pleased with the results of the trip.

The layout of the *Nasookin*'s accommodations was the same as the *Bonnington*'s, described earlier. The main deck was devoted primarily to the ship's boiler and machinery and to cargo space. In addition, on the port side was a galley, a pantry, the crew's mess, cold storage room and cabins for cooks. On the starboard side there was a bathroom, lavatory, storeroom, waiter's room, express room and mail room. Aft of the engine were further crew accommodations with six rooms providing berths for 12 men.

The saloon deck immediately above was devoted almost exclusively to passenger accommodations. The centre was occupied by the *Nasookin*'s dining saloon which was attractively decorated, well lit and spacious. Seating was provided for 60 people, with the six main tables running across the width of the room and each seating ten. The ceiling-well over the dining saloon extended up through the second deck above, as was often done in much larger coastal or ocean steamships. The sideboard for the dining room was an elaborate piece of furniture, built in the shipyard from imported mahogany and featuring ornate, leaded windows and mirror panels in the back. Lighting in the dining room was provided by three electrically-lit chandeliers with electric fans attached as well as smaller electric wall fixtures.

Forward of the dining saloon on the port side was the steward's office and room; to the starboard was the purser's office and stateroom. Also on the saloon deck was the men's bathroom and lavatory. Fourteen staterooms, each with berths for three people were located on this deck. The most luxurious rooms were two family staterooms and one suite which could be used as two staterooms with bath or one stateroom with bath as the passengers required. The forward end of the saloon deck was devoted to the smoking room and was fitted with large windows to facilitate viewing the spectacular scenery on the route. At the after end of the saloon deck was the ladies' saloon.

The ladies' observation room on the *Nasookin*, located forward on the second, or gallery, deck. — PABC, 4950

The *Nasookin*'s smoking room, complete with polished brass cuspidors, was situated on the after end of the second deck behind the gallery overlooking the dining saloon. — PABC, 4951

The third of the magnificent sternwheelers in the CPR's final building program was the elegant *Sicamous*, shown above under construction at Okanagan Landing in 1914. — PABC, 1420

The motor launch *Nelson* was built at the Nelson shipyards to provide a local service on the West Arm of Kootenay Lake. — PABC, 1426

The gallery deck, immediately above, was fitted with 25, three-berth staterooms and men's and women's lavatories. Forward was the ladies' observation saloon with large plate glass windows while aft was another men's smoking and observation lounge. Above the gallery, providing lighting to the dining room below, were coloured clerestory windows. Space was also provided for the chief engineer's quarters on this deck.

The Texas deck above provided 18 further three-berth staterooms as well as the Captain's cabin, officers' quarters and a watchman's room. A large staircase led up from the decks below. Entry to the officers' rooms was gained from the outside decks and the pilothouse was located immediately above the Captain's cabin. Another attractive feature of the steamer was that the outside promenade decks, which were covered and spacious, were also electrically lit so that they could be illuminated at the landings at night and extinguished en route.

For lighting at night when cargo was being loaded, the *Nasookin* carried four 2,000-candlepower boom lights. In addition, she was fitted with two 10,000-candlepower searchlights manufactured by the Benton & Sons Electric Company. Power for the lighting system was provided by a 25-kilowatt Canadian General Electric dynamo.

The last of the three sister ships was the *Sicamous*, built at Okanagan Landing and launched on May 19, 1914, amid celebrations as happy as those at Nakusp and Nelson when the other two steamers had been launched. Like the *Bonnington* and *Nasookin*, she was an immediate success. Some modifications were made to the design so that she differed slightly from her sisters. Most noticeable was the reduced length of her Texas deck, which did not provide any passenger accommodations. Both the *Bonnington* and *Nasookin* tended to be difficult to control in a strong crosswind because of their large, high superstructure, and the reduced size of the *Sicamous* may have helped this problem.

Two other vessels were built for the Lake and River Service just before the outbreak of World War I. The first of these was the motor launch *Nelson* (II), built at Nelson and named to commemorate the veteran sternwheeler *Nelson*, which was retired in 1913. The new *Nelson* was an attractive gasoline-engined boat measuring 61 x 11 feet (18.6 x 3.4 m) and was capable of 15-18 miles per hour (24-29 km/h). She was intended for service on the West Arm of Kootenay Lake for handling local passenger traffic but the service did not develop and in 1920 she was sold.

The second new boat was a fine, steel-hulled tug named the *Naramata*, built for the Okanagan Lake service. She was completed shortly before the *Sicamous* and was to be a particularly valuable vessel. Her steel hull, which was prefabricated by the Western Dry Dock Company of Port Arthur, Ontario, gave her a life expectancy far in excess of any of the

Framed by the huge paddlewheel of the *Sicamous*, just prior to the new sternwheeler's launch, the *Okanagan* stands clear of the slipways. — VERNON BOARD OF MUSEUM AND ARCHIVES

Construction of a vessel the size of the *Sicamous* was a major effort for the CPR shipyards. Her steel hull was prefabricated in Ontario and assembled at the yards, while the cabins were built on site. These two photos show the cabin work progressing. — PABC, 1419, 1421

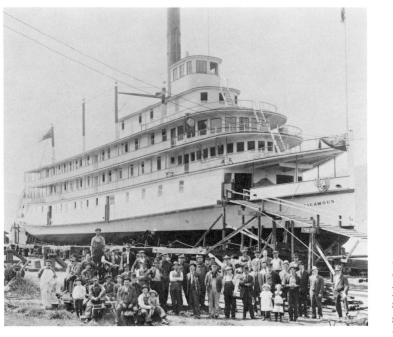

Top right, the engine room of the *Sicamous*.
— JOHN WILLIAMS

The *Sicamous*, lower right, last sternwheeler built for the Canadian Pacific's British Columbia Lake and River Service, has just been launched at Okanagan Landing. Offshore, the *Okanagan* stands clear.
— VERNON BOARD OF MUSEUM AND ARCHIVES

All is ready for the launch of the *Sicamous* as a crowd begins to gather. The lower photo also provides a clear view of the shipyard with its long sliding ways while at left, the shipyard crew, some officials and a few local children pose proudly in front of the towering bulk of the *Sicamous*. — CHARLES VEREY COLLECTION

The *Sicamous* entered service in the summer of 1914 just before the world was plunged into war. On June 12, she made an inaugural excursion to Kelowna and Penticton averaging 20 miles per hour (32 km/h) on the trip. A band played on deck and admiring crowds gathered to view the new steamer as this photo at Kelowna attests. Interestingly, she has not yet been fitted with lifeboats. — KELOWNA MUSEUM

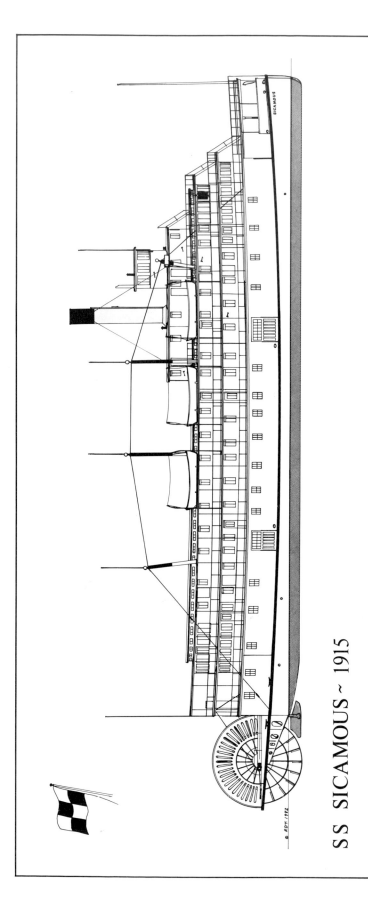

SS SICAMOUS ~ 1915

At Penticton, in 1918, the *Sicamous* poses beside her smaller running mate, the *Okanagan*. — STOCKS FAMILY COLLECTION, IFB

The dining saloon of the *Sicamous* was essentially identical to those on the *Bonnington* and the *Nasookin*. Note the electric fans below the gallery on both sides of the saloon; they helped keep the air moving on a hot Okanagan summer afternoon.
— CHARLES VEREY

Ornate Canadian Pacific initials were etched into the plate glass of the doors in the dining saloon.
— ROBERT D. TURNER

wooden-hulled vessels and she was to remain in service until 1967. The *Naramata* was a powerful boat of 150 gross tons, powered by a two-cylinder compound engine rated at 27.3 nominal horsepower. With two modern tugs, the *Castlegar* and the new *Naramata*, the Okanagan Lake service was prepared for an anticipated steady growth in barge traffic between Okanagan Landing, way points where barge facilities were located, and Penticton which was by that time served by the CPR's Kettle Valley Railway.

The year 1914 looked to be one of promise for the people of the Okanagan and the Kootenays. For the Lake and River Service prospects seemed bright with its major building program nearly complete. But on August 3, 1914 — fruit season in the Okanagan — World War I began and a time of growing prosperity ended abruptly, yielding to a time of war.

The War Years and the Winter of 1916

The war years brought many changes to the country served by the Lake and River Service. Many men left their families and jobs to enlist for fighting in France or to join the Navy; some were never to return. Once promising farms and businesses languished. Experienced engineers, strong young deckhands and stokers, all were needed in the war and many CPR employees volunteered. As the war ground to a stalemate in the trenches, manpower shortages developed and service cuts in the Lake and River Service became necessary. Tourism, which had been counted on to fill the staterooms of the new sternwheelers and rooms of the hotel at Balfour, fell off dramatically. The fine hotel, overlooking Kootenay Lake, was closed during the war, a luxury a country at war could not support.

In the Okanagan, the *Aberdeen* was retired in 1916 and the *Okanagan* was used mainly in the summers during the busy fruit-packing season. The *Sicamous* handled the regular services where, in 1914, two steamers had been needed to handle express and local traffic.

On Kootenay Lake, with the steamers serving as a vital link in the railway system, the service was not as severely affected. The *Nasookin* continued on the Nelson-to-Kootenay Landing run while the *Kuskanook* ran to Kaslo and the *Moyie* handled way points and freight. The *Kokanee*, oldest surviving sternwheeler of the four boats, was available as a relief vessel. On the Arrow Lakes, winter service was normally maintained by the *Minto* and *Kootenay*, with the *Bonnington* and *Rossland* being used in the summers of 1914 and 1915.

The winter of 1916 brought record low temperatures and heavy snowfalls to southern British Columbia and in the southern Okanagan, on Slocan Lake and on the Arrow Lakes route, wrestled the Lake and River Service to a virtual standstill. The cold weather set in early in January and on the eleventh, the *Kootenay* became stuck in the ice at the southern end of the narrows near Cottonwood Island at the head of

Kelowna, April 7, 1916. The boys of "C" Company, 172nd Battalion, Rocky Mountain Rangers, are going off to war amid band music and the excitement and sorrow of farewell.
— KELOWNA MUSEUM

They were leaving Kelowna in 1916 for the trenches of the Western Front. But there were still over two long years of war ahead and many would never return. — KELOWNA MUSEUM

In a happier setting, a group of school children waits at the dock for the *Kuskanook* on Kootenay Lake. — KELOWNA MUSEUM

The narrows between Upper and Lower Arrow Lakes, a tricky stretch of water for sternwheelers. Low water, shifting bars, and occasional fog or ice kept the captains and pilots constantly alert. Top photo, the *Rossland* leaves the narrows at Burton; immediately below, she is steaming through the narrows at low water. Lower, the *Minto* steams upstream past West Arrow Park.
— CHARLES E. TURNER/VPL, 16791/PABC, 1442

Lower Arrow Lake. Her ordeal was a long one for the thaw did not come soon. The next day the *Minto* made her way as far south as possible to take on the *Kootenay*'s few stranded passengers. Presumably, since the *Minto* could not break through to the *Kootenay*, the passengers had to cover the intervening distance on shore or over the ice. The *Kootenay*, with coal running out, had to depend on wood cut on shore for fuel for several weeks until she was able to break her way out, using her paddlewheel to smash open a channel. The *Kootenay* survived her ordeal, but it had taken a toll on her hull, and her future usefulness was limited. She saw little further service and was retired in 1919, leaving only two sternwheelers and two aging tugs on the Arrow Lakes route.

Officially recognizing reality, the Canadian Pacific announced in *The Daily News* at Nelson on January 13, that through service on the Arrow Lakes route was suspended due to the cold. An alternative service via Slocan Lake was provided, three times a week, that bypassed the narrows between the two lakes. Steamers ran from Arrowhead as far south as Burton, but between there and Edgewood, service was suspended. A local service using one of the smaller boats, normally the *Whatshan*, was scheduled between Robson and Edgewood. However, ice built up above Burton and even this reduced service could not be maintained.

On Kootenay Lake, the disruption was less severe although the West Arm froze over and the steamers terminated their runs at Procter. A train service to connect with the boats was maintained so that service was kept up with only minor interruptions.

Drifting ice plugged up the southern end of Okanagan Lake in mid-January. Despite determined efforts, the *Sicamous* was not able to break through to Penticton, and Summerland became the end of the run. By early February, conditions became so bad that for a time she could not make it even that far south. On one run it was nearly midnight by the time she left Kelowna, nearly seven hours late, and by noon the next day she was still three miles (5 km) from Summerland, stuck in the ice. Finally, she backed out of the ice jam and returned to Peachland. Service to Summerland and Penticton had to await the thaw.

Kelowna and some of the smaller communities were particularly hard hit by the cold weather as all their coal was brought in on transfer barges which by February 4, 1916, had been unable to dock for over a week. Prices for firewood rose to $8.00 per cord and it was being hauled in by farmers over 20 miles (32 km) of road.

The Kootenay Lake steamers had run into comparatively little difficulty during the bad weather until early in February, when the *Kokanee* was making a late run to Kaslo. Then, she ran into one of the worst storms on record. Winds from the south, blowing snow and freezing rain whipped up the lake into a fury of waves and spray. After the *Kokanee* left Procter,

175

The Kootenaian noted, "... the next stop was Gray's creek, and heading northeasterly the steamer lounged [*sic*] sideways in a night as dark as pitch, into five miles of frothing waters, lashed into ungovernable fury by a 60 or 70 mile an hour [about 95 to 115 km/h] gale." Water poured in over the low hull and began to flood the stoker's pit, the hold and the engine room. Waves broke over the saloon deck and the spray carried as high as the pilothouse. The stop at Crawford Bay had to be omitted and Captain McKinnon decided to run his boat before the wind, steaming north. So frightening were conditions on board that some passengers became hysterical.

Finally, the *Kokanee* made her way to Pilot Bay and Captain McKinnon steered her straight for the beach, to give the pumps a chance to clear the rising water in the hold. Twenty minutes later she was ready for the storm again and steamed toward her stop, Coffee Creek. There she was to pick up two men, but the weather was so rough that only one could scramble aboard before the steamer was literally blown away from the landing, leaving the marooned man to spend the night in a rawhider's cabin.

The *Kokanee*'s landing at Ainsworth was even less successful. There, a large crowd had been waiting to board the steamer but her two attempts to dock were unsuccessful. Both times the hawsers were secured to the dock they were snapped by the force of the storm. With no way of docking safely at the exposed dock, the boat had to abandon the would-be passengers and beat her way north to Kaslo where she arrived safely some while later, her cabins encrusted with snow and ice. For a coastal steamship designed to withstand storms at sea such weather would not have been so serious but to a shallow draught sternwheeler, it was perilous indeed. With blowing snow and ice and flooding, capsizing had been a real, but fortunately unfulfilled, possibility.

The cold weather continued well into February. A report from Deer Park on the Arrow Lakes on February 13, 1916, indicated that there was 26 inches (66 cm) of snow on the ground and 10 inches (25 cm) of ice on the lake. On the Upper Arrow Lake there were setbacks and the *Minto* was often delayed. So thick was the ice that people could walk across the three-mile (4.8-km) width of Upper Arrow Lake above the narrows. By the middle of the month conditions were improving and above freezing temperatures were recorded. However, even by the 23rd, there was still considerable ice on the lakes, as a report from Rosebery noted, "... causing delay to the boats every day."

By the end of the month, service had been restored between Okanagan Landing and Summerland, while on the Arrow Lakes, on March 2, the *Minto* made a special run from Nakusp to Burton, but it was several days later before conditions returned to normal.

The winter of 1916 was not the only bad year for ice and snow for the boats, but it was one of the worst. In most win-

The *Kokanee* survived the rugged winter of 1916 and continued in service on Kootenay Lake until her retirement in 1923. — PABC, 30035

The *Kootenay* battles winter weather on the Arrow Lakes. Icebreaking barges were pushed ahead to clear the channel but if all else failed, the sternwheelers would steam in reverse, breaking the ice with their paddlewheels. Alternately, they would anchor or run a line ashore and then run the engines full speed in reverse to create a great wash from the surging wheel. The wash could itself break up the ice.
— PABC, 60725

Weather was not the only problem faced by the crews. Here, the *Moyie* with her paddlewheel out of commission will need the attention of the shipyard crew. — GEORGE DONALDSON

When ice built up on the decks and around the paddlewheel there was only one solution — chipping it off by hand. — W. TRIGGS

Thin floating ice did not present serious problems to the steamers. This is the *Okanagan* nearing Kelowna in 1920. — KELOWNA MUSEUM

Winter led to unusual, often gruelling jobs for the crews. When the *Nasookin*'s paddlewheel was damaged in the ice in 1923, crew members had to pull wood over the ice to make repairs.
— JOHN WILLIAMS

The beautiful *Rossland* met her fate in January 1917 when she sank in the ice at Nakusp. Later, she was raised and dismantled. — PABC, 31752

ters, the ice-breaking barges would be called out to clear a channel in front of one of the sternwheelers. The barges, which had steel sheeting on their bows, were pushed ahead of the steamers and did an effective job. Lines were rigged back to the sternwheeler so that by working either the ship's capstan or one on the barge, the barge could be swung to one side or the other to help manoeuvre. If all else failed, the tried technique for ice breaking was to use the paddlewheel. The wooden "buckets" or paddles could be easily replaced but damage to the hull, which might be sustained if the steamer simply rammed her way through, could be fatal. It seemed that none of the boats were immune to getting stuck in the ice although the *Kootenay* probably held the record.

However, in the winter of 1917, ice was to prove the undoing of the *Rossland*. On January 25, after being out of service for some time at Nakusp, she unexpectedly sank at the dock. There was a thin layer of ice along the shoreline, and ice and snow had built up on her decks. It is probable that some of her hull seams opened, or that ports left open in the hull, sank below the water due to the weight of the ice on her decks. She flooded quickly, sinking by the stern. The once-beautiful steamer was a forlorn sight, submerged up to her pilothouse and listing heavily to port. She was raised in March and then stripped of useful materials. The hulk was sold to Captain Albert Forslund, who had commanded her for many years.

In 1923, even the *Nasookin*, with her great size and power, was stuck just off Nelson, when ice wedged around her. She was freed after two days when the *Moyie*, pushing an ice-breaking barge, forced her way down from Procter to open a channel for the big steamer. During the period of her brief imprisonment, the crew had kept her paddlewheel turning slowly to keep a little clear water next to the steamer so that she would not be frozen in solidly.

The war years marked a significant change for the Lake and River Service. The Kettle Valley Railway was completed through to the main line of the CPR. By May 1915, trains could run all the way from Nelson across the southern expanse of the province to Spences Bridge, and in July 1916, the shorter Coquihalla Pass route was completed to Hope, directly east of Vancouver. With direct rail access to the Kootenays, the importance of the Arrow Lakes steamers as a connection with the main line at Revelstoke was diminished. The Arrow Lakes service became much more of a "branch line" as traffic to and from the coast increasingly favoured the railway route.

The war years also saw the passing of two of the pioneers of the Lake and River Service. In January 1916, Thomas J. Bulger, retired master builder, died at Portland at age 89. Since leaving the Lake and River Service in 1903, he had been living with his daughter in the city where he had spent his first 35 years of shipbuilding in the Northwest. Just a year later, on January 18, 1917, Captain John C. Gore, superin-

The war years saw the end to the career of the steamer *Nelson,* shown on the beach at the Nelson shipyard. The new launch *Nelson* is ahead of her while the *Kuskanook* is up on the ways. — CPCA

After the War and in the 1920's

The *Aberdeen* battled her way to Penticton pushing an icebreaking barge ahead but it also took the efforts of men using hand saws to cut through the ice and clear the final channel. This photograph is believed to be from the winter of 1908.
— VERNON BOARD OF MUSEUM AND ARCHIVES

The *Okanagan* steaming slowly through a channel in the ice just off Kelowna on February 25, 1922. — MCEWAN PHOTO, KELOWNA MUSEUM

Even the mighty *Nasookin* and her sisters were not immune from the crush of winter ice on the lakes. In 1923, the *Nasookin* was stuck just off Nelson. — PABC, 1425

tendent of the Lake and River Service, died in Nelson from heart failure. The veteran captain had come to British Columbia from the Willamette River in 1891 and had commanded some of the finest sternwheelers on the Columbia River and Kootenay Lake. He had been appointed Port Captain at Nelson in 1898 when Captain Troup had been sent to the Coast to supervise the construction of the Stikine River fleet. Then in 1901, when Captain Troup had been promoted to become Manager of the Canadian Pacific's newly-acquired coastal steamship operations, Captain Gore had been appointed to the superintendent's position. He was succeeded as superintendent by Captain Douglas Brown, a capable and experienced officer, who also served with the CPR's British Columbia Coast Steamship Service.

In November 1918, World War I ended and a few months later the troops — at least the lucky ones — began to come home. Many returned to the homes they had left, while others moved on to new places and different jobs. For some who returned, the tragic flu of 1919 awaited. But soon southern British Columbia returned to a peacetime economy. Tourism increased and traffic on the sternwheeler and tug and barge routes was steady.

A visit to the Okanagan and Kootenays by the Prince of Wales was the highlight of 1919. The future King Edward VIII travelled across Canada by train and arrived at Penticton on September 30, 1919. The Royal party travelled on the *Sicamous* to Okanagan Landing, stopping at Summerland en route. While the *Sicamous* returned to Kelowna, the Prince visited Vernon and then was driven by car to Kelowna. There, he reboarded the *Sicamous* and returned to Penticton. The Royal party then moved on by train to Nelson, arriving in mid-morning on October 1. There, after a brief visit, the Prince boarded the *Nasookin,* commanded by Captain Walter Seaman, to sail to Balfour where he visited convalescing soldiers at the former CPR hotel which was then serving as a hospital. After a leisurely visit, the Prince continued on the *Nasookin* down Kootenay Lake to Kootenay Landing where the Royal train was waiting. The Prince was served with both lunch and dinner on board. On leaving, he presented Captain Seaman and members of the crew with gifts.

*   *   *

Change was inevitable, and gradually the road and highway system expanded throughout the province and further expansion of the railways began in the Okanagan. In the late 1920's, the long-desired rail link between Procter and Kootenay Landing was begun. Such improvements to the region's transportation system ultimately were to draw away traffic from the Lake and River Service and contribute to its inevitable demise. For the steamboats, the 1920's were like "Indian

The *Kuskanook*'s officers at Kaslo, 1924.
FRONT ROW: Frank Broughton, first officer;
Walter H. Wright, master; John Cameron,
chief engineer.
BACK ROW: Jimmy Hurst, purser; Harold Penny,
assistant purser; William Carr, chief steward;
William Boyd, second engineer; and Walter
Spiller, second officer. — PABC, 86866

Following the completion of the *Nasookin*, the
Kuskanook acted as relief vessel and was used on
the Kaslo service. She eventually lost her elegant
paddlebox but little of her charm.
— W. G. KENNEDY COLLECTION

The wharf at Burton on the Arrow Lakes route was typical of the facilities in use by the 1920's. Water levels of the lakes varied greatly — high in spring, low in winter. The small structures were moved up and down the sloping wharf as water levels dictated. — F. A. BUCHHOLZ, PAC, PA-30829

Engineer John Williams, in his off-duty time, walked along the snow-covered lake front of Penticton and captured this nighttime winter portrait of the *Sicamous*. — JOHN WILLIAMS

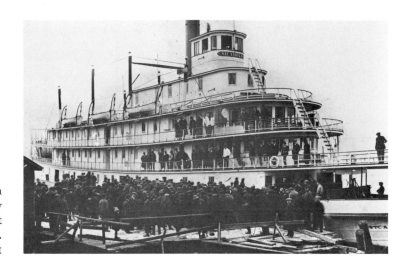

In 1919, when German settlers arrived in Kelowna aboard the *Sicamous*, they were met by an angry crowd of war veterans who did not want them to land. The memories were too fresh. — KELOWNA MUSEUM

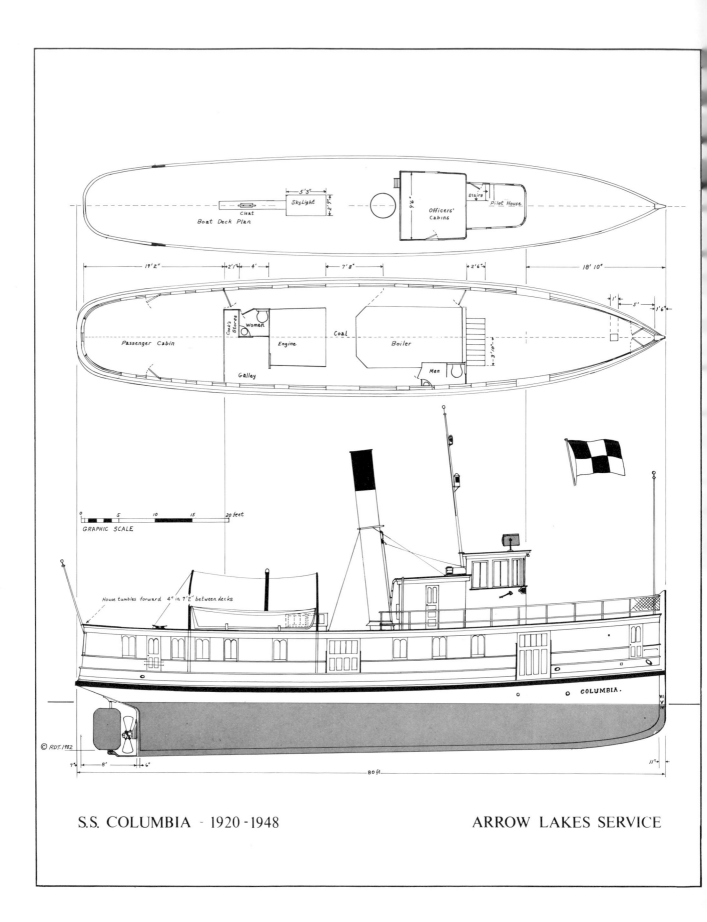

Boat Deck Plan

Cleat

Sky Light

Officers' Cabins

Stairs

Pilot House

Passenger Cabin

Cook's Stores

Women

Galley

Engine

Coal

Boiler

Men

GRAPHIC SCALE

0 5 10 15 20 feet

House tumbles forward 4" in 7'2" between decks

COLUMBIA.

© RDT. 1982

S.S. COLUMBIA · 1920 - 1948

ARROW LAKES SERVICE

The steamer *Columbia* was built at Nakusp in 1920 to replace the tugs *Whatshan* and *Columbia* on the Arrow Lakes route. In winter she maintained the service on Lower Arrow Lake. This photo shows her at the end of her career at Nakusp. — ROBERT W. PARKINSON

She was a useful little vessel and could handle a freight or icebreaking barge effectively. A small passenger lounge was located aft. — PABC, 75871

summer," before the hard years of the Depression and the disposal of nearly all the boats. The summers were warm, the excursions joyful and traffic plentiful, but the end was in sight.

There were a number of changes in the fleet during the 1920's. The sternwheelers *Kokanee* and *Slocan* and the tugs *Ymir*, *Sandon*, *Castlegar*, *Columbia* and *Whatshan* were all retired, but only four new vessels were built for the Lake and River Service. These were the tugs *Kelowna* and *Granthall* and the tug/passenger steamers *Columbia* and *Rosebery*.

The *Kelowna* was built at Okanagan Landing in 1920 to augment the *Naramata* and the aging *Castlegar* on the Okanagan Lake transfer barge service. In size and design, she was typical of the Lake and River Service tugs. She was fitted with the engines from the Arrow Lakes tug *Whatshan* which had been retired in 1919 and dismantled in 1920.

The *Columbia* was built as a replacement for the original tug *Columbia*, built in 1896, and the passenger tug *Whatshan*. Both were scrapped in 1920. The new *Columbia* was intended for passenger and freight service on Lower Arrow Lake, particularly during the winter months when the *Minto* was very often restricted to service north of Burton. The second *Columbia* had a small enclosed passenger cabin and dining room which might be better called a food service area. Altogether, she was an attractive little steamer and measured a modest 80.1 x 15.4 feet (24.4 x 4.7 m). She was licensed to carry 34 passengers and cost approximately $26,500. Her machinery, which gave her a speed of about 11 miles per hour (18 km/h), came from the first earlier *Columbia*.

The other two new vessels were both built in 1928. The *Rosebery* was designed to replace both the sternwheeler *Slocan* and the small steamer *Sandon* on Slocan Lake. Her role was to work the railway transfer barges and provide accommodation for the dwindling numbers of passengers on the route. Increasingly, private automobiles were cutting into passenger travel on the steamers and as revenues declined, so too did the frequency of service.

The *Rosebery* was a useful vessel of 102 x 20 feet (31 x 6.1 m), powered with the engines salvaged from the Okanagan Lake service tug *Castlegar*, which had been scrapped in 1925. Typically, the engines of these steamers outlasted their wooden hulls and were used in several successive generations of vessels. The *Rosebery* was licensed to carry 40 passengers and cost the CPR $35,000. The fine little sternwheeler *Slocan* was withdrawn from service once the *Rosebery* was ready to take over and was sold for use as a warehouse on Slocan Lake. The ungainly tug *Sandon* had been scrapped in 1927.

The finest addition to the Lake and River Service during the 1920's was the steel tug *Granthall*, built by Canadian Vickers of Montreal and assembled in 1928 at the Nelson shipyard. Deep-hulled and powerful, she had new triple-expansion engines rated at 62 nominal horsepower (420 indicated horsepower), which was over twice the output of the

There was time for some fun. Crew members from the tug *Kelowna* demonstrate their climbing skills on the hog chains of a barge.
— JOHN WILLIAMS

The Kootenay Lake tug *Hosmer*, top and middle left, came close to total disaster in 1925 when her cabins were destroyed by fire. She was rebuilt and returned to service. — BILL CURRAN COLLECTION

In 1921, the *York* was transferred to Skaha Lake to move railway barges. After the rail line along Skaha Lake was completed in 1931, she was retired.
— VERNON BOARD OF MUSEUM AND ARCHIVES

The tug *Kelowna* was built at Okanagan
Landing in 1920 to help handle growing traffic
on the transfer barge service on Okanagan Lake.
— CHARLES VEREY

The *Rosebery* was built in 1928 to replace the
aging sternwheeler *Slocan*. — CPCA

The Kootenay Lake Barge Service

The tugs and barges were neither as dramatic nor as picturesque as the sternwheelers, but they certainly were as important. On Kootenay Lake they bridged the critical gap between Nelson, and later Procter, and Kootenay Landing on the CPR's rail line across southern British Columbia.

The Kootenay Landing station.
— L. S. MORRISON COLLECTION

The *Hosmer*, with two 15-car barges, on Kootenay Lake. — R. E. BENEDICT, B.C. FOREST SERVICE

Tugs *Ymir, Valhalla* and *Hosmer*; mainstay of the barge service. — PABC, 213

Switching the barges at Kootenay Landing. Note coke cars from Crowsnest mines. — L. S. MORRISON COLLECTION

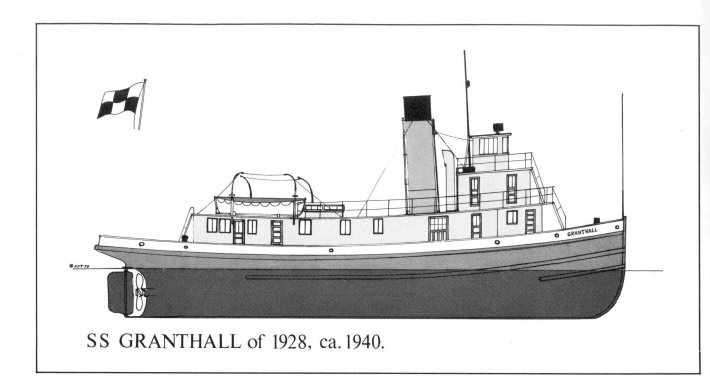

SS GRANTHALL of 1928, ca. 1940.

Canadian National Railways began a service on Okanagan Lake in 1926 using, among other vessels, the passenger carrying tug *Pentowna*, shown in the upper photo. The tug *Canadian National No. 5*, shown above next to the *Okanagan* at Okanagan Landing, was added in 1930. Eventually, barge service was provided to Penticton, Naramata, Summerland, Westbank and Peachland. —

KELOWNA MUSEUM/CHARLES VEREY

The steel tug *Granthall*, built in 1928, was the most powerful tug on Kootenay Lake but she served only two years on the Procter to Kootenay Landing transfer service due to the completion of the long-delayed rail link along the western shore of Kootenay Lake. She had a small passenger lounge aft. — BILL CURRAN

engines in tugs like the *Kelowna*. Unlike the earlier vessels with steel hulls and wooden superstructures, the *Granthall* also had steel cabins. She was licensed to carry 15 passengers and cost $96,170. Her construction however, was ill-timed, for the Kootenay Lake barge service for which she had been built was destined to last only two years after she entered service.

The last active vessel of the old C&KSN fleet was retired in 1923 when the old sternwheeler *Kokanee* was withdrawn from service and stripped of useful components, her days of racing long gone. It was estimated that she steamed about 350,000 miles (563,000 km) on Kootenay Lake. In her last years she had served as a relief vessel, filling in as required for the newer boats. Her old, wooden hull was waterlogged and not worth a long and expensive reconstruction. She was last used while the *Kuskanook*, followed by the *Nasookin*, were given extensive refits. She was sold for use as a lodge at Deanshaven until her hull was not fit for even this undemanding service and she was scrapped in 1930.

In September 1925, Canadian National Railways completed a branch line from Kamloops to Kelowna which gave the central Okanagan direct rail access to both the CNR and CPR main lines. CN built a transfer slip at Kelowna in 1926 and that summer, placed the twin-screw motor vessel *Pentowna* in service on Okanagan Lake. She was prefabricated at the Prince Rupert Dry Dock yards and assembled at Kelowna. The tug *Radius* was purchased and renamed *Canadian National No. 3* in 1928 and a new steel car barge was built. At first, this service was operated as the Okanagan Lake Boat Company, which the CN had purchased, but soon this name was dropped. A new tug, *Canadian National No. 5*, and a second barge were built in 1930. In 1937, the *Pentowna* was rebuilt as a tug and another new steel barge was constructed. By this time, passenger traffic had declined, but freight had increased substantially. While the CNR's tugs and barges competed for the Okanagan Lake traffic, a far more important impact of the CNR's presence in the Okanagan was to come in 1935 when the CPR acquired running rights for passenger trains over the CNR to Kelowna. This expansion of passenger train service, combined with improved highway and declining passenger traffic south of Kelowna signalled the end to steamer passenger service on Okanagan Lake.

For the Lake and River Service, the event that was to have very profound consequences was the announcement in 1928 by the Canadian Pacific that the railway would be completed between Procter and Kootenay Landing. This extension had been planned since the first construction of the Crowsnest Pass line in the late 1890's but had been delayed due to the high costs of blasting out a right-of-way along the mountainsides of the west shore of Kootenay Lake. The completion of the line would mean the end of the "Crow Boat" and the tug and barge service, leaving only the service to Kaslo and Lardeau.

Okanagan Landing

The CPR branch line from Sicamous, on its main line, to Okanagan Landing gave the Okanagan Valley rail access to markets throughout Canada and the United States. The vessels of the Lake and River Service provided the vital connection between the rich agricultural lands to the south and the railway.

The station at Okanagan Landing greeted passengers disembarking from the trains and destined for points along Okanagan Lake. — CPCA

The busy terminal prospered with the steady growth of traffic to and from the Okanagan Valley. — CPCA

A contrast in vessels: from left, the *Aberdeen*, *York*, *Kaleden* and, overshadowing all the others, the *Sicamous*. Absent are the sternwheeler *Okanagan* and the tugs. As on the other routes, the tug and barge service was, in many ways, as critical as the sternwheelers. In the Okanagan during fruit season, the tugs and barges moved hundreds of carloads of perishables to Okanagan Landing for shipment to market. The sternwheelers alone could not have handled the traffic. Barge slips were located at Okanagan Centre, Kelowna, Summerland, Westbank and Penticton. Later, the CPR used the CNR slip at Naramata in exchange for CN access to the CPR's facility at Summerland. After 1926, the barge service was based at Kelowna, following the opening of the CNR's branch line into the city, and the importance of Okanagan Landing declined. With the termination of regular passenger service in 1935 and the withdrawal of the *Sicamous* in 1936 only the shipyard at Okanagan Landing remained important to the Lake and River Service. — PABC, 308

The shipyard at Okanagan Landing, middle photo, built and maintained the fleet of sternwheelers, tugs and barges so important to the Okanagan Valley. The skilled shipwrights and carpenters, in their behind-the-scenes role, kept the vessels in excellent condition. — CPCA

The busy terminal in 1914, looking east past the station towards the shipyard, where the *Sicamous* is nearing completion. — CPCA

193

The Okanagan Valley, with its warm, dry climate and rich soils, prospered as an agricultural region. Settlement and population grew rapidly in the early 1900's. The sternwheelers became very much a part of daily commerce, but more than that, they became part of the social and cultural fabric of the communities they served. Excursions, picnics and special events often focused on the steamers. These were the happy times.

The Okanagan Lake Service

HAPPY TIMES

The *Okanagan* at Kelowna in 1909 at Regatta time.
— G. H. E. HUDSON, KELOWNA MUSEUM

The opening of the Kettle Valley Railway was a time for celebration. Penticton, May 30, 1915.
— VERNON BOARD OF MUSEUM AND ARCHIVES

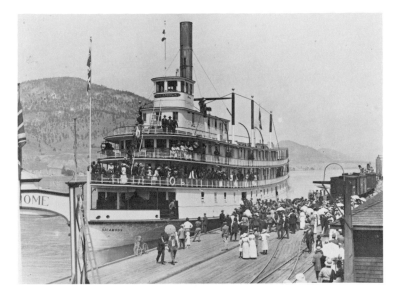

Crowds line the Penticton dock during the summer of 1915. Note the small boat fitted with decorative paddlewheels.
— VERNON BOARD OF MUSEUM AND ARCHIVES

Two vastly different vessels, the tug *Naramata* and the sternwheeler *Sicamous*, rest at the Penticton wharf about 1930. Ultimately, both vessels were preserved after the end of their service with the CPR.
— STOCKS FAMILY COLLECTION, IFB

At the end of September 1919, the Prince of Wales, later King Edward VIII, visited the Okanagan as part of his cross-country tour. The *Sicamous* carried the Prince and his party from Penticton to Okanagan Landing and then from Kelowna back to Penticton. Included was a stop at Summerland pictured at left.
— PABC, 91534

The *Sicamous* at Summerland. The photo also shows the barge slip and packing houses, so important to the local fruit growers.
— SUMMERLAND MUSEUM

For two years, construction crews worked along the sheer rock faces of the mountains on the western shore of Kootenay Lake, blasting a route for the railway between Procter and Kootenay Landing. With each mile gained, with each day's passing, the life of the steamboats drew shorter. The construction itself helped by providing extra traffic, but the end was inevitable.

Traffic across southern British Columbia had grown steadily during the 1920's and, of paramount importance, developments at the Sullivan Mine at Kimberley, leading to outputs of 6,000 tons (nearly 5,450 tonnes) per day, made a direct rail connection with the Trail Smelter essential. Moreover, the fertilizer plant at Trail, installed to make use of waste products from the smelting process, had added significant amounts of freight traffic to the east. The existing service on Kootenay Lake had become a serious bottleneck to the movement of freight. Even adding many new tugs and barges and probably new transfer slips would not have relieved the congestion and would have been expensive and inefficient. The new railroad would have much greater capacity and it would be considerably faster. In itself, the replacement of the tug and barge service by through trains would save nearly a day in handling freight over the route.

Coinciding with the railroad construction were additions to the highway system along Kootenay Lake so that little reason remained to operate steamers south of Procter. The highway route, completed in 1931, followed the eastern shore of Kootenay Lake north from Creston to Gray Creek opposite the West Arm of the lake. Consequently, a ferry was required to carry vehicles across the lake to the end of the road at Fraser Landing. This utilitarian service was to provide a new carreer for the *Nasookin* once her usefulness to the CPR was at an end.

For the B.C. Lake and River Service, December 31, 1930 marked the end of over 30 years of "main line" service between Nelson or Procter and Kootenay Landing. The railway was completed and open for traffic and the sternwheelers and tugs were redundant. The *Nasookin* arrived in Nelson with the last through passengers from Kootenay Landing at approximately 9:00 p.m. ending the once vital "Crow Boat" service. Public attention was directed to the new railway. The retiring steamers and their passing received comparatively little attention.

At the same time, the *Kuskanook*'s tri-weekly service from Nelson to Kaslo was terminated leaving only the *Moyie*'s route from Procter to Crawford Bay, Lardeau and Kaslo as the one remaining sternwheeler service on Kootenay Lake.

The sternwheelers and tugs were tied up at Procter to await their fates. The *Kuskanook* was permitted a brief reprieve, relieving the *Moyie*, which was given an overhaul, but after that was withdrawn. Despite being younger than the *Moyie*, the *Kuskanook* was the steamer considered surplus because of her wooden hull. She was sold in 1931. With her machinery

A Railway Opens;
A Steamer Line Dies

With the completion of the railway between Procter and Kootenay Landing, most of the Kootenay Lake fleet was tied up at Procter. Soon, only the *Moyie* and the *Granthall* would remain in CPR service while the *Nasookin* would be rebuilt as an automobile ferry. — PABC, 53409

The *Kootenay*, retired in 1919 and sold in 1920, ended her days as a rotting hulk at Crescent Bay near Nakusp. — PABC, 62600

The sight of the *Nasookin* or the *Kuskanook* on the "Crow Boat" became but a memory with the completion of the rail line along Kootenay Lake. For the CPR and the Kootenays the railway extension was progress but for the Lake and River Service, it meant the virtual end of the steamboats on Kootenay Lake. For many employees, some with years of service, it was the end of their steamboating careers. — CPCA

and paddlewheel removed, she became a floating hotel. The tugs *Valhalla* and *Hosmer* were both sold, leaving only the new steel-hulled *Granthall* available as a relief vessel for the *Moyie*.

It was in response to prosperity that the Kootenay Lake rail line was first built, but by the time it was finished the Great Depression of the 1930's had begun. The need for a more efficient and faster system of transport had brought about the end of the main steamer service on Kootenay Lake but the Depression would lead to the retirement of more fine vessels in the near future.

The 1930's brought the Depression with its despair, stagnation and hard times for so many people and communities. For the Lake and River Service, the decade saw the final withdrawal of all but two of the remaining sternwheelers. The survivors were the unpretentious *Minto* and *Moyie*; tough and durable boats that would work their way not only through the Depression but through the more demanding years of World War II and the early 1950's. Nearing the end of a career that spanned nearly 60 years, the *Moyie* steams away from Kaslo.

— PERCY ORRELL, MOYIE MUSEUM

CHAPTER VI

THE TWILIGHT YEARS:
1930-1972

The 1930's and 1940's:
Years of Decline

IN THE 1930's, the decline in the Lake and River Service became precipitous. After the completion of the railway between Procter and Kootenay Landing, and the subsequent retirement of most of the boats, only the *Moyie* and the *Granthall* remained in service on Kootenay Lake. They connected the communities along the northern end of the lake with CPR train service at Procter. The *Moyie*, because of her better passenger accommodations and greater capacity for freight, was normally used on the route.

The *Nasookin*, no longer needed by the CPR, had been leased to the British Columbia government to carry motor vehicles across Kootenay Lake between Frasers Landing, on the north side of the West Arm just downstream from Procter, and Gray Creek at Crawford Bay. Initially, she was modified only to the extent of removing the overhanging deck between her bow and the front of her cabins. This was done to facilitate carrying trucks and buses that required high clearance and could not be accommodated on the freight deck.

She was sold outright to the government in 1933 for continued use as an automobile ferry and remained in this service until 1947 when the new ferry *Anscomb* was completed. Since the ferry trip was very short, no overnight accommodations were required on the *Nasookin* for her new role. Her upper cabins had made her difficult to manage in a crosswind, and there was little value in retaining them. She was therefore taken to the Nelson shipyard and extensively rebuilt.

The reconstruction involved removing most of her two upper stateroom decks and relocating the pilothouse and one of the lounges slightly forward of their previous positions. The end result did little for the aesthetic appearance of the steamer, but it certainly made her more functional as a link in the highway system and extended her useful life for another 15 years.

On the Arrow Lakes, by 1930, the fleet had been reduced to only the *Minto*, *Bonnington* and *Columbia*. With the Depression worsening and tourist traffic considerably diminished, the *Bonnington* was tied up at Nakusp after the 1931 summer

Her giant paddlewheel stilled forever, the *Bonnington* lies at Nakusp shipyard, a victim of the Depression and changed travel patterns. It is August 20, 1940. — L. S. MORRISON

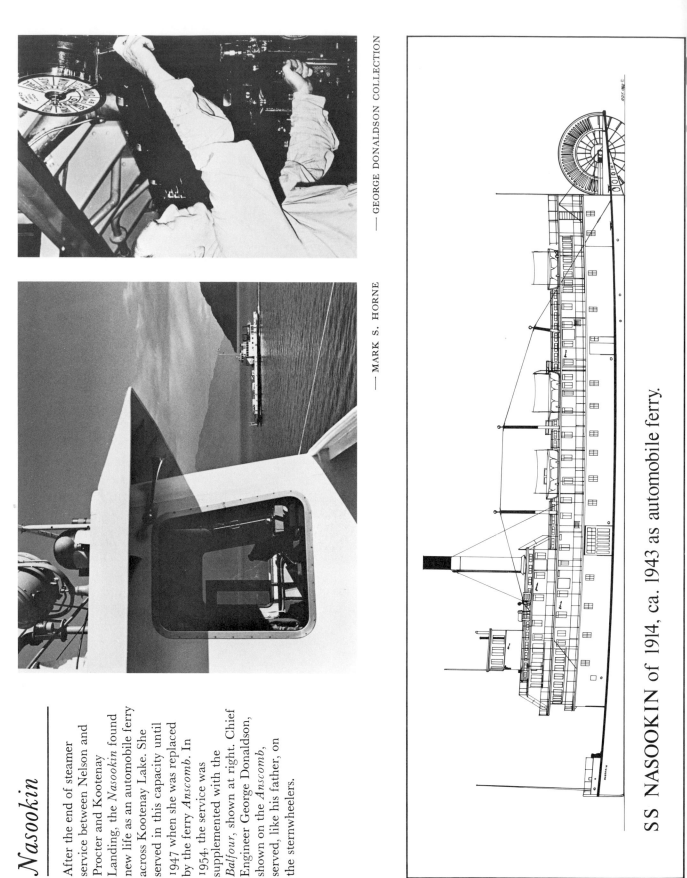

Nasookin

After the end of steamer service between Nelson and Procter and Kootenay Landing, the *Nasookin* found new life as an automobile ferry across Kootenay Lake. She served in this capacity until 1947 when she was replaced by the ferry *Anscomb*. In 1954, the service was supplemented with the *Balfour*, shown at right. Chief Engineer George Donaldson, shown on the *Anscomb*, served, like his father, on the sternwheelers.

SS NASOOKIN of 1914, ca. 1943 as automobile ferry.

The *Nasookin* at Procter in 1947. — ROBERT W. PARKINSON

The *Nasookin* ran between Gray Creek, here on the east side of Kootenay
Lake and Fraser Landing on the west. — ROBERT W. PARKINSON

It is 1947, and the *Nasookin*, carrying a bus across her foredeck, passes the *Anscomb* which will soon replace her. Below, the *Nasookin* steams away from Procter. — ROBERT W. PARKINSON

season, never to see service again. Thereafter, the *Minto* maintained a summer service between Arrowhead and Robson, but, during the winter months, the *Columbia* worked Lower Arrow Lake while the *Minto* confined her service, except on rare occasions, to Upper Arrow Lake.

In the Okanagan, the *Sicamous* and *Okanagan* continued in operation but primarily as freight boats. The completion of the CNR to Kelowna and expansion of the highway system had virtually eliminated the necessity for passenger service on the Lake. In 1934 the *Okanagan* was retired and the following year the CPR acquired passenger train running rights over the CNR line to Kelowna and was able to end passenger boat service in January 1935. The *Sicamous* operated the following two summers primarily carrying fruit, but after that was permanently withdrawn. Freight had remained important, especially during the busy fruit-packing season. However, even this traffic could not sustain the boat indefinitely.

During her last years, the *Okanagan* had remained virtually unchanged, but the *Sicamous*, like the *Nasookin*, underwent an extensive reconstruction. Her upper cabins, no longer needed, were removed. Shorn of her Texas deck and most of her upper saloon deck, she was undoubtedly a more functional vessel, but the conversion did little to lengthen her career. On their retirement, the two sternwheelers were tied up at the Okanagan Landing shipyard. Neither vessel was ever returned to service. The *Okanagan* was sold in 1938 and dismantled. The *Sicamous* was luckier and in August 1951, after lying at Okanagan Landing for 15 years, she was towed to Penticton for preservation on the waterfront as a landmark and reminder of an earlier era of transportation on Okanagan Lake. She was used for a variety of purposes including housing a wax museum and later, a restaurant. But unfortunately, full restoration of the vessel as an historic site and museum has not been accomplished.

The tugs and barges of the Lake and River Service on Okanagan Lake continued to provide important connections for freight for many years after the retirement of the sternwheelers. Until after World War II, the service was handled by the *Naramata* and the *Kelowna*. After 1926, with CPR freight trains running over the CNR to Kelowna, the tug and barge operations had been shifted to Kelowna from Okanagan Landing. However, the shipyard remained open. The change led to more efficient handling of freight, and reduced the distance of the barge runs to the major shipping points along the southern shores of Okanagan Lake.

On Slocan Lake, the small steamer *Rosebery* continued to ply back and forth between Slocan City and Rosebery, calling at New Denver and Silverton en route. Her primary function was moving railway transfer barges and providing a connection with trains to and from Nelson. As passenger volumes declined, the rail service was reduced to a once-a-week mixed train. With little traffic remaining on the isolated trackage

The lovely *Okanagan* spent her last years mostly as a freight boat but was used also to push transfer barges. — CHARLES VEREY

A steel barge being reassembled at Okanagan Landing in 1936. It is barge *No. 4* which was originally built by Canadian Vickers and assembled at Nelson in 1927. — CHARLES VEREY

The CPR maintained shipyards at Nelson, Nakusp, Okanagan Landing and Rosebery. They were essential for the continued operation and overhaul of the steamers and barges even after the busy years of construction. These photos show the *Nasookin*, after her sale for use as a ferry, being pulled up onto the ways at Nelson. Teams of horses turned the capstans to slowly but surely pull the boats out of the water. As a small concession to mechanization, the yard had a small donkey engine as well.
— BILL CURRAN COLLECTION

Captain J. B. Weeks was the last captain of the *Sicamous*. He emigrated in 1893 and became a deck hand on the *Aberdeen* then in 1904 he received his master's certificate. He first commanded the *York* and soon after, the *Aberdeen*. In 1922, he took over the *Sicamous*. He retired in 1942 and died in 1968 at age 91.
— STOCKS FAMILY COLLECTION, IFB

The *Sicamous* made her last scheduled passenger run on January 6, 1935 and soon after, her upper cabins were cut down as she was relegated primarily to freighting. She operated during the 1935 and 1936 summer seasons but was then retired. The photos show the work in progress, top left, on her cabins in 1935 and as she last saw service, middle left, tied up at Okanagan Landing.
— BILL CURRAN COLLECTION/NORMAN GIDNEY

With the introduction of CPR passenger train traffic over the CNR to Kelowna and the suspension of passenger service on the steamers, Okanagan Landing languished although the shipyard remained active. Norman Gidney photographed the railway yard, with rail removed, in September 1942.

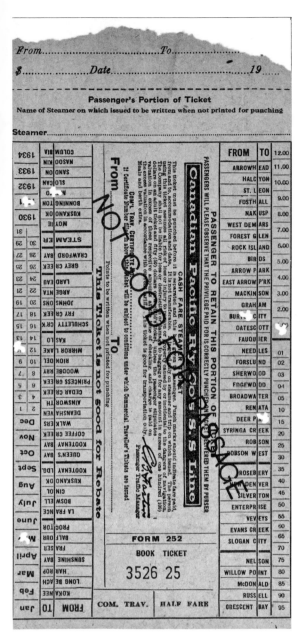

A ticket receipt from the *Minto* for a trip from Burton City to Deer Park. The trip, of May 11, 1931, cost $1.00. — AUTHOR'S COLLECTION

The use by the CPR of the CNR's tracks between Vernon and Kelowna was a severe blow to the Lake and River Service. The base for freight barge operations was moved to Kelowna in 1926 and passenger service was terminated in 1935. Southbound, a train of empty refrigerator cars is rolling along the shore of Kalamalka Lake towards Kelowna. — POPE COLLECTION, IFB

On Kootenay Lake, the only barge services that remained were from Procter to Kaslo and Lardeau serving the two isolated branch lines and a few mines along the lakeshore. With little traffic remaining at Kaslo and Lardeau, the entire train was moved by barge. This saved maintaining equipment on the branch lines.
— PABC, 13012

During fruit season the tug and barge service on Okanagan Lake was particularly busy. Lines of box and refrigerator cars crowd the transfer wharf at Penticton. A typical fruit harvesting season of the 1940's.— CPCA

The *Rosebery*, at left, backing away from the dock at Slocan City, as rebuilt in 1943.
— ROBERT W. PARKINSON

The *Rosebery* at Slocan City as the train crew switches the barge. As on Kootenay Lake, the entire train will be loaded onto the barge.
— JAMES CROOKALL COLLECTION, VCA

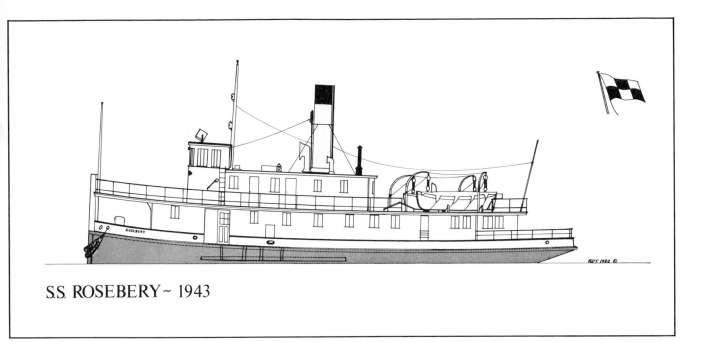

S.S. ROSEBERY ~ 1943

In 1949, the city of Penticton purchased the
Sicamous from the CPR and two years later she
was towed to Penticton by the *Okanagan* for
permanent preservation.
— STOCKS FAMILY COLLECTION, IFB

During the 1930's and 40's, the tugs *Naramata*,
left, and *Kelowna*, right, maintained the barge
service on Okanagan Lake. — CHARLES VEREY

The *Columbia* near Robson. Her replacements were not satisfactory. — W. GIBSON KENNEDY

The tug *Widget* was chartered in 1948 to fill in until a replacement could be acquired for the *Columbia*, whose hull was condemned. The motor launch *Nipigonian* also was used on the route. — BOB SPEARING

from Rosebery to Nakusp it became the practice to move the entire train, including locomotive and caboose, on transfer barges. This proved to be less expensive than stationing a train crew and locomotive at either Nakusp or Rosebery.

Only three vessels were added to the Lake and River Service after 1930. The first of these was a replacement for the *Rosebery*, which had been built for the Slocan Lake route in 1928. The steamer's hull had become waterlogged. Consequently, a new hull was built and the machinery transferred to it. A new boiler, costing over $21,000, was installed and with the cost of the new hull and reconditioning the salvaged cabins, the total cost of the project was nearly $54,000. Appropriately, the new boat was also named *Rosebery* and she made her first run on November 5, 1943. Captain James Fitzsimmons, in retirement for eight years, had the pleasure of putting the trim little steamer through her trials on her maiden voyage. The new hull was slightly longer than the old and there were minor changes to the cabins, but basically the design remained unchanged.

The second new vessel acquired was an all-steel, diesel-powered tug built for the Okanagan Lake service by West-coast Shipbuilders of Vancouver and assembled at Okanagan Landing. Named the *Okanagan*, she was a fine, powerful vessel, well suited to handle the transfer barges, and cost approximately $200,000.

The final vessel purchased turned out to be the least satisfactory. By 1948, the steamer *Columbia*, used on Lower Arrow Lake during the winter and, when required, as a relief for the *Minto*, was in need of replacement. As with the first *Rosebery*, which had been of similar vintage, the *Columbia*'s hull was worn out. A replacement vessel was found in the form of the 50-foot (15-m) M.V. *Surfco* which had operated along Vancouver Island out of Port Alberni. The little vessel was not at all suited for moving any quantity of freight. It was therefore necessary for the *Minto*, under Captain Otto Estabrooks, to operate down the narrows late in the fall to provide as good a service as possible to the isolated ranches and farms in the area.

The Last Steaming Days of the Minto and the Moyie

In their declining years both the *Minto* and the *Moyie* were curiosities as well as functioning links in the transportation system of the Kootenays. They had become, because of their age, a form of living history and consequently received considerable publicity. The *Minto* was written up in *The Saturday Evening Post* and the National Film Board produced a movie on the old sternwheeler. Steamship enthusiasts travelled from distant parts of North America to ride the vessels, which had become the only surviving commercial paddlesteamers in western Canada, south of the Yukon River.

While all passenger services were included in the CPR's system timetables of the period, the Company also produced a

The sternwheelers never lacked in aesthetics and the *Minto*, photographed backing away from the wharf at Burton, was no exception. Her spotless condition belies her advancing years and half century of service on the Arrow Lakes. In the distance are the narrows, leading south to Lower Arrow Lake. — L. S. MORRISON

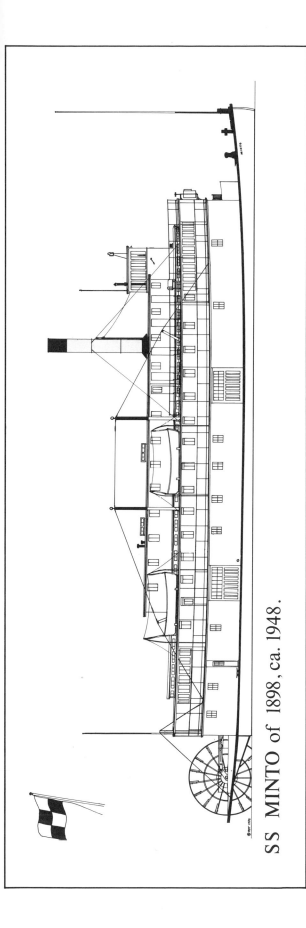

SS MINTO of 1898, ca. 1948.

The *Minto* lacked the graceful paddlebox of some of the other stern-wheelers. It is 1947 and the *Minto* is one year short of her 50th birthday.
— WILBUR C. WHITTAKER

The Arrow Lakes route from Robson in the south to Arrowhead in the north was beautiful and scenic; the *Minto*, aging gracefully, was a photogenic and charming vessel. The photographs on this and the following three pages are by W. Gibson Kennedy who made several trips on the *Minto* during the 1940's and early 1950's.

At Robson West with the *Columbia*, which was purchased in 1948.

Arriving at Robson in 1952.

On Lower Arrow Lake in August 1944.

Northbound on Lower Arrow Lake in July 1941.

Approaching the wharf at Deer Park on the east side of
Lower Arrow Lake in August 1944.

The *Minto* navigates the narrows between Lower and Upper Arrow lakes. For travellers, the passage was a highlight of the trip but for the captain and crew it was a time for particular watchfulness and attention. Although the narrows were difficult, even the *Bonnington* could pass through in summer but during low water — from November to late Spring — they were impassable to the larger boats and a challenge for vessels like the *Minto*. Normally, through service was suspended over the winter and a local service provided from Nakusp south to Carrolls Landing or Burton and from Robson north as far as Needles. This avoided the worst section of the narrows just south of Burton. Gib Kennedy took these beautiful scenes in August 1944.

STATEROOM NUMBER				
TENS	•	2	3	4
UNITS	1 2 3 4 5 6 7 8		9 0	

ISSUED BY
CANADIAN PACIFIC RY. CO. STEAMSHIP LINE   5

British Columbia Lake and River Service

ARROWHEAD, B.C.   .50

TO

NAKUSP, B.C.   .75

On Date Stamped on Back
**FOR ACCOMMODATION
INDICATED BY PUNCH MARKS**   .00

S. S. MINTO   1.50

On S.S. ....

**PASSENGER TO RETAIN
This Portion of Ticket
NOT GOOD FOR PASSAGE**   2.00

This portion of Ticket is of No VALUE
except to the passenger to identify
accommodation.   2.50

NOT TRANSFERABLE

FORM 1374 No. **58623**   3.00

— ROBERT W. PARKINSON COLLECTION

CAN. PAC. RY.
SEP
3
1942
STEAMER MINTO

Arrowhead, top left, framed by snow-capped mountains, remained the northern terminal for the *Minto* for her entire career. The arrival of the steamer was always a welcome event for the town's population. — JIM HOPE COLLECTION

Train service from Revelstoke connected with the *Minto*. The tug, lower left, is the *Beaton* which provided a barge service across the lake. — ROBERT W. PARKINSON

mimeographed information sheet on the Arrow Lakes service to provide additional background notes on the *Minto* and her service. Excerpts from this sheet follow and provide some interesting insights into the service in its last years.

"Vancouver, B.C. May 1st, 1951

ARROW LAKES SERVICE — SS 'MINTO'

The Canadian Pacific Lake Steamship 'Minto' provides service twice a week in each direction on the Arrow Lakes on the following schedule:

NORTHBOUND Read Down		SOUTHBOUND Read Up
Tue. & Fri.	5.30 AM Lv. Robson West	Ar. 2.30 PM Thurs. & Mon.
Tue. & Fri.	3.30 PM Ar. Nakusp	Lv. 4.00 AM Thurs. & Mon.
Wed. & Sat.	8.00 AM Lv. Nakusp	Ar. 5.00 PM Wed. & Sat.
Wed. & Sat.	11.45 AM Ar. Arrowhead	Lv. 1.05 PM Wed. & Sat.

On the Southbound trip, the S.S. 'Minto' connects with Canadian Pacific Railway Train No. 12 Eastbound at Robson West Mondays and Thursdays. Robson West is approximately 485 miles [780 km] east on the Kettle Valley route of the Canadian Pacific."

The sheets also note that trips via the Arrow Lakes route could be included in tours to Lake Louise and Banff and details are provided on the branch line connection between Revelstoke and Arrowhead. Passengers travelling from the east and planning to embark on the *Minto* are advised to arrive at Robson West the day before due to the steamer's 5:30 a.m. departure time. Fare information and a cautionary note follow:

"The steamer fare between Arrowhead and Robson West is $5.35 plus cost of berth ($1.25 to $2.00), or stateroom ($3.00 to $3.25). There are 22 staterooms with two single berths each and 4 staterooms with a double lower berth and a single upper. These latter cabins can accommodate 3 people. Meals are a very reasonable price, breakfast costing 75 cents, lunch and dinner $1.00 each, and are served to children at reduced prices.

"... The 'Minto' was placed in service on the Arrow Lakes to provide passenger and freight service for the people of the district. It was not built with a view to accommodating tourists and therefore interested passengers should be cautioned not to expect luxurious accommodation. Cabins on the 'Minto' are steam heated as are the lounges and although accommodation is not spacious, a comfortable trip can be expected."

There are then notes on the scenic attractions of the route and it is pointed out that passengers travelling southbound on Saturdays can not be accommodated on board at Nakusp and should make reservations at one of the local hotels.

"The 'Minto' has space for seven automobiles which can be carried from one end of the lake to the other. No vehicle exceeding 6′ 4″ [1.9 m] in height 6′ 6″ [2 m] in width and exceeding five tons [4.5 tonnes] in weight can be accepted for transportation. Measurements must include couplings, chimneys and radio antennae or other projections. Reservations for cars are necessary.

Intending passengers would do well to bear the following facts in mind when considering a trip on the 'Minto',

Advance reservations are necessary as the trip is very popular during the summer.

Accommodation is not luxurious but is comfortable.

Meals are plain, but the food is good.

The trip represents wonderful travel value as it is inexpensive, scenic and unusual. The Arrow Lakes journey can easily be incorporated into a trip either Eastbound or Westbound.

Further information can be obtained from Canadian Pacific agents or by writing to:

H. C. James
General Passenger Agent
Canadian Pacific Railway
Vancouver, B.C."

By the late 1940's, the *Moyie*'s operations were reduced to about two trips a week. One run to Kaslo was devoted to handling the CPR way freight from Nelson. The freight normally left Nelson in the morning and ran out along the lakeshore to Procter where the entire train was loaded onto one of the transfer barges. The *Moyie* then took the barge up the lake to Kaslo where the train was unloaded. Here, the train crew performed any local switching required and ran up the line towards Nakusp as far as required. When this work was done, the train was reloaded onto the barge and the *Moyie*, with barge, steamed back to Procter, arriving in the evening. This run was normally made on Fridays, although "extras" also operated. On Saturdays, the *Moyie*'s day began by steaming from the freight slip at Procter to the passenger wharf opposite the Holiday Inn (not affiliated with the modern hotel system). There, she waited for the arrival of CPR train No. 11, the westbound *Kootenay Express*. After passengers boarded and freight was transferred, the *Moyie* steamed on up the lake as far as Argenta and Lardeau, called where required and arrived back at Procter late in the evening.

The *Moyie*'s was a scenic and relaxing service, somehow anachronistic in the post-World War II era of air and automobile travel. But roads to the remote communities along Kootenay Lake were improved only very slowly, and well into the 1950's no real alternative to the *Moyie*'s service existed. The CPR would have liked to replace the *Moyie* with the much newer *Granthall* but the tug had insufficient facilities for passengers and freight. She was, however, better suited to moving the transfer barges than was the old sternwheeler.

After 56 years of almost continuous service on the Arrow Lakes route, time had at last run out for the *Minto*. A vessel can be operated economically for only so long, and changed

Beach Landings

Service on the lakes and rivers was both personal and casual. If a farmer had a crop to ship from an isolated ranch, the steamers would pull into the beach and the deck hands would load the cargo while the purser took care of the paperwork. Waving a flag or lighting two beach fires signaled a steamer to stop.
— ROBERT W. PARKINSON

Farewell to the Minto

Captain Walter Wright looks down from the wheelhouse of the *Minto*. He had been a watchman on the *Minto* on her first voyage.
— L. S. MORRISON

With a practised hand, Captain Wright steers the *Minto*. It is 1944, and after 46 years of use, the handles of the wheel have developed a lustrous patina. — W. GIBSON KENNEDY

Captain Otto L. Estabrooks, whose father, George Ludlow Estabrooks, also commanded CPR sternwheelers for the Lake and River Service, served on all the major routes and before his retirement in 1951 was captain of the *Minto*. After the withdrawal of the second *Columbia*, Captain Estabrooks skilfully took the *Minto* down through the narrows as late in the season as possible during the winters of 1948, 1949 and 1950 to serve the isolated ranchers in the area.
— JOHN WILLIAMS

The sternwheelers had nearly all passed into history by the time colour photography became commonplace. On the left, Arthur Broomhall captured these two views of the *Minto* at Edgewood in 1953, just a year before she was retired. — ARTHUR BROOMHALL

The tug *Okanagan*, top of this page, operating until 1972, photographed from the Kelowna floating bridge by Nicholas Morant. — CPCA

The tugs were normally painted an attractive yellow and green colour scheme in contrast to the sternwheelers' overall white with red trim. This photo, from 1982, shows the retired *Naramata* at Okanagan Landing.
— ROBERT D. TURNER

225

conditions in the West Kootenays precluded any thought of a modern replacement vessel for the old sternwheeler. Road systems were being extended and improved and, significantly, at this time the larger centres were growing and the small outlying communities were not. More and more people chose to live in the major towns where there were more jobs and greater opportunities. The net result was a steadily declining volume of business for the *Minto*; the end was inevitable. When the CPR announced her pending retirement, the Company noted that losses on the Arrow Lakes operations had reached $100,000 annually and, beyond ordinary maintenance, an additional $16,000 would have to be spent on the wharves at Nakusp and Robson West. Moreover, the *Minto* herself would have required an expenditure of $10,000 for an overhaul to pass her next inspection. With an estimated 2,500,000 miles (4,023,000 km) behind her, the *Minto*'s time had come.

The announcement of her retirement was greeted with sadness all along the lakes and far beyond as the old vessel had made many loyal friends and left many memories. Vessels are, of course, inanimate but the *Minto* had become far more than just an old, obsolete piece of machinery. She had been an integral part of life in the West Kootenays since the time when the region was still a frontier.

Several generations had grown up to the sight of her steaming up and down the lakes, hearing the distant sound of her whistle. To people living in the small communities along the lakes she was often the only means of dependable transportation and communication with the rest of the world. The vessel and her crew had become friends to the residents of the lakeside communities.

On Friday, April 23, 1954, the *Minto* began her last voyage on the Arrow Lakes, steaming from Nakusp to Robson West and return. The next day, she made a final return trip to Arrowhead before dropping her fire for the last time at Nakusp. Captain R. S. Manning, who had first joined the CPR in 1911, and just one year from retirement, was Master. All staterooms were sold out for the last trip from Robson West. Reservations to ride the *Minto* for the last time had come from many parts of British Columbia, and far beyond. One passenger of particular note was Mrs. Oliver Maitland from Winnipeg. Fifty-six years before, she had ridden on the *Minto*'s maiden voyage. This time, there was a television crew and several radio and newspaper reporters to see the *Minto* depart from Robson West.

At every community along the route people came down to the dock to see the *Minto* for the last time. At Syringa Creek, the retired postmaster, after 50 years of service, passed the mail aboard for the last time and stood with hat in hand on the wharf as the steamer pulled away. At Fullmore Point, across from Edgewood, Jock Ford, in full regalia, played a lament on the bagpipes to bid farewell. Captain Manning stopped the *Minto*'s engines so the strains of the bagpipes

Time ran out for the *Minto* and the Lake and River Service on the Arrow Lakes by the early 1950's. Serving on the *Minto* on her last run were, from left: Reg Barlow, second engineer; Fred Barlow, first officer; Robert Manning, master; Lawrence Exton, chief engineer; and Jack Edmunds, purser. Reg and Fred Barlow were father and son. Fred transferred to the *Minto* for her last runs. — PABC, 91690

The end came for the *Minto* in 1954 when the CPR announced that she would be retired. Her final voyage was a sad occasion for all on board and for people all along her route.

— L. S. MORRISON

An old friend was leaving, never to return. The *Minto*, decorated in flags and wreaths, backs slowly away from the dock at Arrowhead. Her whistle, echoing from the surrounding hills, was a final farewell. The *Minto*'s whistle was installed later at the Celgar mill at Castlegar.

— JOHN E. GREGSON

could be heard more clearly on board. There was probably not a dry eye on the steamer. Fifty people came down to the dock at Edgewood. Spring flowers were taken aboard to decorate the dining room table at Burton; a cedar wreath was attached to the steamer's bow. In the narrows between the two lakes a dredge crew placed another wreath aboard and the dredge carried the message, "Farewell *Minto*. Well done old girl."

But the voyage was not all sadness. At Nakusp a dance was held for the crew and the spring weather held for the rest of the voyage. The next morning, as she carried on north to Arrowhead, the farewells continued. At Halcyon Hot Springs, retired Brigadier General Burnham, a resident since the 1920's, saw the *Minto* off in his full dress uniform. When the *Minto* returned to Nakusp later that day the end came at last. Only the *Moyie* on Kootenay Lake remained of the once large fleet of sternwheelers.

With such sentiment for the old vessel it was not surprising that some effort should be made to preserve the *Minto*; the town of Nakusp purchased her from the CPR for one dollar. However, the project foundered for lack of funds, for the *Minto* needed much long-term, expensive maintenance to preserve her. Eventually she was sold for scrap and her boiler, engines, brass fittings and paddlewheel were removed. However, in 1956, before demolition could continue further, her hulk was purchased for $800.00 by John Nelson, who had her towed to Galena Bay at the north end of Upper Arrow Lake, not far from where the *Bonnington* had been dismantled. There the elderly man did his best to repair the steamer, replacing some window frames and the flag pole and making a new name plate for the wheelhouse. The next spring, high water enabled Nelson to beach the *Minto* higher on the shore and she remained there for another decade. John Nelson died at age 88 in 1967 and his *Minto* followed him a year later when the sternwheeler was towed out to the middle of the lake and burned. The *Minto* was destroyed to make way for the flooding of the Arrow Lakes as part of the massive Columbia River hydro-electric development program underway at the time. B.C. Hydro had offered to determine the cost of refitting her as a museum. However, the estimate was nearly $100,000 and Walter Nelson, son of the late owner of the vessel, concluded that the effort to save the now badly deteriorated vessel was unwarranted. The *Minto*'s viking funeral was held on August 1, 1968.

Following the retirement of the *Minto* in 1954, the CPR sold the *Columbia*, its last remaining vessel on the Arrow Lakes, along with a barge, to Ivan Horie who continued to provide a freight service on Lower Arrow Lake for a few years. For the CPR, the 67-year history of steamboat operations on the Arrow Lakes was at an end. The *Minto*, built just 18 months after the CPR purchased the service, had survived it all.

After attempts to preserve the *Minto* at Nakusp failed, she was purchased by John Nelson and moved to Galena Bay at the north end of Upper Arrow Lake. But one man with slim resources could not arrest the slow deterioration caused by the weather. When the level of the Arrow Lakes was to be raised as part of the Columbia River hydro project, the fate of the *Minto* was sealed. Moving her was impractical; she was towed offshore and burned. — VPL, 936/PABC, 61232

The End Comes for the Moyie

With the retirement of the *Minto* in 1954 only the *Moyie* remained of the once large fleet of sternwheelers and it was clear that the old vessel's time was running out. Facing the increasingly high maintenance costs of the *Moyie*, coupled with the declining traffic on the Kootenay Lake run and the improvement of the road system between Kaslo, Lardeau, Trout Lake City and Beaton, the CPR had no option but to retire its last sternwheeler. In March 1957, the formal announcement came that the *Moyie* would make her last run on April 27, 1957, to bring to an end the service career of the 59-year-old sternwheeler. The freight service on Kootenay Lake was to be taken over by the tug *Granthall* but passenger service was to be discontinued with the *Moyie*'s retirement.

On Saturday morning, April 27, 1957, the *Moyie* began her last voyage for the Canadian Pacific Railway. She slipped away from the dock at Procter and proceeded on her routine run to small landings and communities along the shore of the northern end of Kootenay Lake. Like the *Minto*'s last voyage, just three years earlier, the *Moyie*'s was to be a sentimental farewell for many residents of the lake communities and friends of the old steamer. For long-time residents of the region, the parting was particularly sad and at every stop she made, people turned out to see the *Moyie*. At Lardeau, 20 cars and trucks gave the steamer a horn-blowing send-off while at Argenta the boat was presented with a decorated wreath. More flowers were presented at Johnson's Landing. At Kaslo, the largest community on the *Moyie*'s route, the pilings of the dock were decorated with red, white and blue bunting and a large sign read: "Better Lo'ed Ye Ne'er Be. Will Ye No Come Back Again." Stores were closed, the Boy Scouts stood at attention in uniform, volunteer fire fighters were on hand and a band played. Captain McLeod was presented with a photograph of his steamer, signed by many of the 100 passengers on board and the crew. During her nine-hour voyage, she called at 13 communities and everywhere the reception was warm yet sad. Captain G. A. West, of Shutty Beach, boarded her carrying three dozen daffodils for the passengers as he and his wife had always done for the past 38 years on their spring trip up the lake. Andrew Scott, aged 89, who had been at her launching, was on board as were many other long-time residents of the area. When she was tied up to the wharf at Procter late in the afternoon, the end to Canadian Pacific sternwheeler service had come.

The *Moyie*'s crew transferred to the tug *Granthall* which was to take over the service on the lake the next week. Fortunately, efforts were already well advanced to preserve the *Moyie* and on May 1, 1957, the CPR announced that she had been sold to the town of Kaslo for one dollar. The Kootenay Lake Historical Society, with a membership of 500, was behind the project and the provincial government promised a grant of $7,500 towards the vessel's preservation. Later, the *Moyie* was towed to Kaslo during high water on the lake and

With the retirement of the *Minto*, only the *Moyie* remained of the once proud fleet of sternwheelers. — ROBERT W. PARKINSON

The *Moyie's Final Years*

The *Moyie*, in company with the *Nasookin* which was by then owned by the provincial government, rests at Procter in 1946. The once busy rail yards are quiet. At left, the *Moyie* is steaming up the lake on a crisp autumn day.

— ROBERT W. PARKINSON/CPCA

The service to Kaslo and Lardeau was the reason for the *Moyie's* survival long after all the other CPR sternwheelers on Kootenay Lake had been retired. In the photos at right she is docked at Kaslo with a transfer barge.

— ROBERT W. PARKINSON

beached on the lakeshore where she became the community museum and a fine monument to the role played by the stern-wheelers in the history of the Kootenays.

Saving the *Moyie* from scrap was only the beginning of the continuing process of preserving the old vessel. When she was retired, the *Moyie* was in generally good condition, but the CPR had not lavished excessive maintenance on a vessel of that age, due for retirement. Moreover, any vessel of pre-dominantly wooden construction requires continuing mainte-nance. For the dedicated volunteers of the community, the painstaking task of keeping the *Moyie* sound began.

Painting, cleaning and repairs were routine, ongoing re-quirements, and at the same time the boat had to be open to the public in order to generate more support for the project, as well as to provide revenue from donations and admissions. The survival of the *Moyie* is a great tribute to the efforts of all those involved and the work will continue as long as she endures. The two greatest threats to her survival are fire and the weather. The former is a constant danger to any structure and to an old wooden one in particular. The latter takes its toll more slowly, causing rot and gradual deterioration. Com-pounding the problems, as the years go by, is the difficulty of obtaining skilled labour. The tools and techniques of working with wooden ships — of recaulking a hull, or applying new canvas to the decks — are not being passed on and the trades associated with the old technologies are dying out.

In a heartening move, Parks Canada announced in 1982 that the *Moyie* was to be taken over as a National Historic Park. This was an important recognition of the significance of the vessel to the history of western Canada. A town the size of Kaslo should not be expected to preserve a vessel like the *Moyie* entirely from its own resources, particularly when the vessel has significance far beyond the local community.

After the *Moyie*'s retirement, the tug *Granthall* continued on the Kootenay Lake routes through 1957, but then she, too, was retired. The barge service was then operated for the CPR by Ivan Horie. Under contract, he took over the tug and barge operations on both Kootenay and Slocan Lakes. For the Kootenay Lake service the small diesel-powered tug *Melinda Jane* was built. In this way, a vestige of the former service continued until December 16, 1977 when the CPR was granted permission by the federal government to discontinue the rail service to Kaslo and Lardeau. Traffic had fallen off dramatically by this time; in 1974, only six loaded cars were barged up the lake to Kaslo and Lardeau while only 121 loads were shipped out. The volume was simply not enough to justify maintaining the expensive transfer slips and related trackage and to pay for the operation of the tug and barges.

After being withdrawn from service, the *Granthall* remained at Nelson until 1964 when she was sold. Various proposals to use her did not come to fruition and she was eventually rebuilt as a fish barge on the Pacific coast.

The mine at Riondel remained an important shipper of ore after the retirement of the *Moyie* in 1957. As there was no barge slip there, the barge was simply tied up to the dock and the lead-zinc concentrates were loaded directly aboard. The chartered tug *Melinda Jane* replaced the *Moyie* and *Granthall*, ending CPR ownership of steamboats on Kootenay Lake.
— CPCA

The *Moyie* had become such a familiar and important part of life in Kaslo that the community raised a successful campaign to preserve the veteran sternwheeler on the lakefront. While she would never again steam into Kaslo Bay, she would remain a lasting historical monument to the sternwheeler era in British Columbia.
—ROBERT W. PARKINSON/ROBERT D. TURNER

By the late 1960's traffic on the tug and barge service on Okanagan Lake had declined significantly over earlier years. Rail traffic generally had dwindled over the CPR's Kettle Valley route and some commodities, particularly fruit and other perishable agricultural produce, had been all but lost to the railway in favour of truck transport. The excellent highway system throughout the southern part of British Columbia and the availability of fast, mechanically refrigerated trucks, left the railways a poor second choice for shippers.

The tug *Okanagan* was the regular vessel on the service at this time and she could comfortably handle the traffic between Kelowna and Penticton and way points. The *Kelowna*, the last wooden-hulled tug owned by the CPR on Okanagan Lake, had been laid up in 1956 and sold the following year. The *Naramata* remained as the relief tug for the *Okanagan*. However, the *Naramata* was not used again after substituting for the *Okanagan* on May 18, 1965. In 1969, she, too, was sold.

The *Okanagan* remained in service on the lake until May 31, 1972 when she made her last run. Captain Sam Podmoroff, a veteran of 31 years service with the CPR, was her skipper and when he brought his tug into the wharf at the end of the run, it marked the closure of the last Canadian Pacific operated service on the inland lakes and rivers of British Columbia. While tugs and barges were still running on Kootenay and Slocan Lakes carrying CPR rail cars, they were, as already noted, operated under contract for Canadian Pacific. The retirement of the *Okanagan* ended the CPR's direct ownership of vessels on the lakes and rivers of southern British Columbia and, at the same time, 80 years of service on Okanagan Lake.

A factor contributing to the demise of the service was the rapidly escalating value of waterfront property in the Okanagan. At both Kelowna and Penticton, the transfer slips and approach tracks occupied some of the finest lakeshore property in British Columbia. Since the service had declined to a point where it was no longer essential and could be replaced, it was logical to put the property to more profitable uses. In Penticton, within a few years, the site of the transfer slip was occupied by a major hotel complex.

The impact of the Lake and River Service on the Okanagan Valley and its people had been immense. Settlement, agricultural development, tourism and industry had all benefited from the regular and reliable transport that the sternwheelers and tugs and barges had brought to the region. As happened elsewhere, the very success of the services in first making settlement and agriculture possible and then, contributing to its prosperity, planted the seeds of ultimate demise. The demand for fast, efficient, low-cost transport and the acceptance of new technologies brought about such dramatic changes in the transportation system of the Okanagan that the lake boats simply became obsolete and unable to cope with the needs of the region.

The Okanagan Service Ends, 1972

The *Naramata* became the last operational steam-powered tug in the Lake and River Service. She was last used in 1965 while the diesel tug *Okanagan* was temporarily out of service. — CPCA

Captain Walter Spiller at the wheel of the
Okanagan on February 28, 1963. After 46 years
with the Lake and River Service, Captain Spiller
was retiring. He had worked on all the major
routes during his career and had obtained his
master's certificate in 1930. — R. MORRISON, IFB

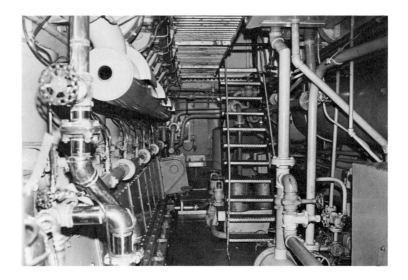

The *Okanagan*, top right, had the distinction of
being the last operational tugboat in the Lake
and River Service. She was a powerful vessel,
capable of handling two loaded transfer barges
with no difficulty. — ERIC SISMEY

The spotless engineroom of the *Okanagan*.
— ERIC SISMEY

Captain Sam Podmoroff became the last master of the *Okanagan* in CPR service. He started with the Lake and River Service in 1941 on Kootenay Lake before transferring to the Okanagan in 1947. The relief captain on the *Okanagan* during the final years of service was Norman Nordstrom who in 1971 had 25 years with the CPR. Captain Podmoroff had 31 years total CPR service.

— ERIC SISMEY

It is early evening of an overcast spring day in 1970 as a CP Rail diesel switches the car barges at Penticton. The crew of the *Okanagan* waits patiently to shift the second barge into position.

— ROBERT D. TURNER

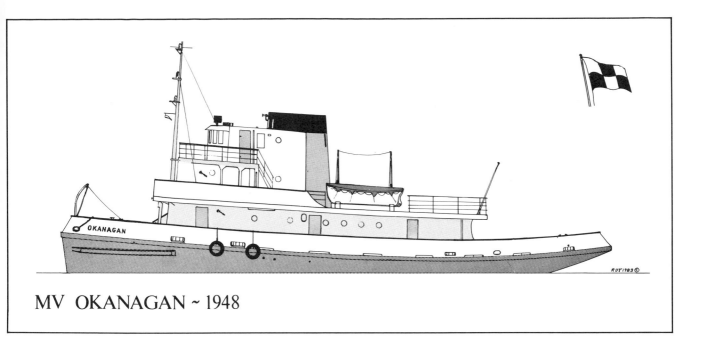

MV OKANAGAN ~ 1948

With work at Penticton completed, the *Okanagan* backs away from the transfer slip for the return trip to Kelowna in 1961.
— PHILIP C. JOHNSON

The floating bridge across Okanagan Lake at Kelowna was built with a large lift span to permit navigation. In this photograph, the span is raised for the passage of the *Okanagan* and her two barges. — ERIC SISMEY

237

Late in 1972, the *Okanagan* and the one remaining barge, *No. 8*, were sold to Fintry Estates. The ferry slips and related facilities were eventually dismantled and the service became a memory. At Okanagan Landing, the site of the shipyards became a park and some of the buildings were saved. After her sale by the CPR, the tug *Naramata* remained at Okanagan Landing and was eventually acquired by the local Sea Cadets. Like the *Moyie* and *Sicamous*, her preservation is certainly justified but it will not be an easy or inexpensive task.

Canadian National Railways continued to operate its tug and barge service on Okanagan Lake after the CPR retired the *Okanagan*, hoping that the remaining traffic might sustain the one service even if it had been insufficient to justify two. However, after one more year, Canadian National also found it could not justify running the tugs any longer and ended its Kelowna-based operation. The tugs *Pentowna* and *Canadian National No. 6* and the remaining barges were sold. The *No. 6* was acquired by Fintry Estates which had also purchased the *Okanagan*. The *Pentowna* found a home on the waterfront at Peachland.

CNR barge services on Okanagan Lake continued to decline and on February 15, 1973 *Canadian National No. 6* handled the last barge load of rail cars and operations ceased.
— ERIC SISMEY

The barge service on Slocan Lake outlived all other remnants of the once extensive CPR British Columbia Lake and River Service. Its longevity was a result of its being a link in the rail line to Nakusp. Abandoning the transfer barge service on Slocan Lake would have meant the cessation of all rail service to Rosebery and, more significantly, Nakusp.

Service on Slocan Lake changed very little during the post-World War II years. Depending on traffic requirements, a train crew departed from Nelson in the morning with whatever traffic had accumulated for the Nakusp branch (more properly called the CPR's Kaslo Subdivision). On arrival at Slocan City, the entire train including the locomotive was switched onto the barges. The *Rosebery* then ferried the barges to Rosebery where the train was unloaded and run over the 26.9 mile (43.3 km) distance to Nakusp. The train crew usually spent the night at Nakusp and then returned to Rosebery early the next morning. From there the operation was just a reversal of the previous day's. Mixed train service was offered on the branch until 1959.

The *Rosebery* remained active on Slocan Lake until 1956 when she was withdrawn from service. She was sold, and scrapped soon after, in 1958. It was at this time that Ivan Horie took over the tug and barge service on a charter basis. The tug *Iris G.* was built for the service and assembled at Slocan City and has continued to handle the barges into the 1980's. Because of the low traffic volumes on both Kootenay and Slocan Lakes, it was possible for one crew to operate each tug in turn as required. In the 1970's, the Slocan Lake barge service normally operated once or twice a week. In 1978, Canadian Pacific sought permission to abandon the line to

Barge Service Epilogue: Slocan Lake

The barge service was not always routine. Accidents did occur through weather, groundings, or other mishaps. For example, a carload of ore was lost overboard at Slocan City in 1903 and a brakeman was killed. In 1916 a car was lost at Silverton. A more dramatic incident involved the loss of most of the train on the Slocan Lake barge on December 31, 1946. While some of the freight cars remained on the barge which stayed partly afloat, the locomotive (No. 3512), a snowplow and some steel rolling stock sank to the bottom of the lake. Some years later, in February 1970, a barge, loaded with over six carloads of concentrates valued at $60,000, sank in Kootenay Lake at Riondel. Fortunately, the barge and concentrates were recovered.

The *Rosebery*, shown at Slocan City in June 1947, maintained the passenger, freight and barge service on Slocan Lake until 1956 when she was retired. — ROBERT W. PARKINSON

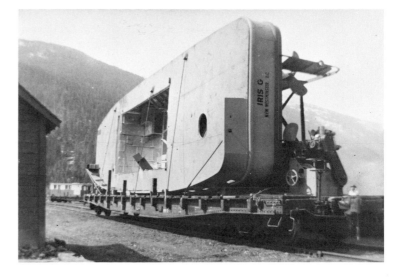

The replacement for the *Rosebery* was the diesel tug *Iris G*, which was moved by rail from New Westminster for final assembly at Slocan City. She was owned by Ivan Horie and operated under contract to the CPR. — BILL CURRAN

The Last Survivor

The Slocan Lake barge service, operating on a contract basis by Ivan Horie's Interior Lake Services, became the last of the old Lake and River Service routes. A once, or occasionally, twice a week service continued to maintain rail service to Nakusp. At lower left, the *Iris G* pulls her single steel barge away from the transfer slip at Rosebery for the run down Slocan Lake to Slocan City in August 1973. — ROBERT D. TURNER

Slocan Lake
Barge Service

The train crew, top right, adjusts the apron of the transfer slip at Rosebery.
— ROBERT D. TURNER

The diesel, middle right and below left, carried on the barge, eases the caboose off the transfer slip and onto the approach tracks. The pole, evident beside the diesel, was used for pushing the slip farther out into the lake as the water level fell. — ROBERT D. TURNER

Lower right, the *Iris G* and the transfer slip at Slocan City. — ROBERT D. TURNER

Nakusp, as well as the barge service, but was unsuccessful. So the Slocan Lake operation survives, a last, somewhat curious, reminder of steamboating days in the Slocan Valley.

The Sternwheelers in Retrospect

The entire history of the Canadian Pacific's sternwheelers and steam tugs in British Columbia spanned just one lifetime. Even adding the early days of the Columbia and Kootenay Steam Navigation Company the time is really quite short. But it was a period of vast and sweeping changes. These changes affected virtually every aspect of life in British Columbia and greatly altered the landscape itself. In 1889, when George Dawson journeyed up the Columbia on the primitive sternwheeler *Dispatch*, the Kootenays were still a largely-unexplored wilderness. Just ten years later, cities had grown and a reliable and frequent transportation system was in place. During this same period, the Okanagan Valley saw an equally significant transformation, as the agricultural potential of this warm, fertile region began to be realized.

The steamboats themselves evolved and advanced from primitive, unreliable examples of frontier carpentry to elegant, sophisticated vessels of the finest standards. They became symbols of local pride. The sternwheelers were often the only means of communication for people living in the small, isolated communities in the Okanagan and West Kootenays. Mail, supplies, visitors and news of the world all came in by steamer. For settlers seeking a new, brighter future, travelling on the sternwheelers was often the final stage in a long journey to their new homes. The arrival of the steamboats on their routes from the outside world always brought people down to the docks. Like the small town railway station, the steamer landings and the vessels provided a community focus.

On holidays and special occasions, or sometimes just for the fun of it, the steamers could be counted on for excursions, moonlight cruises or sometimes races. What could have been more exciting for a youth growing up at Nelson in 1896 than to watch the *Kokanee* and the *International*, with smoke and steam pouring from their stacks, race down the West Arm of Kootenay Lake?

The sternwheelers, tugs and barges were no less important to the larger communities than they were to the small towns. They provided the basic, reliable transportation system that was essential for the prosperity of any commercial or industrial activity. The mines and mills of the Kootenays could not have developed without a consistent, reasonably priced system of delivering their products to market.

In nearly every waterside location in the Okanagan and Kootenays, the steamboats preceded the railways. The mountains formed such formidable barriers to railroad construction that in some cases rail connections were never built and the steamers remained in service until roads made them unnecessary. Elsewhere, as on Kootenay Lake, they bridged major

By the 1950's, the sternwheelers were anachronisms surviving in a world their builders could not have foreseen. A younger generation would grow up, perhaps remembering them, but no longer able to experience them. But that, of course, is the way with all things that pass into history. — JOHN E. GREGSON

This story of the sternwheelers has spanned less than 70 years from the construction of boats like the *Dispatch* and the *Aberdeen* to the final runs of the *Minto* and *Moyie*. The steam tugs and their successors, the newer diesel craft, survived longer. While it is easier and perhaps more romantic to recall the hectic days of the pioneer era with the steamboat races and frenzy of mining development, the essence of the story lies in the essential, day-to-day service the crews and their boats provided to a vast and thinly populated land. This, and their undeniable beauty, are what make the steamboats truly memorable. — ED VIPOND / KELOWNA MUSEUM

gaps in the railways, providing an efficient alternative to railroad construction for many years. The railway has often been thought of as one of the great forces in opening British Columbia to settlement and development, and indeed it was, but the sternwheelers and tugs played a role whose importance should not be underestimated.

The short-lived Stikine service was an anomaly in an otherwise careful and considered development of a steamboat service. But the Stikine route had been predicated on what appeared to be solid promises of later connecting rail development that simply did not come about. A fine fleet of vessels was built only to be sold off, many of them wasted. The Stikine produced some of the most exciting and saddest moments in the history of the Lake and River Service. It also provided, by default, two vessels — the *Moyie* and the *Minto* — whose careers spanned nearly the entire history of the CPR's sternwheelers.

Another aspect of the steamboats — both the sternwheelers and the tugs — that cannot be overlooked is their aesthetic quality. It would have taken a hard heart, or at least a very busy mind, not to have paused to watch the *Moyie* steam into Kaslo Bay or listen to the whistle of the *Sicamous* echoing from the Okanagan hills. The boats were certainly picturesque as the prints of many fine photographers attest. They also represented an unobtrusive technology — quiet and rhythmic. They left no lasting scars on the landscape, only the lasting memories of the people who knew them and the ripples of their wakes that were soon gone with their passing.

NOTES ON SOURCES
OF REFERENCE

ONLY TWO BOOKS have been written on the history of sternwheelers in British Columbia although the steamers have been mentioned and described in many regional and local histories. Art Down's *Paddlewheels on the Frontier* (2 Volumes, 1967 and 1971), provides an excellent, well illustrated overview of sternwheelers in British Columbia and the Yukon. Of a more regional scope, E. L. Affleck's detailed account *Sternwheelers, Sandbars and Switchbacks* (1973), focuses on steamers and railway development in southeastern British Columbia and is a rich source of information on the Columbia and Kootenay Steam Navigation Company and the CPR. Both of these works were consulted throughout the preparation of this book. Norman Hacking wrote an excellent series of articles relating primarily to the Fraser River steamers in the *British Columbia Historical Quarterly*. Additionally, his 1947 paper, "British Columbia Steamboat Days, 1870-1883," was informative in providing details of J. A. Mara's early steamers. *The Princess Story* by Norman Hacking and W. Kaye Lamb (1974) also contains considerable material on early sternwheelers, particularly those of the Canadian Pacific Navigation Company on the lower Fraser River. Captain James Fitzsimmons (1937) wrote a brief but very useful account of steamers on the Columbia which is particularly relevant to this study of the CPR's Lake and River Service.

Beyond these sources, there are *Lewis & Dryden's Marine History of the Pacific Northwest* (Wright, 1965) and *The H. W. McCurdy Marine History of the Pacific Northwest* (Newell, 1966), which are basic sources for the entire region. Also invaluable, is the fleet list and discussion in George Musk's *Canadian Pacific, The Story of the Famous Shipping Line* (1981), which provides excellent material on the Lake and River Service. Kaye Lamb's *History of the Canadian Pacific Railway* (1977) and John Fahey's *Inland Empire, D. C. Corbin and Spokane* (1965) were both basic references to railway development in the Kootenays. Fahey's book is particularly useful in understanding the extension of American lines from Spokane into the Kootenays.

Several unpublished sources proved valuable in compiling the history of the Lake and River Service. The detailed report on operations in 1918-1919 by J. S. Byron provides an insightful review of the service in the post-World War I era and is unique. A summary financial review of the vessels, by the CPR, dated December 31, 1953 was helpful in determining details of vessel history and construction.

A basic source for compiling the fleet lists and technical details of the vessels was the annual reports of the Steamship Inspection Branch of the federal Department of Marine and Fisheries published each year in the *Sessional Papers*. Similarly, the lists of shipping published in the federal *Sessional Papers* gives basic dimensions and ownership of all vessels in Canada. Particularly valuable were the original notebooks of the steamboat inspectors for the period 1880-1918 now held at the B.C. Provincial Archives. These and surviving registry documents were treated as the primary sources of statistics on the vessels. Supplementing these sources was *Lloyd's Register of Shipping*, although many of the steamers are not listed. Additionally, some CPR records have survived, including a 1915 alphabetical list of vessels with technical information on the sternwheelers and tugs, and several records of floating equipment from the 1940's. The notebooks and service records of the late John Williams, retired Lake and River Service chief engineer, also provided much useful technical detail. The White Pass and Yukon Route Papers (at the Yukon Archives), while dealing with Yukon River vessels, included information on some of the former CPR Stikine service boats. Articles by Elsie Turnbull (1966) and W. Gibson Kennedy (1943 and 1949) also provided overviews of the CPR steamer operations.

Retired Lake and River Service employees and residents of the districts served by the steamers provided much useful information and personal recollections. Interviews helped fill in many details for the period after about 1910. Additionally, in the Imbert Orchard Collection at the Provincial Archives of British Columbia are recorded interviews with Captain Otto Estabrooks (Accession No. 1076) and Captain J. B. Weeks (Accession No. 1075).

Fundamental to this study were the files of newspapers from the communities in the Kootenay, Okanagan and Stikine districts. Most of the newspapers noted below are available on microfilm at the Provincial Archives. The names and sometimes even the town where the papers were published, often were changed but the following is a general guide, based on Archives holdings: From the Kootenays, the *Nelson Daily Miner* (originally, *The Miner*), and Nelson's *The Daily News*, Kaslo's *The Kootenaian* and *The Kaslo Claim* and New Denver's *The Ledge* were particularly informative. Revelstoke papers, including *The Kootenay Star* (from June 1890 to March 1894), *The Kootenay Mail* and *The Revelstoke Mail* (from April 1894-1905), were essential. From the Okanagan, *The Vernon News* and Kelowna's *The Orchard City Record* were of particular value. Other newspapers consulted included *The Trail Creek News*, Sandon's *The Paystreak*, the *Silverton Silvertonian*, the *Slocan City News*, *The Slocan Drill*, *The Rossland Miner*, and *The Penticton Herald*.

I was also fortunate in being able to read almost complete files of *The Stikeen River Journal*, published at Wrangell in 1898 and 1899, and the unfortunately incomplete, but still valuable, files of the *Glenora News* for 1898. These provided excellent material on the Stikine River service.

Victoria's *The Daily Colonist* and Vancouver's *The Daily Province* were excellent sources since their reports often covered events in other parts of British Columbia and neighbouring areas. These papers and Vancouver's *Daily News-Advertiser* and *Daily World* provided coverage of the construction of the Stikine River steamers and gave lengthy accounts of the Klondike Gold Rush. Normally, newspaper references have been included in the text.

Two particularly useful periodicals were *The British Columbia Mining Record* and *Canadian Railway and Marine World*. The former journal provided detailed accounts of mining development throughout British Columbia from the late 1890's to the early 1900's and also included descriptions of transportation improvements. The latter journal, more technical in nature, reported regularly on railway and shipping developments in Canada after 1905. *Poor's Manual of Railroads* was an important source of information on railway development in British Columbia.

For Chapter I, dealing with the Columbia and Kootenay Steam Navigation Company, in addition to the standard references of Affleck (1973), Downs (1971) and Musk (1981), Captain Fitzsimmons' article (1937) was a valuable starting point. News-

paper accounts from Revelstoke were helpful in detailing the operations of the *Lytton* and outlining the formative period of the C&KSN. Similarly the early issues of *The Miner*, from Nelson, had many references to the early steamboat operations. The steamers were so critical to life and commerce in these frontier areas that they received great attention in the press. Details of the career of Captain Troup came from Wilson and Stewart's (1969) publication on steamers on the Columbia, clippings and correspondence provided by Earl Marsh, formerly of the B.C. Coast Steamship Service, and records from the Oregon Historical Society. Another source was a report of a speech given by Troup in Nelson in *The Daily Miner*, April 16, 1901. *The Oregonian* of January 2, 1897 published an account, focusing on the career of Captain Troup, of the purchase of the C&KSN by the CPR.

Chapter II, which carries the story through the first year of Canadian Pacific control of the steamboats and the new building program, also was based heavily on the early papers including those published in the Slocan Valley and at Kaslo. Great Northern (International Navigation and Trading Company) material came from the files of the Great Northern Railway at the Minnesota Historical Society as well as newspaper accounts. Canadian Pacific *Annual Reports* were consulted for this entire period and provided official Company viewpoints and details of transactions relating to the railway developments and the purchase of the C&KSN.

The story of the Stikine River service, described in Chapter III, was an obscure one since the service was so short-lived. *The Stikeen River Journal* published at Wrangell provided much valuable information, as did the *Glenora News*. Vancouver's *Daily Province*, *Daily World* and *Daily News-Advertiser* and Victoria's *Daily Colonist* were all full of news of the Klondike Gold Rush. Fortunately, these papers provided good coverage of the construction of the first of the Canadian Pacific steamers built at False Creek and also provided details of the *Tartar* and *Athenian*. *The Princess Story* (1974) by Hacking and Lamb also discusses the Stikine service. Excellent general background on the Klondike Gold Rush is provided by Berton in *Klondike* (1958) and by Zaslow in his detailed treatment, *The Opening of the Canadian North* (1967). Further information on the Stikine railway project is provided in the Federal *Sessional Papers* for 1898 and 1899. Jennings' 1898 report on routes to the Yukon is particularly interesting, as is Louis Coste's report of 1899. The proposed railway from the Stikine River to Teslin Lake for the all-Canadian route to the Klondike was debated frequently in 1898 in the House of Commons and received major attention by the legislators on February 8 and March 16, 1898. Details of the settlement with Mackenzie and Mann are outlined in the *Debates* of May 13, 1902. The *British Columbia Mining Record* carried frequent stories on the Yukon and one notable article, in 1898, entitled, "the Stikine on Ice, by One Who Has Been and Done It." The CPR guidebook *Klondike and Yukon Gold Fields via Canadian Pacific Railway* (1898) revealed the type of information made available to the public at the time of the Klondike Gold Rush. References to the White Pass and Yukon's construction and operations were Lavallée (1972) and Clifford (1981). Finally, Loken's article on Stikine River sternwheelers (1979) included a listing of all steamers known to have operated on the Stikine. Other articles in this issue of the *Alaska Geographic* helped place the Stikine service in better context.

Chapters IV and V which encompass the peak years of the Lake and River Service were based extensively on the CPR documents and publications noted in the bibliography and CPR public and employee timetables from both public and private collections. Newspaper accounts continued to be important particularly for details of the vessels. *Canadian Railway and Marine World* described in some detail the *Kuskanook* in July 1906 and the *Bonnington* in November 1910. The material on the operations of the Kootenay Railway and Navigation Company was based on the KR&N papers held by the Minnesota Historical Society and was supported by newspaper accounts from both Nelson and Kaslo. Interviews with Bill Curran, whose father was an engineer on the steamers, and with Dr. R. S. Goodwin who, as a young man, worked as assistant superintendent at Kaslo, were also helpful. Barrie Sanford's book *McCulloch's Wonder* (1977) was an excellent source on the Kettle Valley Railway route from the Kootenays through to the coast.

The war years and the 1920's, detailed in Chapter V, were aided particularly by Byron's (1919) extensive report on the service and its floating equipment. Interviews with Lake and River Service personnel were also helpful in this section. All those noted in the acknowledgements contributed insights and recollections to this section. Chapter VI, which records the decline of the service, was based on these sources and the general references noted as well as CPR timetables and notices. The last runs of the *Minto* and *Moyie*

were reported in the newspapers of all the communities in the areas served, as well as being noted by Victoria and Vancouver newspapers. Articles by Sismey (1965 and 1972), Neuberger (1949) and Parkinson (1948) were used, as were the notes and letters of Robert W. Parkinson, on his trips to the Kootenays where he rode and photographed the *Moyie, Minto* and *Nasookin.*

Approximate metric equivalents of most measurements have been included for clarity. Gross and net tonnage figures, which are measures of volume, have not been converted since metric equivalents have not been adopted for use in Canada. Gross tonnage is determined by computing the volume, in square feet, of a ship's enclosed spaces with certain exceptions and then dividing by 100 to arrive at the tonnage. Net tonnage is the vessel's gross tonnage minus deductions for space occupied by the crews' quarters, machinery, bunkers, galley and toilets, below decks anchors, etc. Tonnage for vessels are useful for comparative purposes but should not be confused with weights.

BIBLIOGRAPHY

1. General References

Affleck, E. L. 1973. *Sternwheelers, Sandbars and Switchbacks* (Revised Edition). The Alexander Nicolls Press, Vancouver, B.C.

Affleck, E. L. 1973. *The Kootenays in Retrospect* (Four Volumes). The Alexander Nicolls Press, Vancouver, B.C.

Balf, Mary. 1973. *Ship Ahoy! Paddlewheelers of Thompson Waterway.* Kamloops Museum, Kamloops, B.C.

Berton, Pierre. 1958. *Klondike.* McClelland & Stewart Limited, Toronto, Ont.

Burrows, Roger G. 1981. *Railway Mileposts: British Columbia. Volume 1: The CPR Mainline Route: From the Rockies to the Pacific.* Railway Milepost Books, North Vancouver, B.C.

Canada. Department of Marine and Fisheries. 1880-1920. *Annual Reports*, Steamboat Inspection Branch (Also the *List of Shipping*, published regularly by this and later departments). Sessional Papers, Ottawa, Ontario.

Canadian Pacific Railway. 1890-1972. *Annual Reports.* CPR, Montreal, P.Q.

Canadian Pacific Railway. 1898. *Klondike and Yukon Gold Fields via Canadian Pacific Railway* (5th and 6th editions). CPR, Montreal, P.Q.

Canadian Pacific Railway, General Publicity Department (Editors). 1937. *Canadian Pacific Facts and Figures.* Canadian Pacific Foundation Library. CPR, Montreal, P.Q.

Canadian Pacific Railway, Department of Public Relations (Editors). 1946. *Canadian Pacific Facts and Figures* (Revised Edition). Canadian Pacific Foundation Library. CPR, Montreal, P.Q.

Carey, Roland. 1983. "Four Steamboats Built for Captain Troup," *Marine Digest.* June 11, 1983.

Carter, Norman. 1975. "When Boys Were Boys . . . and Worked for the C.P.R.!" *Western Living*, September 1975: pp. 6, 8 and 27.

Chapman, Peter. 1981. *Where the Lardeau River Flows.* (Sound Heritage Series No. 32), Provincial Archives of British Columbia, Victoria, B.C.

Clapp, Frank A. 1981. *Ministry of Transportation and Highways Inland and Coastal Ferries.* Ministry of Transportation and Highways, Victoria, B.C.

Clifford, Howard. 1981. *Rails North, The Railroads of Alaska and the Yukon.* Superior Publishing Company, Seattle, Wash.

Coste, Louis. 1899. "Coste Report on Teslin Lake Route," *Sessional Papers.* 62 Victoria, No. 66A. Queen's Printer, Ottawa, Ont.

Downs, Art. 1967. *Paddlewheels on the Frontier.* Volume 1. B.C. Outdoors Magazine, Cloverdale, B.C.

Downs, Art. 1971. *Paddlewheels on the Frontier.* Volume 2. B.C. Outdoors Magazine, Cloverdale, B.C.

Estabrooks, Captain Otto L. 1968. *Why a Century of Sternwheel Boats in British Columbia.* The Author, Penticton, B.C.

Estabrooks, Captain Otto L. 1968. "Some Reasons for Stern Wheel Boats on Okanagan Lake." *32nd Report of the Okanagan Historical Society*: pp. 27-31.

Fahey, John. 1965. *Inland Empire. D. C. Corbin and Spokane.* University of Washington Press, Seattle, Wash.

Fitzsimmons, James. 1937. "Columbia River Chronicles," *British Columbia Historical Quarterly*, Vol. 1(2): pp. 87-100.

Fowler, S. S. 1939. "Early Smelters in British Columbia," *British Columbia Historical Quarterly*, Vol. 3 (3): pp. 183-201.

Hacking, Norman R. 1947. "British Columbia Steamboat Days, 1870-1883," *British Columbia Historical Quarterly*, Vol. 11(2): pp. 69-112.

Hacking, Norman R. and W. K. Lamb. 1974. *The Princess Story, A Century of West Coast Shipping.* Mitchell Press Ltd., Vancouver, B.C.

Hilton, G. W., R. Plumer, and J. Jobe. 1976. *The Illustrated History of Paddle Steamers.* The Two Continents Publishing Group Ltd., New York, N.Y. (Edita Lausanne).

Jennings, W. T. 1898. *Routes to the Yukon.* (Printed by Order of Parliament), Queen's Printer, Ottawa, Ont. (also published in *Sessional Papers*. 61 Victoria, No. 30, 1898).

Johnson, K. 1951. *Pioneer Days of Nakusp and The Arrow Lakes.* The Author, Nakusp, B.C.

Kennedy, W. Gibson. 1943. "Shallow Draft, The Story of Seventy-Seven Years of Steamboating," *Cominco.* Vol. 4(1): pp. 1-7, 24-28.

Kennedy, W. Gibson. 1949. "Veteran Sternwheelers Are Links With Romantic Past . . . ", *Spanner.* June 1949: pp. 8-10, July-August 1949: pp. 8-10, 34.

Kennedy, W. G. 1983. *Canadian Pacific's Rossland Subdivision.* British Railway Modellers of North America, Calgary, Alta.

Lamb, W. Kaye. 1977. *History of the Canadian Pacific Railway*. Collier Macmillan Canada, Ltd., Toronto, Ont.

Lavallée, Omer. 1972. *Narrow Gauge Railways of Canada*. Railfare, Montreal, P.Q.

Loken, Marty. 1979. "107 Years of Stikine Riverboating." *Alaska Geographic*, Vol. 6(4): pp. 52-65.

Martin, Albro. 1976. *James J. Hill and the Opening of the Northwest*. Oxford University Press, New York, N.Y.

Musk, George. 1968. *Canadian Pacific Afloat 1883-1958. A Short History*. Canadian Pacific Railway, London, U.K.

Musk, George. 1981. *Canadian Pacific. The Story of the Famous Shipping Line*. Holt Rinehart and Winston of Canada Ltd., Toronto, Ont.

Neuberger, Richard L. 1949. "There's No Boat Like the Minto." *The Saturday Evening Post*, April 30, 1949: pp. 36-37, 105-06, 108.

Newell, Gordon. 1966. *The H. W. McCurdy Marine History of the Pacific Northwest*. Superior Publishing Company, Seattle, Wash.

Newell, Gordon and Joe Williamson. 1958. *Pacific Steamboats*. Superior Publishing Company, Seattle, Wash.

Newell, Gordon and Joe Williamson. 1959. *Pacific Coastal Liners*. Superior Publishing Company, Seattle, Wash.

Ormsby, Margaret. 1958. *British Columbia; a History*. Macmillan Company of Vancouver Ltd., Vancouver, B.C.

Parkinson, Robert W. 1947. "Steamboatin' in the Kootenays." *Steamboat Bill of Facts*, August 1947: pp. 30-31, and March 1948: pp. 10-11.

Poor, Henry V. 1890-1924. *Poor's Manual of Railroads*. (Published annually), M. V. Poor Co., New York, New York.

Sanford, Barrie. 1977. *McCulloch's Wonder. The Story of the Kettle Valley Railway*. Whitecap Books Ltd., West Vancouver, B.C.

Sanford, Barrie. 1981. *The Pictorial History of Railroading in British Columbia*. Whitecap Books Ltd., West Vancouver, B.C.

Sismey, Eric D. 1962. "Okanagan Queen, Old Sicamous is Resting." *The Daily Colonist, Islander*, July 29, 1962.

Sismey, Eric D. 1965. "Thomas Dolman Shorts." *30th Report of the Okanagan Historical Society*: pp. 145-51.

Sismey, Eric D. 1972. "MV. Okanagan, Last of an Era." *The Daily Colonist, Islander*, August 27, 1972: pp. 10 and 13.

Smith, R. Munro. 1924. *The Design and Construction of Small Craft*. The Technical Section, Association of Engineering and Shipbuilding Draughtsmen, London, U.K.

Stevens, G. R. 1973. *History of the Canadian National Railways*. Collier Macmillan Canada Ltd., Toronto, Ont.

Thompson, Wilbur B. 1978. "The Canadian Pacific Railway Comes to Port Blakely." *Sea Chest*, Vol. 12 (1): pp. 19-20.

Troup, R. W. 1978. *The Storybook Life of Capt. James W. Troup*. The Author, Portland, Ore.

Turnbull, Elsie G. 1964. *Topping's Trail. The First Years of a Now Famous Smelter City*. Mitchell Press Limited, Vancouver, B.C.

Turnbull, Elsie G. 1966. "Steamboating." *Cominco Magazine*, Vol. 27(3): pp. 1-4; (4): pp. 6-8; (5): pp. 6-8; (6): pp. 9-11.

Turner, Robert D. 1977. *The Pacific Princesses. An Illustrated History of the Canadian Pacific Railway's Princess Fleet on the Northwest Coast*. Sono Niss Press, Victoria, B.C.

Turner, Robert D. 1981. *The Pacific Empresses. An Illustrated History of the Canadian Pacific Railway's Empress Liners on the Pacific Ocean*. Sono Nis Press, Victoria, B.C.

Wilson, Alfred W. G. 1913. *The Copper Smelting Industries of Canada*. Mines Branch (No. 209). Canada Department of Mines. Government Printing Bureau, Ottawa, Ont.

Wilson, Fred W. and Earle K. Stewart. 1969. *Steamboat Days on the River*. Oregon Historical Society, Portland, Ore.

Wright, E. W. (Editor). 1967. *Lewis and Dryden's Marine History of the Pacific Northwest*. Superior Publishing Company, Seattle, Wash. (Originally published by Lewis and Dryden Printing Co., 1895).

Zaslow, Morris. 1967. *The Opening of the Canadian North 1870-1914*. McClelland & Stewart Limited, Toronto, Ont.

2. *Unpublished Sources and Limited Circulation CPR Publications*

Byron, J. S. 1919. *Report on the B.C. Lake & River Service, 1918-1919*. 44 page Ms., PABC, Victoria, B.C.

British Columbia Department of Public Works. Papers relating to the operations of the steamship *Nasookin*. PABC, Victoria, B.C.

Canada. Board of Steamboat Inspection. 1872-1918. *Records of the Office of Steamboat Inspector*. PABC, Victoria, B.C.

Canada. Department of Transport. 1867-1962. *Port of Victoria, Steamship Registry Papers*. PABC, Victoria, B.C.

Canadian Pacific Railway. 1915. *Alphabetical List of Steamers in the B.C. Lake and River Service*. Nelson, B.C., June 1, 1915.

Canadian Pacific Railway. 1916. *Rules and Regulations for the Government of Employees of the B.C. Lake and River Steamers*. CPR, Montreal, P.Q.

Canadian Pacific Railway. 1920. *British Columbia Lake and River Service Passenger Tariff 11*. CPR, Montreal, P.Q. Issued September 9, 1920.

Canadian Pacific Railway. 1953. *Property Investment in B.C. Lake and River Service at December 31, 1953*. 92 page Ms., PABC, Victoria, B.C.

Dawson, G. M. 1889. *Private Diary*, Department of Rare Books and Special Collections, McGill University Libraries, Montreal, P.Q.

Duchesnay, E. J. 1897. *Diary* (Survey expedition to the Stikine River-Teslin Lake region). PABC, Victoria, B.C.

Great Northern Railway. (Kootenay Railway and Navigation Company, Kaslo and Slocan Railway and Kaslo and Lardo-Duncan Railway) *Papers and Correspondence*. Minnesota Historical Society, St. Paul.

Hume, John F. 1973. *Some Highlights in the Life of J. Fred Hume, A Pioneer of Revelstoke and Nelson*. Ms., PABC, Victoria, B.C.

Sismey, Eric D. 1976. *Estabrooks — Father and Son*. 13 page Ms.

Weeks, Captain J. B. ca.1942. *The History of Steamboats on Okanagan Lake as Written by J. B. Weeks, 1886-1942*. 28 page Ms., PABC, Victoria, B.C. and Kelowna Centennial Museum, Kelowna, B.C.

White Pass and Yukon Route. *Papers* (including sternwheeler notebooks by Jones and Gaudin), Yukon, Archives, Whitehorse, Yukon.

Williams, John. 1918-1931. Personal papers, notebooks, and service record re: B.C. Lake and River Service.

The crew of the *Sicamous* pose in 1928 for the photographer. Also on board is John Stobo, master builder for the Lake and River Service, visiting from the headquarters at Nelson. It was on the occasion of the retirement of Le Dye, chief cook, who was returning to China after many years of service with the CPR.

Front Row, left to right: Fred Hodges, deckhand; Douglas Elliott, deckhand; George Churchill, deckhand; Bill Ramsay, deckhand; Captain Joseph Weeks; Jack McRae, chief engineer; Charles Pittingrel, coal passer; Ira Brinson, fireman; Douglas Tucker, fireman; Cecil Hiltz, fireman; W. Edward Walker, coal passer.

Second Row, left to right: John Thomson, quartermaster; Jack Vass, quartermaster; Henry Smith, deckhand; Bill White, stevedore; Otto Estabrooks, first mate; John A. Williams, second engineer; Jack Johnson, mail clerk; Ernest Hodges, mail clerk; George Gordon, express clerk; Charles Watson, night watchman.

On the stairs, left to right: Alfred Watson, purser; Roy McCall, second mate.

Above on deck, left to right: four Chinese cooks whose names have not been recorded; Le Dye, chief cook; Bill Ferguson, chief steward; John Stobo, master shipbuilder from Nelson; Fred Bourne, freight clerk; Bill McDonald, waiter; Fred Ford, waiter; John Thomas, waiter; and an unidentified waiter.
— PABC, 91912 with names supplied by the late John Williams, who was second engineer.

APPENDIX I

VESSELS OF THE COLUMBIA AND KOOTENAY STEAM NAVIGATION COMPANY AND THE CPR'S BRITISH COLUMBIA LAKE AND RIVER SERVICE*

* For the routes served by each steamer, see Appendix II.

The CPR purchased the Columbia and Kootenay Steam Navigation Company in 1897, acquiring the following vessels: *Lytton, Nelson, Illecillewaet, Nakusp, Kokanee, Trail* and *Columbia* (1896).

** Registered dimensions (in feet). See note on sources at end of this Appendix.

*** Key to Abbreviations: Cy., cylinder(s); Tr. Exp., Triple Expansion; C., Compound; nhp, Nominal Horsepower; bhp, Brake Horsepower; Sc., screw(s); Pass., Passenger carrying vessel; All measurements in inches.

NAME	YEAR BUILT (launching date and/or maiden voyage [mv] date where known)	BUILDER	LENGTH/ BREADTH/ DEPTH**	TONS: GROSS NET	VESSEL TYPE; ENGINES: BORE/STROKE (Builder or Origin)***	NOTES
1. Columbia and Kootenay Steam Navigation Company						
Dispatch (sometimes *Despatch*)	1888	Columbia Transportation Co., Revelstoke	54.0 10.8 x 2 4.5	37.1 23.4	Wooden, catamaran hull Sternwheeler 2 — 8x24 2.1 nhp	1
Lytton	1890 mv. July 1	A. Watson, Revelstoke	131.0 25.5 4.8	451.7 284.6	Wooden hull Sternwheeler 2 — 16x62 10 nhp	2
Kootenai	Aug. 25, 1885	Henderson & McCartney, Little Dalles	140 25	557.7 351.3	Wooden hull Sternwheeler 2 — 14x72 13 nhp	3
Columbia	1891 mv. Aug.	A. Watson, Little Dalles	152.5 28.0 6.3	534	Wooden hull Sternwheeler 2 — 18x72 Harlan & Hollingsworth, Willmington, Delaware (1877)	4
Nelson	June 11, 1891 mv. Aug.	D. Stephenson, C&KSN, Nelson	131.6 26.4 6.0	496.0 312.5	Wooden hull Sternwheeler 2 — 14x54 13.0 nhp ex *Skuzzy* (II)	5
Illecillewaet	Oct. 30, 1892	C&KSN, Revelstoke	78.0 15.0 4.0	97.9 61.7	Wooden hull Sternwheeler 2 — 8x24 4.3 nhp ex *Dispatch*	6

NAME	YEAR BUILT (launching date and/or maiden voyage [mv] date where known)	BUILDER	LENGTH/ BREADTH/ DEPTH**	TONS: GROSS NET	VESSEL TYPE; ENGINES: BORE/STROKE (Builder or Origin)***	NOTES
Spokane	1891	G. R. Gray, Bonners Ferry	125.8 24.8 5.3	399.8 251.7	Wooden hull Sternwheeler 10.6 nhp	7
Nakusp	July 1, 1895	T. Bulger, C&KSN, Nakusp	171.0 33.5 6.3	1083.2 831.8	Wooden hull Sternwheeler 2— 20x72 26.6 nhp Iowa Iron Works	8
Kokanee	Apr. 7, 1896	T. Bulger, C&KSN, Nelson	142.5 24.8 5.7	347.5 164.8	Wooden hull Sternwheeler 2 — 17x72 19.26 nhp	9
Trail	May 9, 1896	T. Bulger, C&KSN, Nakusp	165.0 31.0 4.9	662.8 417.6	Wooden hull Sternwheeler 2 — 14x60 13.0 nhp ex *Kootenai*	10
Columbia	1896 rebuilt 1912	T. Bulger, C&KSN, Nakusp	77.0 14.5 6.4	49.8 33.9	Wooden hull Sc. Tug C.2Cy., 9&18x12 19.5 nhp, 1 Sc. John Daly, Toronto	11

2. *Canadian Pacific Railway, British Columbia Lake and River Service*

NAME	YEAR BUILT	BUILDER	LENGTH/ BREADTH/ DEPTH	TONS: GROSS NET	VESSEL TYPE; ENGINES	NOTES
Aberdeen	May 22, 1893	E. G. McKay, CPR, Okanagan Landing	146.2 29.9 6.8	544.0 349.1	Wooden hull Sternwheeler 2 — 16x72 27.3 nhp B.C. Iron Works	12
Kootenay	April, 1897 mv. 6/1897	CPR, Nakusp	183.5 32.6 6.2	1117.1 732.5	Wooden hull Sternwheeler 2 — 18x72 21.6 nhp ex *William Irving*	13
Slocan	May 22, 1897	CPR, Rosebery	155.7 25.2 6.5	578.0 364.2	Wooden hull Sternwheeler 2 — 16x72 17.1 nhp B.C. Iron Works	14
	rebuilt 1905 and registered as new vessel		155.7 27.5 6.7	604.7 337.7	— engines retained	

NAME	YEAR BUILT (launching date and/or maiden voyage [mv] date where known)	BUILDER	LENGTH/ BREADTH/ DEPTH**	TONS: GROSS NET	VESSEL TYPE; ENGINES: BORE/STROKE (Builder or Origin)***	NOTES
Rossland	Nov. 18, 1897	CPR, Nakusp	183.4 29.1 7.0	883.5 531.5	Wooden hull Sternwheeler 2 — 22x96 32.2 nhp B.C. Iron Works, Vancouver	15
	rebuilt 1910				— engines retained	
Denver	1896	New Westminster; Assembled, Slocan City	36.0 8.5 3.8	9 6	Wooden hull Sc. tug C.2Cy., 4.5&5 x6	16
William Hunter	Nov. 7, 1892	New Denver	58.5 12.9 3.2	50.7 34.5	Wooden hull Sc. Pass. Simple, 2 — 7x9 3.3 nhp	17
Hamlin	Apr. 21, 1898 Apr. 1898	CPR, Vancouver	146.2 30.0 4.6	514.9 453.5	Wooden hull Sternwheeler 17.0 nhp	18
Ogilvie	Apr. 23, 1898 Apr. 30, 1898	CPR, Vancouver	146.8 30.0 4.6	741.9 453.5	Wooden hull Sternwheeler 2 — 16x72 17.0 nhp B.C. Iron Works, Vancouver. Boiler: Polson	19
McConnell	Apr. 23, 1898 May 1898	CPR, Vancouver	142.2 30.0 4.6	728.5 444.5	Wooden hull Sternwheeler 2 — 16x72 17 nhp Albion Iron Works, Victoria	20
Duchesnay	Apr. 1898	CPR, Vancouver	120.0 20.8 4.0	276.7 184.34	Wooden hull Sternwheeler 2 — 12x54 9.6 nhp	21
Tyrrell	June 6, 1898	Polson Iron Works, Toronto; prefab. hull. Assembled, Vancouver; Cabins, CPR	142.0 30.2 4.8	678.3 408.1	Composite hull Sternwheeler 2 — 16x72 17.1 nhp Polson Iron Works	22
Constantine	1898	Hall Bros.,† Port Blakely	146.0 30.0 5.0	484.1 291.8	Wooden hull Sternwheeler Engines ex *Mary Morton*	23

NAME	YEAR BUILT (launching date and/or maiden voyage [mv] date where known)	BUILDER	LENGTH/ BREADTH/ DEPTH**	TONS: GROSS NET	VESSEL TYPE; ENGINES: BORE/STROKE (Builder or Origin) ***	NOTES
Schwatka	1898	Hall Bros.,† Port Blakely	146.0 30.0 5.0	484.1 291.8	Wooden hull 2 — 16x72 Willamette Iron & Steel, Portland, Ore. 2 boilers	24
Dalton	1898	Hall Bros.,† Port Blakely	150.2 32.0 5.0	522.8 348.2	Wooden hull Sternwheeler	25
Walsh	1898	Hall Bros.,† Port Blakely	150.2 32.0 5.0	522.8 348.2	Wooden hull Sternwheeler	26
G. M. Dawson	Mar. 7, 1901	CPR, Vancouver	151.4 31 5.4	550? 350?	Wooden hull Sternwheeler 2 — 17x72 19.2 nhp Hamilton Engine Works	27
Sandon	Oct. 1898	CPR, Rosebery	76.0 16.9 6.2	97.2 66.4	Wooden hull Sc. Pass./Tug C.2Cy., 10&22x16 19.5 nhp, 1Sc. Polson Iron Works	28
Moyie	Oct. 22, 1898	Bertram Iron Works, Toronto; prefab. hull. Assembled, Nelson; Cabins, CPR	161.7 30.1 5.1	834.8 525.9	Composite hull Sternwheeler 2 — 16x72 17.1 nhp Bertram Iron Works	29
Minto	Nov. 18, 1898	Bertram Iron Works, Toronto; prefab. hull. Assembled, Nakusp; Cabins, CPR	161.7 30.1 5.1	828.9 522.2	Composite hull Sternwheeler 2 — 16x72 17.1 nhp Bertram Iron Works	30
Ymir	Feb. 27, 1899	CPR, Nelson	77.7 16.7 6.5	69.7 47.4	Wooden hull Sc. Tug C.2Cy., 12&26x18 1Sc. 27.3 nhp	31
Procter	1900	CPR, Nelson	65.0 14.4 5.2	43.1 29.3	Wooden hull Sc. Pass./Tug C.2Cy., 9&18x12 1-Sc. 13.6 nhp ex *Kaslo*	32
Victoria	1898	N. P. Roman, Trout Lake	75.0 15.0 3.7	107	Wooden hull Sternwheeler 2 — 8x36	33

NAME	YEAR BUILT (launching date and/or maiden voyage [mv] date where known)	BUILDER	LENGTH/ BREADTH/ DEPTH**	TONS: GROSS NET	VESSEL TYPE; ENGINES: BORE/STROKE (Builder or Origin)***	NOTES
Valhalla	1901	CPR, Nelson	102.5 20.8 9.0	153.2 34.1	Wooden hull Sc. Tug C.2Cy., 14&30x20 36.5 nhp, 1Sc. Polson Iron Works, Owen Sound, Ont.	34
York	Jan. 18, 1902	Bertram Iron Works, Toronto; prefab. hull. Assembled, Okanagan Landing; Cabins, CPR	88.0 16.2 4.9	134.0 91.1	Steel hull Sc. Pass./Tug 2 — C.2Cy., 7&12x8 12.9 nhp, 2Sc. Bertram Iron Works	35
Slocan	Sept. 30, 1905	CPR, Rosebery	157.7 27.5 6.7	604.7 337.7	Wooden hull Sternwheeler 2 — 16x72 17.1 nhp B.C. Iron Works, Vernon. ex *Slocan* (1897)	36
Kuskanook	May 5, 1906	CPR, Nelson	193.5 30.9 7.0	1008.2 547.6	Wooden hull Sternwheeler 2 — 22x96 32.8 nhp Polson Iron Works	37
Okanagan	Apr. 16, 1907	CPR, Okanagan	193.2 32.3 7.7	1077.8 679.0	Wooden hull Sternwheeler 2 — 22x96 32.3 nhp Polson Iron Works	38
Hosmer	1909	CPR, Nelson	109.8 20.9 8.4	153.9 104.7	Wooden hull Sc. Tug C.2Cy., 14&30/20 36.5 nhp. 1Sc. Polson Iron Works, Toronto	39
Whatshan	1909	CPR, Nakusp	89.8 19.0 8.1	105.5 71.8	Wooden hull Sc. Pass./Tug C.2Cy., 12&26/18 27.3 nhp, 1Sc. Polson Iron Works, Toronto	40
Kaleden	July 23, 1910	CPR, Okanagan Landing	94.0 18.4 4.6	180.1 113.5	Wooden hull Sternwheeler 2 — 8x36 4 nhp ex *Victoria*	41

NAME	YEAR BUILT (launching date and/or maiden voyage [mv] date where known)	BUILDER	LENGTH/ BREADTH/ DEPTH**	TONS: GROSS NET	VESSEL TYPE; ENGINES: BORE/STROKE (Builder or Origin)***	NOTES
Castlegar	Apr. 12, 1911	CPR, Okanagan	94.4 19.4 8.2	104.2 70.8	Wooden hull Sc. Tug C.2Cy., 12&26x18 27.3 nhp, 1Sc. Collingwood Shipbuilding Co.	42
Bonnington	Apr. 24, 1911	Polson Iron Works, Toronto; prefab. hull Assembled, Nakusp; Cabins, CPR	202.5 39.6 7.5	1700.0 954.9	Steel hull Sternwheeler 2C.2Cy., 16&35x96 98.7 nhp (Tandem compound) (Builder)	43
Nasookin	Apr. 30, 1913	Western Dry Dock & Ship-building, Port Arthur, Ont.; prefab. hull. Assembled, Nelson; Cabins, CPR	202.2 40.0 8.0	1869.0 1035.2	Steel hull Sternwheeler 2C.2Cy., 16⅜&35⅜x96 101.3 nhp (Tandem compound) (Builder)	44
Nelson	1914	CPR, Nelson	60.7 11.0 3.8	24.5 16.7	Wooden hull Launch Gas engine, 1Sc.	45
Naramata	Apr. 20, 1914	Western Dry Dock & Ship-building, Port Arthur; prefab. hull. Assembled, Okanagan Landing; Cabins, CPR	89.8 19.5 8.0	149.9 73.7	Steel hull Sc. Tug C.2Cy., 12&26/18 27.3 nhp, 1Sc. (Builder)	46
Sicamous	May 26, 1914	Western Dry Dock & Ship-building, Port Arthur; prefab. hull. Assembled, Okanagan Landing; Cabins, CPR	200.5 40.0 8.0	1786.7 994.3	Steel hull Sternwheeler 2C.2Cy., 16⅜&35⅜x96 101.3 nhp (Tandem compound) (Builder)	47
Kelowna	1920	Nickson Construction Co., Okanagan Landing	89.0 19.4 8.0	96.0 34.7	Wooden hull Sc. Tug C.2Cy., 12&26x18 27.3 nhp, 1Sc. ex *Whatshan* Polson Iron Works, 1909	48

NAME	YEAR BUILT (launching date and/or maiden voyage [mv] date where known)	BUILDER	LENGTH/ BREADTH/ DEPTH**	TONS: GROSS NET	VESSEL TYPE; ENGINES: BORE/STROKE (Builder or Origin)***	NOTES
Columbia	1920	CPR, Nakusp	80.1 15.4 8.4	89.5 44.2	Wooden hull Sc. Pass/Tug C.2Cy., 9&18x12 19.6 nhp, 1 Sc. ex *Columbia* (1896) John Daly, Toronto	49
Rosebery	Apr. 19, 1928 rebuilt 1943 (see below)	CPR, Rosebery	102.0 20.0 7.3	132.6 51.7	Wooden hull Sc. Pass/Tug C.2Cy., 12&26x18 27.3 nhp, 1Sc. ex *Castlegar* Collingwood Shipbuilding (1911)	50
Granthall	Mar. 7, 1928	Canadian Vickers, Montreal; Assembled, CPR, Nelson	102.0 24.1 10.0	164.2 54.6	All Steel Sc. Pass/Tug Tr. Exp., 12¾,21½&35x24 62.7 nhp, 1Sc. (Builder)	51
Rosebery	1943	CPR, Rosebery	97.7 20.2 7.4	165.8 79.8	Wooden hull Sc. Pass/Tug C.2Cy., 12&26x18 17.3 nhp, 1Sc. ex *Rosebery* (1928), ex *Castlegar*, (1911)	52
Okanagan	Feb. 18, 1947	Westcoast Shipbuilders Vancouver; Assembled, Okanagan Landing	101.5 23.8 10.6	204 139	All Steel Sc. Tug Diesel, 1Sc. 8Cy., 16x20 800 bhp @ 257 rpm Washington Engine Works	53
Nipigonian	1929	Penetang, Ont.	39.9 9.2 4.5	10 7	Wooden hull Launch. Sterling Gas Engine, 150 bhp	54
Widget (chartered)	1944	Vancouver, B.C.	36.5 9.5 4.8	9 6	Wooden hull Sc. Tug Diesel, 1Sc. 70 bhp, Buda	55
Columbia ex *Surfco*, ex *Uchuck*	1928	Vancouver, B.C.	50.1 11.4 5.6	22 15	Wooden hull Sc. Pass/Tug Diesel, 1Sc. 85 hp	56

3. Tugs, Operating Under Contract with CPR for Barge Service on Slocan and Kootenay Lakes

NAME	YEAR BUILT	BUILDER	LENGTH/ BREADTH/ DEPTH	TONS: GROSS NET	VESSEL TYPE; ENGINES	NOTES
Iris G	1956	J. Manly Ltd., New Westminster	45.8 15.1 7.1	39 27	Steel Tug Diesel, 2Sc. 228 bhp Gardner diesels	57
Melinda Jane	1958	J. Manly Ltd., New Westminster	53.7 17.0 6.7	56 38	Steel Tug Diesel, 2Sc. 304 bhp	58

SOURCES: The standard sources were the yearly reports of the Steamship Inspection Branch, Department of Marine and Fisheries, published in the federal Sessional Papers; the same department's (and its successor's) List of Shipping; the original steamship inspection notebooks held in the Provincial Archives of British Columbia; and the steamship registration files for the port of Victoria also held by the PABC. Where differences occurred, the latter two sources were given preference. Other sources were surviving CPR documents and reports, contemporary published reports, and finally, published secondary sources, noted in the Bibliography. It should be noted that sources often disagreed on vessel characteristics. Some variation undoubtedly resulted from changes to the vessels themselves during their careers and also the many different ways used to measure vessels.

† These four vessels are believed to have been built at the Hall Brothers yards, but apparently they were not included in Hall Bros. lists of vessels. It may be that they were built by the CPR at the Hall Bros. yards by arrangement. Captain Troup was noted on United States Customs records as owner of the vessels but he was acting for the CPR.

Notes

1 Built by J. Fred Hume, W. Cowan and Captain Robert Sanderson for their Columbia Transportation Company. Last used as a snag boat. Dismantled by 1893. Engines to *Illecillewaet*. Registered at New Westminster.

2 Cost $38,000. Out of service, 1902, and dismantled. Average speed, 12.5 knots. Registered at New Westminster.

3 Originally built by contractors for CPR construction. Damaged in grounding, 1895; to Nakusp and dismantled. Engines and equipment to *Trail*. Purchased by C&KSN for $10,000.

4 Cost $75,000. Burned in 1894; a total loss. Registered in U.S.A.

5 First major steamboat on Kootenay Lake. Withdrawn from service, 1913; hulk burned in carnival celebrations at Nelson, July 16, 1914.

6 Designed for operation in shallows and during low-water periods. Bow reinforced for ice-breaking. Sold for scrap, 1902.

7 Built for supply work on the Great Northern Railway; purchased from G. W. Gray by C&KSN, and lengthened, 1893. Registry changed to Canadian (New Westminster). Burned at Kaslo, March 21, 1895; a total loss.

8 Destroyed by fire at Arrowhead, December 23, 1897.

9 Dismantled, 1923. In her prime, capable of over 18 mph (29 km/h). Original cost: $22,000.

10 Built primarily for freight service to Trail from Revelstoke (Arrowhead). Burned at Trail, 1900; a total loss.

11 Built for barge service between Arrowhead and Nakusp and also used during winter months on Lower Arrow Lake for passengers and freight service.

12 Rebuilt, 1902. Withdrawn, 1916 and sold to B. Johnson, 1919. Registered at Vancouver.

13 Under contract before CPR purchase of C&KSN was completed. Withdrawn in 1919 and sold, 1920, to Captain Sanderson for houseboat. In existence until 1940's.

14 Built for passenger and barge service on Slocan Lake. Rebuilt with new hull and registered as a new vessel in 1905; assigned a new official number (121,680). Withdrawn from service, 1928. Superstructure, engines and boiler were retained in reconstruction.

15 Built for express passenger service on the Arrow Lakes. A lake boat design with deep hull. Noted for her speed. Additional cabins built on Texas deck 1908 (cost of $2,290). Rebuilt with new hull and further staterooms, 1910. Original cost $86,000. Sank

in ice at Nakusp, January 1917, raised, and later stripped and sold.

16 Purchased to move transfer barges on Slocan Lake. Later transferred to Shuswap Lake to serve as tender for CPR houseboat. Sold, 1907.

17 Built by Hume, Hunter and McKinnon from locally sawn lumber for service on Slocan Lake (Slocan Trading & Navigation Company of Nelson, B.C.). Withdrawn from service by 1900, scrapped, 1903.

18 Freight steamer for Stikine River; first CPR vessel in service on Stikine. Sold, 1901, to British Yukon Navigation Co.; to McCallum, Banser and Reider, 1903; to T. J. Kickham, 1904; to E. J. Coyle, 1910; to Hamlin Towing Co., 1911; to J. H. Green, 1917; to Defiance Packing Co., 1918. Converted to oil burner, 1910. On registry to mid-1920's.

19 Sold in January 1901, to British Yukon Navigation Company (White Pass & Yukon), dismantled for parts, Skagway later that year. The components of the *Ogilvie, McConnell* and *G. M. Dawson* were used in the White Pass steamers *Dawson, White Horse* and *Selkirk.*

20 Sold in January 1901, to British Yukon Navigation Company (White Pass & Yukon), dismantled for parts at Skagway later that year. See also note 19.

21 Sold in June 1899, to E. J. Rathbone, later to United States Army Quartermaster Corps and renamed *General Jeff C. Davis*; finally to Alaska Railroad.

22 Sold in July 1898, to British American Corporation, Ltd., for $40,000. Operated on the Yukon River into the early 1920's. Derelict near Dawson. Registered at Portland, Oregon.

23 Never used by CPR. Sold, May 31, 1898, to British American Corporation. Sank en route to Yukon River from Puget Sound while under tow on July 4, 1898. Registered at Portland, Oregon.

24 Never used in CPR service; laid up on completion. Freight steamer, sold by CPR August 1904, for $12,000 to Charles W. Thebo for Yukon River trade. Later to Northern Navigation Company (White Pass & Yukon Route). Laid up by 1916. Derelict near Dawson. Registered at Portland, Oregan.

25 Never used in CPR service; laid up on completion. Sold, 1901, to British Yukon Navigation Company, resold to S. Willey Navigation Company for Puget Sound trade and renamed *Capital City.*

26 Never used by CPR; laid up on completion. Sold, September 1902, for $14,500 for Seattle-Bremerton service. Destroyed by fire at Bremerton, July 1903. Registered at Portland, Oregon.

27 Left incomplete at False Creek yards until sold to British Yukon Navigation Company. Launched in 1901 and towed to Skagway where she was dismantled. See also note 19. Hull used as a barge and later as a basis for a floating bunkhouse on the Queen Charlotte Islands. Also known as *Dawson.*

28 Built for transfer barge service on Slocan Lake. Licensed to carry 50 passengers. Used as relief vessel for *Slocan.* Dismantled in 1927 after having steamed approximately 120,000 miles (193,000 km).

29 Probably the best known sternwheeler in Western Canada. Retired in April 1957; preserved at Kaslo, B.C., after 59 years of service. New boiler, 1929.

30 Twenty additional staterooms built in 1910. New boiler, 1929. Retired from Arrow Lakes service, April 1954. Sold to Nakusp for preservation, resold to John Nelson who moved her to Galena Bay. Burned in 1968 by B.C. Hydro.

31 Rebuilt in 1912. Withdrawn in 1929 and sunk in Kootenay Lake.

32 Originally for service on Kootenay Lake. Used for towing barges and also as tender for CPR houseboat. Transferred to Trout Lake in 1904. Sold 1917 to W. A. Foote and retired in 1921. Sometimes spelled *Proctor.*

33 Built by Neils Pierson Roman for service on Trout Lake. A barge-like hull with primitive cabins. Purchased by CPR in 1900. After transfer of *Procter,* used as a wharf at Trout Lake City. Engines to *Kaleden.*

34 Rebuilt, 1910. Withdrawn from service by completion of Procter to Kootenay Landing railway extension, December 31, 1930. Sold, 1931, to R. Dill for houseboat.

35 A small, steel-hulled, tunnel-screw steamer originally ordered to replace the *Victoria* on Trout Lake but diverted to the Okanagan to relieve the *Aberdeen,* then the only CPR steamer in service there. In 1921, transferred to Skaha (Dog) Lake to move transfer barges. Retired in 1932 after completion of railway along Skaha Lake to Okangan Falls. (During this period she was technically the property of the Kettle Valley Railway, having been sold to the KVR in March 1920 for $12,000.) Hull sold to C. S. Leary and moved to Nakusp but not used.

36 Rebuilt from *Slocan* (1897) using engines, boiler and cabins on a new hull. Sold, May 1928, for warehouse.

37 1906-1914 used primarily between Nelson and Kootenay Landing. Replaced by *Nasookin,* then used Nelson to Kaslo. Retired, 1930, and sold for use as a hotel, 1931.

38 Sistership to *Kuskanook.* Relegated to freight service by late 1920's, laid up, 1934, and sold in 1938 for dismantling.

39 Cabins burned, 1925, but rebuilt. Retired following Procter-Kootenay Landing railway extension on December 31, 1930. Sold, 1934. Salvage value of $762.

40 Used in transfer barge service and also as a passenger and freight steamer on Lower Arrow Lake during the winter months. Passenger cabin added aft. Out of service, 1919, scrapped, 1920. Machinery and boiler to *Kelowna.*

41 Engine from *Victoria*. Retired, 1917 and scrapped, 1920.

42 Removed from service, 1925. Engine and boiler to *Rosebery* (1928).

43 Usually laid up in winter months at Nakusp. Retired, 1931, and sold in 1942 to B.C. government. Boiler and smokestack transferred to *Nasookin*. Dismantled at Beaton, 1948.

44 Built for Nelson-Kootenay Landing passenger-express service. Laid up following railway completion between Procter and Kootenay Landing, December 31, 1930. In 1931 leased to B.C. government as an automobile ferry. Sold to government for this service and extensively rebuilt, 1933. Retired, 1947, to Navy League but damaged at Nelson and scrapped 1948.

45 Passenger launch for service on West Arm of Kootenay Lake. Sold, 1920, for $1,200.

46 Retired in 1967 and sold, 1969. Preserved at Okanagan Landing.

47 In 1935 cabins cut down and afterwards used primarily for freight service. Retired, 1936. Sold, 1949, to Penticton for preservation and moved to Penticton, 1951. Originally cost over $160,000.

48 Out of service, 1956, and sold May 13, 1957, to P. Ellergodt.

49 Passenger and freight steamer for Arrow Lakes service. Used particularly in winter months on Lower Arrow Lake, replacing the *Whatshan*. New boiler, Paterson Iron Works, 1938. Withdrawn, 1947; sold, 1948.

50 Replaced *Slocan* on passenger and barge service. Rebuilt with new hull, 1943.

51 After Procter-Kootenay Landing rail line completed used as relief boat for *Moyie* on Kaslo service. Retired in 1958 and sold 1964 to Earl Harcourt (Yellowknife Transportation Co.). Dismantled and shipped to Hay River but not used. Eventually shipped to New Westminster, hull reassembled at Manly yards. Finally rebuilt as fish barge and renamed *G.N. Transporter* owned by Francis Millerd & Co. Ltd., Vancouver.

52 Retired, 1956, following takeover of barge service by charter operator using tug *Iris G*. Scrapped, 1958.

53 Retired, 1972, and sold to Fintry Estates.

54 Built for passenger service on Lake of the Woods, Ontario. When hull of *Columbia* was condemned, 1947, shipped to Lower Arrow Lake as a temporary replacement. Used February 1 to late April 1948.

55 Used with barge, February 1 to late April 1948, as replacement for the *Columbia*. Ivan Horie, owner. Operated under charter.

56 Purchased, 1948, to replace *Columbia* (1920). Cabins modified for service on Lower Arrow Lakes. Sold to Ivan Horie on April 24, 1954. Sank in 1968, salvaged and returned to Coast in 1969.

57 Replaced *Rosebery* (II) on Slocan Lake barge service. Owned by Ivan Horie (Interior Lake Services) and operated under contract.

58 Replaced *Granthall* on Kootenay Lake barge service. Built for Ivan Horie and operated for his Kootenay Water Transport Ltd. under contract to CPR. Service for CPR ended in 1977. Sold, 1980, to Shields Navigation Ltd., and moved to Vancouver. Renamed *Storm Spray*.

APPENDIX II

MAJOR LAKE AND RIVER SERVICE ROUTES AND THE VESSELS SERVING THEM*

* Columbia Transportation Company and Columbia and Kootenay Steam Navigation Company vessels are included. Fraser River routes operated by the CPR's B.C. Coast Steamship Service and CPR construction era vessels are included for purposes of completeness and comparison only. All tugs are steam powered unless noted otherwise. Dates shown are years in service, while dates in parentheses are years of sale or dismantling where different from last date shown.

1. *Columbia River-Arrow Lakes Route*

Columbia Transportation Company, 1888-1889

Columbia and Kootenay Steam Navigation Company, 1889-1897

Canadian Pacific Railway, B.C. Lake and River Service, 1897-1954

Dispatch, sternwheeler, 1888-1892 (1893)
Lytton, sternwheeler, 1890-1902
Kootenai, sternwheeler, 1890-1895
Columbia, sternwheeler, 1891-1894
Illecillewaet, sternwheeler, 1892-1902
Nakusp, sternwheeler, 1895-1897
Trail, sternwheeler, 1896-1900
Columbia, tug, 1896-1919 (1920)
Kootenay, sternwheeler, 1897-1919 (1920)
Rossland, sternwheeler, 1897-1917
Minto, sternwheeler, 1898-1954
Whatshan, passenger tug, 1909-1919 (1920)
Bonnington, sternwheeler, 1911-1931 (1942)
Columbia, passenger tug, 1920-1947 (1948)
Nipigonian, motor launch, 1948
Widget, diesel tug, 1948 (under charter)
Columbia, motor passenger tug, 1948-1954

2. *Kootenay Lake Service*

Columbia and Kootenay Steam Navigation Company, 1891-1897

Canadian Pacific Railway, B.C. Lake and River Service, 1897-1958 (contractor operated tug and barge service continued 1958-1977**)

Nelson, sternwheeler, 1891-1913 (1914)
Spokane, sternwheeler, 1893-1895
Kokanee, sternwheeler, 1896-1923
Moyie, sternwheeler, 1898-1957 (preserved at Kaslo)
Ymir, tug, 1899-1929
Procter, passenger tug, 1900-1904 (transferred to Trout Lake)
Valhalla, tug, 1901-1930 (1931)
Kuskanook, sternwheeler 1906-1931
Hosmer, tug, 1909-1930 (1934)
Nasookin, sternwheeler, 1913-1930, (1931-1933 on charter; 1933-1947 as automobile ferry for B.C. government) (1948)
Nelson, motor launch, 1914-1919 (1920)
Granthall, passenger tug, 1928-1958 (1964)
Melinda Jane, diesel tug, 1958-1977** (under charter)

3. *Okanagan Lake Service*

Canadian Pacific Railway, B.C. Lake and River Service, 1893-1972

Aberdeen, sternwheeler, 1893-1916 (1919)
York, passenger and freight/tug 1902-1921 (1921-1931, Skaha Lake service) (1932)
Okanagan, sternwheeler, 1907-1934 (1938)
Kaleden, sternwheeler, 1910-1917 (1920), (also used 1910 on Skaha Lake)
Castlegar, tug, 1911-1925
Naramata, tug, 1914-1967 (1969) (preserved at Okanagan Landing)
Sicamous, sternwheeler, 1914-1936 (1949) (preserved at Penticton, 1951)
Kelowna, tug, 1920-1956 (1957)
Okanagan, diesel tug, 1947-1972

4. *Slocan Lake Service*

Slocan Trading and Navigation Company, 1892-1897

Canadian Pacific Railway, B.C. Lake and River Service, 1897-1957 (service maintained by charter operator,*** post 1957).

William Hunter, passenger, freight/tug, 1892-1900 (1903)

Denver, tug, 1897-1903 (transferred to Shuswap Lake until 1907)

Slocan, sternwheeler, 1897-1905

Sandon, passenger tug, 1898-1927

Slocan, sternwheeler, 1905-1928

Rosebery, passenger tug, 1928-1943

Rosebery, passenger tug, 1943-1956 (1958)

Iris G., tug 1956*** (chartered vessel)

5. *Stikine River Service*

Canadian Pacific Railway, B.C. Lake and River Service, 1898

Hamlin, sternwheeler, 1898 (1901)

Ogilvie, sternwheeler, 1898 (1901)

McConnell, sternwheeler, 1898 (1901)

Duchesnay, sternwheeler, 1898 (1900)

Tyrrell, sternwheeler, not used (1898)

Constantine, sternwheeler, not used (1898)

Schwatka, sternwheeler, not used (1904)

Dalton, sternwheeler, not used (1902)

Walsh, sternwheeler, not used (1901)

G. M. Dawson, (*Dawson*), sternwheeler, not used (1901)

6. *Trout Lake Service*

Captain Neils P. Roman, 1898-1900

Canadian Pacific Railway, B.C. Lake and River Service, 1900-1917

Victoria, sternwheeler, 1900-1904

Procter, passenger tug, 1904-1917 (service maintained until 1921)

7. *Lower Fraser River Service*

Canadian Pacific Navigation Company, 1883-1901

Canadian Pacific Railway, B.C. Coast Steamship Service, 1901-1919

R. P. Rithet, sternwheeler, 1883-1909

Transfer, sternwheeler, 1893-1909

Beaver, sternwheeler, 1898-1913 (1918)

8. *Fraser River (CPR Construction Era)*

Andrew Onderdonk, Contractor — Fraser River, 1882-1884

Skuzzy, sternwheeler (first), 1882-1884

Myra, sternwheeler, 1882-1883?

9. *Thompson River-Shuswap Lake (CPR Construction Era)*

Andrew Onderdonk, Contractor

Skuzzy, sternwheeler (second), 1885-1886 (1890)

APPENDIX III

LAKE AND RIVER SERVICE STEAMER CREWS AND ACCOMMODATIONS

* carried during fruit season only

** in freight and barge service

SOURCE: J. S. Byron (1919) *Report on the B.C. Lake & River Service, 1918-1919*. The report notes that the *Bonnington* carried the same crew as the *Sicamous*. The passenger-carrying tug *Whatshan* was also in service, but her crew was not noted. Presumably it would have been equivalent to the *Valhalla* and *Hosmer*. She did not carry extra crew members for passenger service.

† The principal vessels carrying automobiles were the *Nasookin* and *Kuskanook* between Nelson and Kuskonook, just north of Kootenay Landing. The *Bonnington* and *Minto* also carried vehicles mostly between Arrowhead and Nakusp. The addition of large doors on the forward sides of the cargo deck on steamers including the *Minto* and *Moyie* was to facilitate handling automobiles as traffic increased in the 1920's.

1. *Crews of British Columbia Lake and River Service Steamers: Winter 1918-1919*

VESSEL	CAPT.	MATE	PILOT	DECK HANDS	ENGIN'RS	FIRE-MEN	COAL PASSERS	PURSER	FRT. CLERK	CHIEF STEW-ARD	ASSIS-TANTS (INCL. COOKS	BARGE-MAN	TOTAL
Sicamous	1	1	—	9	2	3	2	1	1	1	10	—	31
Naramata	1	1	1*	2	2	2	—	—	—	—	1	1	11
Minto	1	1	1	9	2	3	2	1	1	1	11	—	33
Slocan	1	1	—	5	2	2	1	1	—	1	3	—	17
Sandon	1	1	—	2	1	2	—	—	—	—	1	—	8
Nasookin	1	1	—	9	2	3	1	1	1	1	10	—	30
Kuskanook	1	1	—	8	2	2	1	1	1	1	10	—	28
*Moyie***	1	1	—	7	1	2	—	1	—	—	1	—	14
Valhalla	1	1	1	2	2	2	—	—	—	—	1	—	10
Hosmer	1	1	1	2	2	2	—	—	—	—	1	—	10

2. *Vessel Accommodations, ca. 1920*

VESSEL	DINING ROOM TABLES	SEATS	NUMBER OF STATEROOMS	DOUBLE LOWER	SINGLE LOWER	SINGLE UPPER	TOTAL PASSENGER CAPACITY	VEHICLE† CAPACITY BY MID-1920's
Bonnington	6	48	59	59	—	59	400	17
Kokanee	3	18	11	11	—	11	200	—
Kuskanook	4	32	39	14	25	39	400	8
Minto	4	32	31	4	27	31	225	8
Moyie	4	24	13	3	12	14	400	6
Nasookin	6	48	54	58	—	58	400	23
Okanagan	5	30	32	16	16	32	400	8
Sicamous	6	48	36	40	—	40	400	17
Slocan	4	24	2	2	—	2	300	2

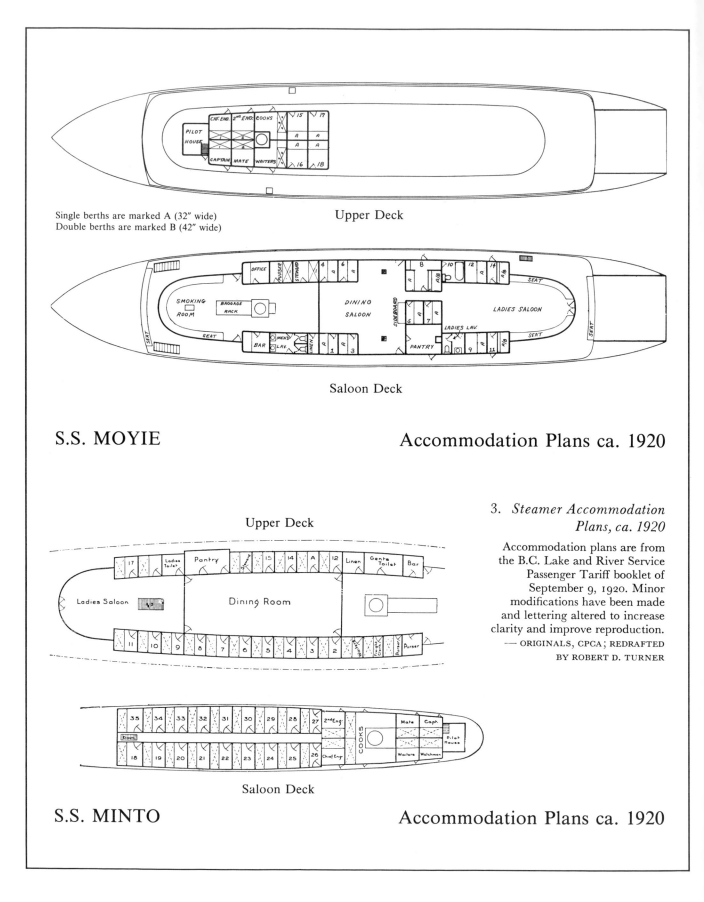

Upper Deck

Single berths are marked A (32″ wide)
Double berths are marked B (42″ wide)

Saloon Deck

S.S. MOYIE

Accommodation Plans ca. 1920

Upper Deck

3. *Steamer Accommodation Plans, ca. 1920*

Accommodation plans are from the B.C. Lake and River Service Passenger Tariff booklet of September 9, 1920. Minor modifications have been made and lettering altered to increase clarity and improve reproduction.

— ORIGINALS, CPCA; REDRAFTED BY ROBERT D. TURNER

Saloon Deck

S.S. MINTO

Accommodation Plans ca. 1920

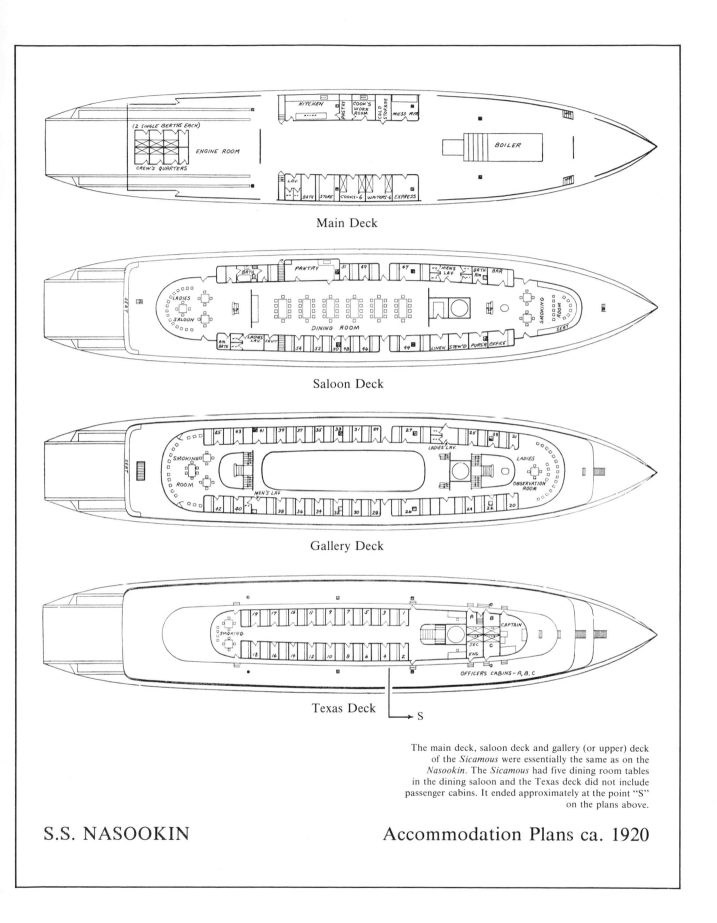

Main Deck

Saloon Deck

Gallery Deck

Texas Deck

→ S

The main deck, saloon deck and gallery (or upper) deck
of the *Sicamous* were essentially the same as on the
Nasookin. The *Sicamous* had five dining room tables
in the dining saloon and the Texas deck did not include
passenger cabins. It ended approximately at the point "S"
on the plans above.

S.S. NASOOKIN

Accommodation Plans ca. 1920

APPENDIX IV

RAILWAY TRANSFER BARGES OF THE LAKE AND RIVER SERVICE, LATE 1940's

* Registered dimensions in feet.

** Originally built for Kootenay Lake service as 15 car barge, dimensions 224 x 43 x 8.5 feet of 625 gross tons. Dismantled and shipped at a cost of over $21,000, replacing wooden transfer barge, No. 3.

*** Estimated depth.

BARGE NUMBER	SERVICE	YEAR BUILT	TYPE	LENGTH/ BREADTH/ DEPTH*	REG. TONNAGE	CAPACITY CARS/ TONS	BUILDER/ COST
1	Kootenay	1911	Steel/transfer	224.0 42.0 7.9	695	15/900	Polson Iron Works $68,200
16	Kootenay	1928	Steel/transfer	231.3 43 8.5	778.0	15/1300	$95,000
4	Okanagan	1927 rebuilt 1936**	Steel/transfer	231.0 38.1 8.5	680.6	10/990	Canadian Vickers $86,286
8	Okanagan	1919	Wood/transfer	181.6 36.5 6.9	304.6	8/650	CPR $27,250
9	Okanagan	1920	Wood/transfer	186.3 36.5 7.0	396.3	8/660	CPR $32,000
12	Okanagan	1924	Wood/transfer	187.5 36.5 7.4	420.4	8/700	CPR $24,920
19	Okanagan	1934	Wood/transfer	190.4 36.5 7.4	359.4	8/700	CPR $23,710
3	Okanagan	1940	Wood/transfer	190.4 36.5 7.4	374.5	8/700	CPR $22,000
11	Arrow	1923	Wood/ice breaker	60.4 20.0 6.0	53.3	0/50	CPR $3,400
15	Arrow	1926	Wood/ice breaker	70.0 38.9 6.0	94.1	0/125	CPR $5,700

BARGE NUMBER	SERVICE	YEAR BUILT	TYPE	LENGTH/ BREADTH/ DEPTH*	REG. TONNAGE	CAPACITY CARS/ TONS	BUILDER/ COST
17	Arrow	1930	Wood/ice breaker	70.0 38.9 6.0	102.7	0/125	CPR $7,500
14	Slocan	1926	Wood/transfer	187.1 36.5 7.4***	364.5	8/700	CPR $25,000
18	Slocan	1930	Wood/transfer	187.1 36.5 7.4***	355.9	8/700	CPR $27,000

The *Castlegar* was built in 1911 for the CPR barge service on Okanagan Lake. Barge *No. 39* was typical of the wooden transfer barges used on Okanagan and Slocan lakes and could normally carry eight cars. Of 420 gross tons, it was built in 1910-11 and removed from service in 1934. Plans of a similar barge appear on the following page. — VERNON BOARD OF MUSEUM AND ARCHIVES

The powerful tug *Valhalla* was used on the Kootenay Lake barge service. Normally, she pushed two 15-car barges. — JOHN WILLIAMS

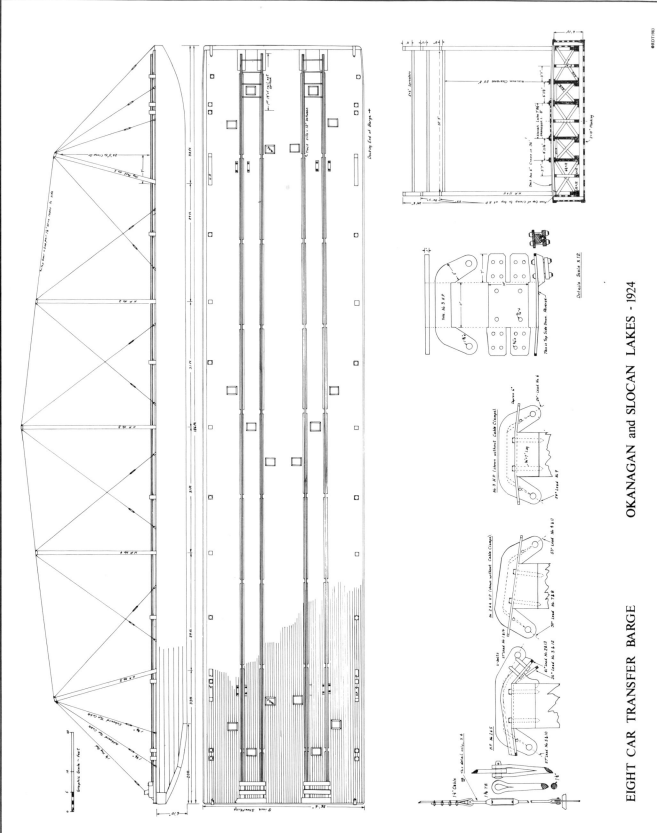

EIGHT CAR TRANSFER BARGE   OKANAGAN and SLOCAN LAKES - 1924

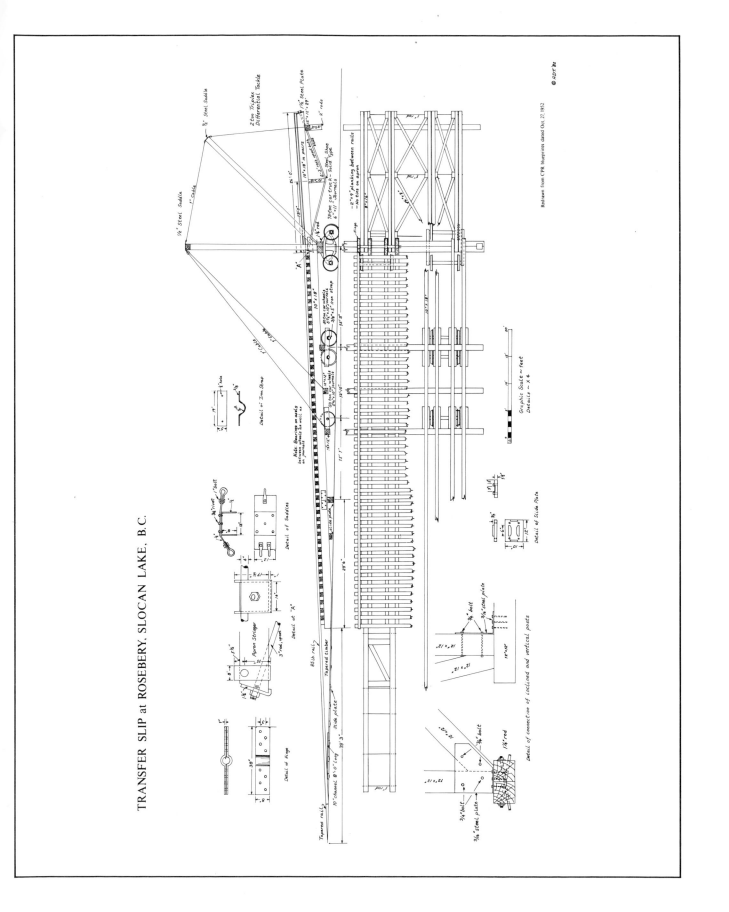

TRANSFER SLIP at ROSEBERY, SLOCAN LAKE, B.C.

APPENDIX V

CPR RAILWAY CONSTRUCTION ERA AND FRASER RIVER STERNWHEELERS

* Registered dimensions in feet.

** Engine dimensions in inches.

The primary source of these statistics was the records of the office of the Inspector of Steamboats, British Columbia Division, (1872-1928) at the Provincial Archives of British Columbia. See also sources for Appendix I.

† These vessels were not owned by the CPR but were owned by Andrew Onderdonk or his associates in the construction of the CPR through British Columbia. Since they have long been associated with the Canadian Pacific, they are included here for completeness.

1. Railway Construction Era Sternwheelers†

NAME	YEAR BUILT (launch date where known)	BUILDER	LENGTH BREADTH DEPTH*	TONS: GROSS NET	VESSEL TYPE; ENGINES BORE/STROKE (Builder or Origin)	NOTES
Skuzzy (I)	May 4, 1882	Wm. Dalton, 14 mi. North of Yale on Fraser River	127.0 24.2 4.5	319.5 254.4	Wooden hull Sternwheeler 2 — 14x54	1
Myra (ex Pacific Slope)	1882	Victoria	92.0 22.7 3.3	81.2 71.9	Wooden hull Sternwheeler 2 — 16x54	2
Skuzzy (II)	1885	J. F. T. Mitchell, Savona's Ferry	133.3 28.0 6.5	471.7 297.2	Wooden hull Sternwheeler 2 — 14x54 ex Skuzzy (I)	3

2. CPR Fraser River Sternwheelers (British Columbia Coast Steamship Service)

NAME	YEAR BUILT	BUILDER	LENGTH BREADTH DEPTH*	TONS: GROSS NET	VESSEL TYPE; ENGINES BORE/STROKE	NOTES
R.P. Rithet	Apr. 20, 1882	A. Watson, Victoria	177.0 33.6 8.5	816.7 686.2	Wooden hull Sternwheeler 2 — 20x60	4
Transfer	May 6, 1893	A. Watson, New Westminster	122.0 24.5 5.6	264.2 97.7	Wooden hull Sternwheeler 2 — 12x60 18 nhp Iowa Iron Works	5
Beaver	April 1898	Albion Iron Works, Victoria	140.0 28.0 5.1	545.4 343.5	Steel hull Sternwheeler 2 — 14x72 13 nhp Albion Iron Works	6

The *Skuzzy* (I) earned lasting fame by being the only sternwheeler to steam upstream through Hells Gate canyon of the Fraser River. Her engines and boiler were used in the second *Skuzzy* which, like the first *Skuzzy*, was used in carrying supplies for the construction of the Canadian Pacific Railway in British Columbia.

— VCA

Photos of the *R. P. Rithet, Transfer,* and *Beaver* appear in *The Pacific Princesses* (1977).

Notes

1 Built to aid in the construction of the CPR through the Fraser Canyon in British Columbia (Andrew Onderdonk contracts). In 1882, John Trutch noted as owner; 1883 Andrew Onderdonk & Co. Hull constructed with at least 20 watertight bulkheads. Noted as the only sternwheeler to steam upstream through Hells Gate Canyon of the Fraser River. This was accomplished with considerable difficulty and required the full power of her engines, the vessel's steam capstain working lines through ring bolts secured into the canyon walls and the muscle power of 125 Chinese railway labourers. Her primary function was to carry construction materials and supplies along the line from the end of track. This vessel was owned by the contractors and not the CPR.

2 A small, shallow-draught sternwheeler built for Captain William Moore for service on the Fraser. Purchased by Andrew Onderdonk for supply work on CPR contracts in 1882.

3 Built to aid in CPR construction along the Thompson River in British Columbia (Andrew Onderdonk contracts). Used boiler and engines from *Skuzzy* (I). Finished in 44 days after keel laid. John Trutch and J. A. Mara listed as owners; laid up soon after construction work completed and eventually scrapped. Engines to Columbia and Kootenay Steam Navigation Company's *Nelson* (1891) and boiler (which was built by Joseph Spratt) to C&KSN's *Lytton* (1890).

4 Built for Captain John Irving's Pioneer Line for service between Victoria and Yale. In 1883 became part of Canadian Pacific Navigation Company's fleet. In 1901 to Canadian Pacific Railway; re-registered to CPR in 1903. Sold in 1909 to Terminal Steam Navigation Company and renamed *Baramba*. Rebuilt to a barge in 1917. Unlike many other sternwheelers, the *R.P. Rithet* operated regularly across the open waters of Georgia Strait, although most frequently during the summer months of better weather conditions. Passenger capacity: 250.

5 Built for the Canadian Pacific Navigation Company for Fraser River service between New Westminster and Chilliwack. Replaced on this route by the *Beaver* in 1898 and then used between New Westminster and Steveston. To CPR, 1901 and re-registered to CPR officially in 1903. Sold in 1909 for $6,000 to Robert Jardine; last used at Redonda Bay, B.C. as the power plant for a cannery. Passenger capacity: 120.

6 The first steel-hulled vessel built in British Columbia. Built for the Canadian Pacific Navigation Company for Stikine River service. Used instead on Fraser River route from New Westminster to Chilliwack. Laid up September 1913 with the completion of the B.C. Electric Railway interurban line to Chilliwack. Sold in 1918 to the British Columbia government for $10,000 and modified for use as a ferry across the Fraser River between Ladner and Woodwards Landing. Scrapped in 1930 when new sternwheel ferry built using the *Beaver*'s engines and boiler. Passenger capacity: 150.

APPENDIX VI

KOOTENAY RAILWAY AND NAVIGATION COMPANY VESSELS

Also including the Nelson and Lardo Steam Navigation Company's *City of Ainsworth*.

* Registered dimensions in feet.

** Licensed Passenger Capacity.

NAME	YEAR BUILT (Launch date where known)	BUILDER	LENGTH/ BREADTH/ DEPTH*	TONS: GROSS NET	VESSEL TYPE ENGINES: BORE/STROKE NOMINAL HORSE-POWER (nhp)	L P C**	NOTES
1. *Kootenay Railway and Navigation Company*							
Alberta (ex *State of Idaho*)	1895	Depuy, Lannen & Rutter, Bonners Ferry	140.0 23.0 6.0	508.2 320.1	Wooden hull Sternwheeler 2 — 12x72 9.6 nhp	200	1
International	July 7, 1896	IN&T Co., Mirror Lake	142.0 24.9 5.6	525.3 280.8	Wooden hull Sternwheeler 2 — 16x72 17.0 nhp	300	2
Argenta	Feb. 17, 1900	KR&N, Mirror Lake	92.2 20.3 4.2	206.3 130.0	Wooden hull Sternwheeler 2 — 8x72 4.3 nhp	40	3
Kaslo	Sept. 17, 1900	KR&N, Mirror Lake	173.5 27.0 7.4	764.8 369.8	Wooden hull Sternwheeler 2 — 20x84 26.0 nhp	500	4

Notes

1 Originally *State of Idaho* of the Bonners Ferry and Kaslo Transportation Company, wrecked on November 10, 1893 and acquired by Alberta and B.C. Exploration Company, renamed *Alberta*. To International Navigation & Trading Co., which became part of Kootenay Railway and Navigation in 1898. Sank at her dock at Kaslo on March 1, 1905. Raised and machinery sold to Columbia & Okanogan Steamboat Co. of Seattle. Hull to G. B. Mathews.

2 Built by International Navigation & Trading Co. as challenge to C&KSN's *Kokanee*. Boiler gave out in 1909; vessel laid up. Sold January 1912 to G. B. Mathews.

3 Built by KR&N for service from Kaslo to Duncan River points. Used primarily in freighting. Dismantled at Mirror Lake.

4 At the time of her completion, she was the finest steamer on Kootenay Lake. Sank at Ainsworth on May 27, 1910. Raised and taken to Mirror Lake shipyard, but not repaired. Dismantled.

5 Built by citizens of Ainsworth to improve transportation to their community. Foundered off Pilot Bay, November 29, 1898.

NAME	YEAR BUILT (Launch date where known)	BUILDER	LENGTH/ BREADTH/ DEPTH*	TONS: GROSS NET	VESSEL TYPE ENGINES: BORE/STROKE NOMINAL HORSE-POWER (nhp)	L P C**	NOTES

2. *Nelson and Lardo Steam Navigation Company*

NAME	YEAR BUILT	BUILDER	LENGTH/ BREADTH/ DEPTH	TONS: GROSS NET	VESSEL TYPE	L P C	NOTES
City of Ainsworth	1892	Brenner, Watson & Jevous, Ainsworth	84.0 21.0 4.2	193.5 121.9	Wooden hull Sternwheeler 6.6 nhp Willard & Co., Chicago	80	5

APPENDIX VII

CANADIAN NATIONAL RAILWAYS VESSELS IN OKANAGAN LAKE SERVICE*

* Service operated 1926-1973.

** Registered dimensions. All measurements are in feet.

*** Key to abbreviations: Sc., screw; Cy., Cylinder.

NAME	YEAR BUILT	BUILDER	LENGTH / BREADTH / DEPTH**	TONS: GROSS NET	VESSEL TYPE. ENGINES: TYPE BUILDER***	NOTES
Pentowna	1926	Prince Rupert Dry Dock Co. Assembled at Kelowna	121.7 22.0 8.9	145 61	Steel hulled Passenger Tug. 2 Sc. Semi-Diesel, 2 — 12 Cy. L. Gardner & Sons	1
Canadian National No. 3 ex *Radius*	1923	Dawe Shipyard, New Westminster	53.5 14.6 6.7	33 ?	Wooden hulled Tug. 1 Sc. Diesel 125 hp Atlas-Imperial	2
Canadian National No. 5	1930	Prince Rupert Dry Dock Co. Assembled at Kelowna	67.3 17.3 8.8	68	Steel hulled Tug. 1 Sc. Diesel. 300 hp. L. Gardner & Sons	3
Canadian National No. 6	1948	Yarrows Ltd. Esquimalt	83.8 22.1 10.2	158 50	Steel hulled Tug. 1 Sc. Diesel, 1 — 6 Cy. 575 hp. Enterprise Eng. & Foundry Co.	4

Notes

1 Built for passenger and freight service. After 1937, used as a tug, moving one 10-car transfer barge. Preserved at Peachland.

2 Built for J. A. Cates; sunk off Prospect Point, 1925; salvaged and sold to CNR as *Canadian National No. 3*. Assembled, Kelowna by Vancouver Drydock and Salvage Co.

3 Sold February 1965.

4 Out of service, 1973. Sold to Fintry Estates.

INDEX

Page references in italics indicate photographs or illustrations. The following index is limited to the narrative and illustrations in *Sternwheelers and Steam Tugs.* Readers are referred to the accompanying appendices for further details of the vessels and their technical features.